THEORIA ➜ PRAXIS

THEORIA ⇨ PRAXIS

HOW JEWS, CHRISTIANS, AND MUSLIMS CAN TOGETHER MOVE FROM THEORY TO PRACTICE

LEONARD SWIDLER

PEETERS

1998

© 1998 Uitgeverij Peeters, Bondgenotenlaan 153, B-3000 Leuven

ISBN 90-429-0022-9
D. 1998/0602/39

CONTENTS

FOREWORD
Cardinal Franz König

1 JEWISH-CHRISTIAN-MUSLIM DIALOGUE
Leonard Swidler

2 THE DIALOGUE DECALOGUE
Leonard Swidler

3 INTERNATIONAL SCHOLARS' ANNUAL TRIALOGUE
Leonard Swidler

4 DO WE ALL WORSHIP THE SAME GOD?
John Hick

5 THE ABRAHAMIC RELIGIOUS TRADITIONS:
MAKERS OF PEACE OR CONTRIBUTORS
TO HUMAN ANNIHILATION?
Gordon Kaufman

6 HUMAN DIGNITY AND THE CHRISTIAN TRADITION
John B. Cobb, Jr.

7 THE QUR'AN AND THE "OTHER"
Abderrahmane Lakhsassi

8 JUDAISM AND THE GOOD
Arthur Green

9 A NEW PHASE IN JEWISH SELF-UNDERSTANDING?
Nancy Fuchs-Kreimer

10 CHRISTIAN VIEWS ON HOW TO CONCEIVE
AND IMPLEMENT THE GOOD: A
SELF-CRITICAL REFLECTION
Paul Mojzes

11 THE "GOOD" IN THE SOURCES OF ISLAM AND
ITS CONCEPTION AND IMPLEMENTATION
BY MUSLIMS
Fathi Osman

12 SYNTHESIS OF THE CONCEPTION AND
IMPLEMENTATION OF THE GOOD IN
THE THREE ABRAHAMIC TRADITIONS
Denise & John Carmody

13 TOWARD A UNIVERSAL DECLARATION
OF A GLOBAL ETHIC
Leonard Swidler

14 A UNIVERSAL DECLARATION
OF A GLOBAL ETHIC
Leonard Swidler

15 A JEWISH REFLECTION
Pinchas Lapide

16 A CHRISTIAN REFLECTION
John Hick

17 A MUSLIM REFLECTION
Khalid Duran

18 HOW TO USE THIS BOOK
Denise & John Carmody

AUTHORS

FOREWORD

In January, 1993, the yearly dialogue of the "International Scholars' Annual Trialogue" (ISAT) took place for the first time in Europe. This group was formed six years before at the initiative of Professor Leonard Swidler, Temple University, Philadelphia. Pennsylvania, and until now has held all its dialogues in the United States. Thanks to the joint invitations by three organizations—the *Akademie Graz* (Graz Academy) with its President Emil Breisach, and the *Afro-Asiatisches Institut Graz* (Afro-Asian Institute of Graz) with it head Stefan Doblhofer, as well as the *Sektion Graz ökumenischen Stiftung PRO ORIENTE* (Graz Section of the Ecumenical Foundation Pro Oriente) with its head Professor Philipp Harnoncourt—the 1993 dialogue could take place here in Austria. As Founder and Protector of the Foundation Pro Oriente, which has made the dialogue with the Churches of the East its purpose, and also as a Professor Emeritus of Religious Studies, I gladly accept the invitation to write a foreword for the publication of the proceedings of the dialogue.

With its meeting in Graz, Austria, ISAT was close to the border of those areas of former Yugoslavia where members of different nations and religions face each other in war—in contradiction to their holy scriptures, but with newly inflamed nationalist emotions which not seldom appear to be strengthened by religion. Likewise in the Near East as well as in many other places in the world, members of different faiths live in conflict with one another; moreover, it is often difficult to discern whether nationalist, social or religious tensions are the cause thereof. Indeed, with some peoples the enmities seem to be essential elements of their historical heritage. In the past and in the present religions and religious movements of the world were—and still are—misused and the ideals in the respective holy scriptures were and are often misunderstood or distorted. Without patient dialogue between the conflicting parties no lasting peaceful resolutions can be arrived at, and without respectful tolerance and peace between the religions no lasting peace among the peoples and cultures are to be attained.

But it did not need these catastrophes in order to lift up the importance, indeed, the necessity, of dialogue between the religions: Our age is experiencing an encounter, and not seldom even a mixing, of peoples, cultures and religions of the whole world as never before in the entire history of humankind. The new possibilities of transportation and mass communication have relativized all distances and made the world small. Everywhere, whether happily or unhappily, we experience the surprising variety of languages, ways of thinking, traditions, cultures, confessions and religions in the nations and continents of the earth. Many experience this encounter with what was until then unknown and strange as a gift, but others experience it as unsettling or threatening to their identity and react with anxiety, defensiveness and exclusion. The question of living with each other in one world manifests itself in stark clarity as a question of survival for the future of humankind.

Our world, our living space has become more and more consciously a space of common fate for all women and men. We are all affected jointly and thus joined together by the same problems, like that of the just distribution of the goods of this earth. And ultimately we all are likewise especially challenged by the burning question of the protection of a livable environment—not only for us but also for coming generations. Some of these problems can be solved by agreements and treaties and others can draw on scientific advice. To resolve ethical problems, to establish a common responsibility and to recognize a meaning and value in the whole of life the religions both individually and jointly are drawn into the plan. Without a dialogue together, however, that will not be possible.

In the history of the three Abrahamic religions—Jewish, Christian, Muslim—which through their belief in the one God are bound together in a special way, there have been epochs and places of peaceful living together and mutual great respect. Ashamedly, however, we must confirm that much more often have there been conflicts and enmities, indeed, even wars and murderous persecutions in which always the weaker ones were the victims. True, we cannot undo those events, but we can and must admit our guilt, forgive one another and ask for reconciliation. And we can and must learn from history in order to discern our responsibility today toward God, humanity and creation and to step forward for justice, reconciliation and peace.

The "ISAT" Jewish-Christian-Muslim dialogue group has already taken important steps toward this goal in its dialogues up to now. It was first concerned to come to know each other so that then concrete theological as well as historical and contemporary questions could be fundamentally reflected on. The theological reflection in Graz on what Jews, Christians and Muslims each designate as "the good," and the discussions on a "Universal Declaration of a Global Ethic" seem to me to be particularly important precisely in the present world situation.

For all those who believe in the one God of Abraham, indissolubly bound up with the pressing ethical questions is the question of the meaning of human existence. In the search for the authentic meaning and ultimate purpose of all life, in the search for what is truly good and evil, in the search for the meaning of suffering and of death, humanity awaits an answer from the various religions. The Second Vatican Council (1962-65) opened up for the Roman Catholic Church new perspectives in these matters: the disdainful judgment of Christianity toward all non-Christian religions and the parallel colonial, political and cultural expansion of the "Christian West" have now given way to an opening towards those of other faiths which is characterized by tolerance and an appreciative evaluation. In the conciliar decree on non-Christian religions, *Nostra aetate*, we read: "The Church has also a high regard for the Muslims. They worship God, who is one, living and subsistent, merciful and almighty, the Creator of heaven and earth, who has also spoken to men. They strive to subject themselves without reserve to the hidden decrees of God, just as Abraham submitted himself to God's plan, to whose faith Muslims eagerly link their own." (*Nostra aetate* 3) And concerning the Jews the same Council said: "Sounding the depths of the mystery which is the Church, this sacred Council remembers the spiritual ties which link the people of the New Covenant to the stock of Abraham." (*Nostra aetate* 4) Jews, Christian and Muslims call upon a common Father, on Abraham, whom the Apostle Paul in the fourth chapter of his Letter to the Romans called the "Father of Belief."

In dialogue it is possible to discern better those things which are common, similar and different. The temptation is great to maintain that one's own conviction is the only correct one and that one's own faith community is the best, and thus ascribe to one's own confessional, religious and cultural identity an absolute validity, thereby denying truth and the right of existence to the other. Dialogue, however, demands modesty and patience and a readiness to see that one's fellow humans also have a living faith, a high culture and traditions worth holding onto.

Yet another reflection appears to me to be important: Not infrequently one hears, even from representatives of religious communities, that interreligious dialogue leads to a relativization of the truth, to

3

an unsettlement of one's own faith and to lazy compromises. For all who have competently participated in the dialogue of the religions, without a doubt the encounter and discussion with men and women of other traditions constitutes a powerful challenge. This can, however, at once also bring with it a deepening of one's own faith. To be sure, interreligious dialogue demands of all participants a thorough factual knowledge, a developed life of faith, the readiness to listen, and even the courage to leave well worn paths and to think in a new manner. Through the faith witness of the other, each will be required on the one hand to place her/his own claim of absoluteness in question; on the other hand, however, new riches of religious life will also be opened up. Not seldom encounters with other religious traditions lead to a more thorough reflection on one's own theology and a more intensive living of one's own spirituality.

A change of the deposit of the faith, of the *depositum fidei*, however, is not in question; that would be the equivalent of a betrayal of one's own religious community.

Everyone who participates in interreligious dialogue must naturally be firmly rooted in his/her own faith and likewise be capable of distinguishing between central and peripheral elements. So that the dialogue and its results might have a realistic prospect of acceptance, every participant should also be a credible and authentic representative of the religious community or church to which s/he belongs. In the common search for the truth the theologians must nevertheless also be prepared and willing to listen to each other with no pre-judgments in order to come to know better the other tradition and likewise allow other convictions prove themselves. Once mutual mistrust has been dismantled and a climate of trust between religions has been established, this latter can then richly reward each side. The mystery and truth of God are so endlessly rich and deep, transcending all human conceptual power and all possibilities of linguistic expression that no religion, no theology and no spiritual tradition can even approach completely exhausting them. All who—with all correctness and firmness of faith conviction—realize their own inability exhaustively to grasp and express the mystery and the truth of God will also be eagerly ready to respect other ways of religious life, thought and speaking, indeed, even to adapt elements thereof to their own way of viewing.

Common consultations and conferences alone, however, cannot fulfill all these tasks. Hence, it gives me a special joy that the participants in this dialogue here in Austria for the first time went beyond their intellectual theological reflections and found their way together to the Stiegen Church in Graz in common prayer for reconciliation and peace. Jews, Christians and Muslims can also jointly call upon, praise and worship "their" one God—the God of Abraham, creator of heaven and earth, loyal God of the Covenant. They are also accustomed to hear the word of God and follow it. Peace-*Shalom-Eirene-Salam* is for Jews, Christians and Muslims not in the first instance the fruit of human efforts, but a holy, graced gift of God for which we pray—at once a gift of God and a task for God's people. That the establishment of understanding, reconciliation and peace is also bound up with great striving was clearly and strikingly symbolized in the fitting together of the heavy steel sections of the altar during the service.

This Jewish-Christian-Muslim prayer took place between two events which sprang from initiatives of the Roman Catholic Church: The World Day of Prayer for Peace on January 1, 1993, and the Interreligious Prayer for Peace at Assisi, Italy. on January 9-10, to which Pope John Paul II and representatives of all the European Conferences of Catholic Bishops had issued the invitation. Representatives of the three monotheistic religions—the Jewish and the Muslim faith communities as well as all the Christian Churches—were come together above all to pray for the end of wars and violence on the European continent. With faith in the one God and aware that they must give a reckoning before God, Jews, Christians and Muslims cannot withdraw themselves from their responsibility for a world that is becoming one.

Whoever looks to the future and wishes to take their obligation toward the world and humanity in the third millennium seriously will grant to the dialogue of the religions and its joint contribution to the resolution of global problems the greatest significance. I therefore enthusiastically greet the fact that the present proceedings culminating in the 1993 dialogue of ISAT in Graz will be published in English and in German, and wish these publications wide distribution and continued dialogues on all sides. And I wish with all my heart the committed efforts of ISAT God's blessing.

Cardinal Franz König, Vienna, Austria

I. JEWISH-CHRISTIAN-MUSLIM DIALOGUE

Leonard Swidler

Dialogue as the term is used today to characterize encounters between persons and groups with different religions or ideologies is something quite new under the sun. In the past when different religions or ideologies met it was mainly to overcome, to teach, the other, because each was completely convinced that it alone held the secret of the meaning of human life.

More and more in recent times sincerely convinced persons of different religions and ideologies have slowly come to the conviction that they did not hold the secret of the meaning of human life entirely unto themselves, that in fact they had something very important to learn from each other. As a consequence they approached their encounters with other religions and ideologies not primarily in the teaching mode—holding the secret of life alone—but *primarily* in the learning mode—seeking to find more of the secret of the meaning of life. That is dialogue.

The question I wish to address here is why it is important for specifically Jews, Christians and Muslims to enter into dialogue—beyond the general reason just mentioned—starting with the underlying reasons.

The impetus for dialogue in the contemporary world in general has come, and continues to come, mainly from Christians, and then secondly from Jews. Thus it is natural that when Islam enters into dialogue, it is most likely to first be with Christians and then Jews. To be sure, the need for dialogue between Islam and Hinduism and even Buddhism as well is underlined almost daily in the newspaper reports of mutual hostility and killings. But it is overwhelmingly the encounter with the other two Abrahamic religions, Judaism and Christianity, that has been the motor driving Islam toward dialogue.[1]

---

[1] For a brief history of one of the most organized Trialogues, see Eugene Fisher, "Kennedy Institute Jewish-Christian-Muslim Trialogue," *Journal of Ecumenical Studies*, 19,1 (Winter 1982), pp. 197-200. It consisted of twenty Jewish, Christian, and Muslim scholars, was sponsored by the Kennedy Institute of Ethics, Georgetown University. It started in 1978 and ran until 1984, meeting twice a year for three days each time. In April, 1989, another ongoing trialogue, this time international, sponsored by the *Journal of Ecumenical Studies* and the National Conference of Christians and Jews, held its first, very successful three-day meeting; a fifth was held in Graz, Austria, 1993, a sixth in Jerusalem in 1994; after a hiatus,

As a prolegomenon to understanding why this is true, it is important to list at least some of the major elements these three Semitic or Abrahamic religions have in common.

1. Elements in Common

1) They all come from the same Hebraic roots and claim Abraham as their originating ancestor: the historical, cultural and religious traditions all flow out of one original source, an *Urquelle*.

2) All three traditions are religions of ethical monotheism, that is, they all claim there is one, loving, just, creator God who is the Source, Sustainer, and Goal of all reality and that s/he expects all human beings, as images of God, to live in love and justice; in other words, belief in the One God has ethical consequences concerning oneself, other persons, and the world. This is a *common* heritage of the three Abrahamic religions, which is by no means shared by all elements of the other major world religions.

3) The three traditions are historical religions, i.e., they believe that God acts through human history, communicates through historical events, through particular human persons, preeminently Moses, Jesus, and Muhammad. Historical events, like the exodus, crucifixion, and *hijrah*, and human persons do not at all play the same central role in many other world religions, as, for example, in Hinduism and Taoism.

4) Judaism, Christianity, and Islam are religions of revelation, i.e., they are persuaded that God has communicated, revealed, something

---

the seventh will be held in Loccum, Germany in 1998.

A dialogue between Muslims and Hindus has been launched, but only on a small scale. One such between Riffat Hassan and Kana Mitra was sponsored by the *Journal of Ecumenical Studies* in 1985. See Leonard Swidler, ed., *Religious Liberty and Human Rights in Nations and Religions* (NYC & Philadelphia: Hippocrene & Ecumenical Press, 1986), pp. 109-142. A miniature dialogue between Islam and Buddhism also took place at the same conference between Mohammed Talbi and Masao Abe and published in ibid.; both are reprinted in Leonard Swidler, ed., *Muslims In Dialogue* (Lewiston, NY: Edwin Mellen Press, 1992). For further details see, Leonard Swidler, "International Annual Scholars' Trialogue (ISAT)," *Journal of Ecumenical Studies* 33,3 (Summer, 1996), pp. 360-368, and the essay on ISAT below.

of God's self and will in special ways through particular persons, but for the edification, the salvation—or said other, for the humanization, which is also the divinization—of all humankind. In all three religions this revelation has two special vehicles: prophets and scriptures.

a. Clearly in Judaism the men prophets Isaiah, Amos, Hosea, Jeremiah, and the women prophets Miriam and Huldah, etc. are outstanding "mouthpieces" of Yahweh (*pro-phetes*, one who speaks for another), and the greatest of all the prophets in Judaism is Moses. For Christianity Moses and the other prophets are God's spokespersons—but also numbered among the Christian prophets are Anna (Lk. 2:36-8), and the two daughters of Philip (Eusebius, *Eccl. Hist.* III.31), and most of all Jesus—though most Christians later came to claim something beyond prophethood for him. For Islam all these Jewish and Christian prophets are also authentic prophets, God's revealing voice in the world—and to that list they add Muhammad, the Seal of the Prophets.

b. For these three faiths God's special revelation is also communicated in "The Book," the "Bible." For Jews the Holy Scriptures are the Hebrew Bible, for Christians it is the Hebrew Bible and the New Testament, and for Muslims it is those two, plus the Qur'an, which is corrective and supplemental to the first two. For Muslims, the Jews and Christians have the special name: "People of the Book."

There are many more things that the three Abrahamic faiths have in common, such as the importance of covenant, of law and faith, of the community (witness in the three traditions the central role of the terms "People," "Church," and "Ummah," respectively). But just looking at the list of commonalities already briefly spelled out will provide us with an initial set of fundamental reasons why it was eventually perceived as imperative for Jews, Christians and Muslims to engage in serious, ongoing dialogue.

First, if Jews, Christians and Muslims believe that there is only one, loving, just God in whose image they are and whose will they claim to try to follow, they need to ask why there are three different ways of doing so—obviously that question can be faced only in dialogue.

Second, if Jews, Christians and Muslims believe that God acts through human history, that God communicates through historical events and particular human persons, they need to face the question of whether all religiously significant historical events and persons are limited to their own histories—put colloquially: Do Jews, Christians and Muslims really believe that they have God in their own historical boxes, or that, by their own principles, God transcends all limitations, including even their sacred historical events and persons?

Third, if Judaism, Christianity and Islam believe that God communicates, reveals, her/himself to humans not only through things, events, and humans in general, but also in special ways through particular events and persons, they are going to have to face the question of whether God's will as delivered through God's spokespersons, i.e., prophets, and the recording in writing of their teachings and kindred material in what is known as Holy Scriptures, is limited to their own prophets and scriptures. Concretely, Jews will have to reflect on whether Jesus and the writings of his first—Jewish—followers (the so-called New Testament) have something to say about God's will for humankind to non-Christians (and themselves?). Jews and Christians will have to reflect on whether the prophet Muhammad and his "recitation," i.e., "Qur'an," have something to say about God's will for humankind to non-Muslims (including themselves?!). Muslims of course already affirm the importance of the Jewish and Christian prophets and scriptures.

Obviously these questions, and others of serious importance concerning the ultimate meaning of life, can be addressed only in dialogue among Jews, Christians and Muslims.

Once this is recognized, however, it also immediately becomes clear that all the questions just listed which challenge the absoluteness and exclusivity of the three Abrahamic traditions' claims about having all the truth, about God being found only in the boxes of their history, prophets, scriptures, and revelation, also apply to the non-Abrahamic religions and ideologies, such as Hinduism, Buddhism and Marxism.

2. Different Dialogues—Different Goals

Pragmatically, however, one cannot engage in dialogue with all possible partners at the same time. Moreover, all the goals of one dialogue with a certain set of partners can never be fulfilled by another set of dialogue partners. For example, the goal of working toward denominational unity between the Lutheran Church in America and the American Lutheran Church would never have been accomplished if Catholics had been full partners in that dialogue with Lutherans. Or again, Jews and Christians have certain items on their mutual theological

9

agenda, e.g., the Jewish claim that the Messiah has not yet come and the Christian counter-claim, which will not be adequately addressed if Muslims are added as full partners. And so it goes with each addition or new mix of dialogue partners.

There is a special urgency about the need for Christians to dialogue among themselves to work toward the goal of some kind of effective, visible Christian unity: the absurdity and scandal of there being hundreds of separate churches all claiming "one foundation, Jesus Christ the Lord," is patent. The need for intra-Jewish dialogue I will leave to my Jewish sisters and brothers to inform me about in specifics, but it nevertheless appears apparent in general. However, for Christians, dialogue with Jews has an extraordinarily high priority that cannot be displaced, and where it has not been both initiated and continued, that exigency demands to be addressed with all possible speed and perseverance. If nothing else, the twentieth-century Holocaust of the Jews in the heart of Christendom makes this dialogue indispensable.

Nevertheless, there is something like—though not precisely—a relationship of parent and offspring which should incline Jews to enter into dialogue with Christians, and Jews and Christians with Muslims. Furthermore, there are today all the external reasons for Jewish-Christian dialogue with Islam that flow from the reality of the earth now being a global village and the unavoidable symbiotic relationship between the Judeo-Christian industrialized West and the partly oil-rich, relatively non-industrialized Islamic world.

3. Expectations from the Trialogue

A special word of caution to Jews and Christians entering into dialogue with Muslims is in order. They will be starting such a venture with several disadvantages: 1) the heritage of colonialism, 2) ignorance about Islam, 3) distorted image of Muslims, and 4) culture gap.

The vast majority of Muslims trained in Islamics are non-Westerners, which means they very likely come from a country that was until very recently a colony of the West. Many Muslims are still traumatized by Western colonialism and frequently identify Christianity, and to a lesser extent, Judaism, with the West. Jewish and Christian dialogue partners need to be aware of this and move to diffuse the problem.

10

Jews and Christians will need to make a special effort to learn about Islam beyond what was required for them intelligently to engage in the Jewish-Christian dialogue, for in the latter they usually knew at least a little about the partner's religion. With Islam they will probably be starting with a negative quantity compounded from sheer ignorance and massive misinformation.

Most often the current Western image of a Muslim is a gross distortion of Islam. Indeed, it is frequently that of some kind of inhuman monster. But the Khomeni distortion of Islam is no more representative of Islam than the Rev. Ian Paisley of Northern Ireland is of Christianity in general or Richard Nixon was of the pacifist Quaker tradition.

Most difficult of all is the fact that a huge cultural gap exists between the great majority of Muslims and precisely those Jews and Christians who are open to dialogue. In brief: Islam as a whole has not yet really experienced the "Enlightenment" and come to terms with it, as has much of the Judeo-Christian tradition, although obviously not all of it. Only a minority of Muslim Islamics scholars will share the "deab-solutized" understanding of truth needed to be able and want to enter into dialogue with "the other," that is, to converse with the religiously "other" primarily to learn religiously from her or him—which means that many efforts at dialogue with Muslims will in fact be prolegomena to true interreligious dialogue. Frequently such attempts will be not unlike "dialogue" with many Orthodox Jews or evangelical Christians—or with Roman Catholics before Vatican II.

But the prolegomena must be traversed in order to reach authentic dialogue. In this case surely the words of the Vatican and Pope Paul VI apply to all Christians and Jews and Muslims, who "must assuredly be concerned for their separated brethren...making the first approaches toward them.... dialogue is *demanded* nowadays .... by the pluralism of society, and by the maturity man has reached in this day and age."[2] It is toward that end all Christians, Jews and Muslims are urged to strive, first among themselves and then with each other in pairs and all together.

---

[2] *Ecclesiam suam*, no. 78, quoted in Austin Flannery, *Vatican Council II* (Collegeville, MN: Liturgical Press, 1975), p. 1003.

11

4. Muslim Critical Thinkers

Despite the facts of the cultural gap and that only a minority of Muslim Islamicists have a "deabsolutized" view of truth, there are today many more of them than is usually recognized. Often, however, they live outside the Muslim world. Let me recall a personal experience exemplifying why:

An Egyptian Muslim Islamicist spent a number of years studying and teaching in America. At that time he made his own the historical critical mentality and was very open to interreligious dialogue. We spoke quite specifically about a "dialogic" article he wished to write for the *Journal of Ecumenical Studies*. Suddenly for family reasons he had to return to Egypt and shortly thereafter took a position teaching Islamics at a university in Saudi Arabia. After two years of correspondence and coaxing he wrote me in despair that he could not write the article we had worked out together so long as he was in the Arabian world; the intellectual atmosphere was just too restrictive for him to be able to think the thoughts he would have to in order to write the article.

The Muslim scholar in question was Fathi Osman who taught with me at Temple University in 1975\76, during which time he wrote a review article on Christology that was published in *JES* in 1977.[3] He most recently returned to the United States, and joined the Jewish-Christian-Muslim trialogue sponsored by JES and the NCCJ—and is again his former liberated self—and then some (more on this below).

The same point was made poignantly by Fazlur Rahman: "Free thought and thought are synonymous, and one cannot hope that thought will survive without freedom.... Islamic thought, like all thought, equally requires a freedom by dissent, confrontation of views, and debate between ideas is assured."[4]

Professor Rahman, who until his death in 1988 was for many years at the University of Chicago, knew well whereof he spoke. He was the Minister of Education of the newly created Pakistan from 1947

---

[3] Fathi Osman, Zalman Schachter, Gerard Sloyan, and Dermot Lane, "Jesus in Jewish-Christian-Muslim Dialogue," *Journal of Ecumenical Studies*, 14,3 (Summer, 1977), pp. 448-65.

[4] Fazlur Rahman, *Islam* (New York: Doubleday, 1968), p. 125.

to 1957, and from 1962 to 1968 he was Director of a newly formed Islamic Research Institute (established by President Ayub Khan).

> But even as the institute was a little less than halfway through to the initial stage of its goal, it became the victim of a massive attack of the combined forces of the religious right and the opposition politicians. I resigned in September 1968 and the Ayub Khan government fell six months later, and, although this group of progressive scholars has done its best to maintain itself, it has since been overwhelmed by the forces of reaction.[5]

Nevertheless, critical thinking among Muslim Islamicists has broken through. The Yugoslavian Muslim Smail Balic wrote that,

> In regard to research into the real occasions for the individual revelations of the Qur'an, and the consequent legal philosophy, not enough is done seriously to distinguish the time-bound elements from the enduring. The knowledge that the Qur'an is in part also a collection of time-related documents from the early history of Islam has not yet been able to move beyond pure theory.[6]

The Indian Muslim Asaf A. A. Fyzee stated that,

> For me it is clear that we cannot "go back" to the Qur'an. Rather, we must go forward with it. I want to *understand* the Qur'an as the Arabs of the time of the Prophet did only in order *to interpret it anew*, in order to apply it to my living conditions and to believe in it insofar as it speaks to me as a human person of the twentieth century.[7]

---

[5] Ibid.

[6] Smail Balic, *Ruf vom Minareth* (Berlin, 1979), p. 90.

[7] Cited in Rotraud Wielandt, *Offenbarung und Geschichte im Denken moderner Muslime* (Wiesbaden: F. Steiner, 1971), p. 159.

The Professor of Arabic Language and Islamic Culture at the University of Paris and, for a time, Temple University, Muhammad M. Arkoun, severely criticized at a Christian-Muslim dialogue in Bonn in 1981 the kind of dialogue wherein the conservative and fundamentalist elements of each side simply reenforced each other; rather, he wanted modern critical scholarly thought brought to bear on both religions and their dialogue: "For this reason I demand in what concerns me a critically new reading of the Scripture (Bible, Gospels, Qur'an) and a philosophical critique of exegetical and theological reason."[8] Professor Arkoun recently argued this point even more forcefully and with great stress on the need to study religions together:

> In this context where struggling ideologies are at work, it seems totally romantic, irrelevant, and useless to engage in debates between religions about traditional faiths, values, or dogmas. Positive and efficient initiatives should be taken in the field of education: primary and secondary schools, universities, the mass media, nongovernmental organizations and other private and public institutions, so as to promote a new teaching of history, *comparative* cultures, *comparative* religions, *comparative* philosophies and theologies, *comparative* literature and law.[9]

After spelling out in some detail how this comparative study should be carried out with the aid of modern critical scholarly tools, Arkoun concluded:

> This is, in very short allusive terms, my proposal as a Muslim scholar—not to contribute, I repeat to an encounter that would mean that we think and work within the framework of *I and we vs. you and them* but to the creation of a new space of intelligibility and freedom. We

---

[8] Cited in M. S. Abdulla, ed., *Der Glaube in Kulture*, Recht und Politik (Mainz: Hase & Koehler, 1982), p. 142.

[9] Mohammad Arkoun, "New Perspectives for a Jewish-Christian-Muslim Dialogue," *Journal of Ecumenical Studies*, 25,3 (Summer, 1989).

need to be emancipated from inherited traditions not yet studied and interpreted with controlled methods and cognitive principles.

Muslims are currently accused of being closed-minded, integrists, fundamentalists, prisoners of dogmatic beliefs. Here is a liberal, modern, humanist, Muslim proposal. I await the response of Jews, Christians, and secularists to my invitation to engage our thoughts, our endeavors, and our history in the cause of peace, progress, emancipation, justice through knowledge, and shared spiritual values.[10]

Perhaps the most thorough-going exponent of the historical-critical method's being indispensable to ascertaining the correct meaning of the foundation of Islam, the Qur'an, was Fazlur Rahman. He clearly argued that the text can be understood only in context:

> The Qur'an is the divine response, through the Prophet's mind, to the moral-social situation of the Prophet's Arabia.... It is literally God's response through Muhammad's mind (this latter factor has been radically underplayed by the Islamic orthodoxy) to a historic situation (a factor like wise drastically restricted by the Islamic orthodoxy).[11]

Like Asaf Fyzee, Rahman too wished to get to the original meaning of the Qur'an so it can be applied, *mutatis mutandis,* now:

> There has to be a two-fold movement: First one must move from the concrete case treatments of the Qur'an—taking the necessary and relevant social conditions of that time into account—to the general principles upon which the entire teaching converges. Second, from this general level there must be a movement back to specific legisla-

---

[10] Ibid.

[11] Rahman, *Islam,* pp. 5, 8.

15

tion, taking into account the necessary and relevant social
conditions now obtaining.[12]

This is very much like the "two-pole" theology of many
contemporary Christian theologians (e.g., Hans Küng and Edward
Schillebeeckx). From this there follows another logical step—again like
that of many progressive Christian theologians, and similarly criticized
from the respective bastions of orthodoxy—namely, that "the tradition
will therefore be more an object of judgment of the new understanding
[of the Scripture] than an aid to it."[13]

Moreover, Rahman rejected the notion that, "any significant
interpretation of the Qur'an can be absolutely monolithic.... the
Prophet's companions themselves sometimes understood certain
Qur'anic verses differently, and this was within his knowledge."[14]
Further, "It is obviously not necessary that a certain interpretation once
accepted must continue to be accepted; there is always both room and
necessity for new interpretation, for this is, in truth, an ongoing
process."[15]

It is precisely this last point that was raised to the level of a
critical hermeneutical methodological principle in dealing with the
Qur'an by Ustaz Mahmud Muhammad Taha from the Sudan. Taha was
an engineer and a sufi mystic who worked tirelessly for the reform of
Islam both inwardly and outwardly. He was tragically executed at age
75 in January of 1985 in a final outburst of violence by General Nimieri
before his overthrow a number of weeks later. However, Taha's thought
continues in his followers, such as the jurist Abdullahi Ahmed An
Na'im.

Taha argued that the shift from the earlier revelation of
principles in Mecca to the later one in Medina is essentially reversible.
The Mecca principles are fundamentally open, liberal, liberating
principles, whereas the Medina principles are specific and restrictive.

---

[12] Ibid., p. 20.

[13] Ibid., p. 7.

[14] Ibid., p. 144.

[15] Ibid., p. 145.

The shift was made because in the concrete circumstances—both the external ones and the then internal capabilities of the Muslims—the Mecca principles could not yet be implemented in all their openness. They were the ideal, on the way to which Medina was but a way-station; it is now time for the Muslims to leave the Medina way-station and move forward toward fulfilling the liberating Mecca ideal. This in brief is the heart of the teaching of Taha, filled out with Qur'anic citations and argumentation of course.[16]

Mohammed Talbi of the University of Tunisia at Tunis has for years been active both nationally and internationally in dialogue with Christians, receiving the Lukas Prize for his contributions to interreligious dialogue from the Protestant Theological Faculty of the University of Tübingen in May, 1985 (the funding for the Lukas Prize comes from the family of Rabbi Lukas, who had been a student at Tübingen). Representative of Talbi's self-critical, yet islamically-committed, thought are his reflections on "Religious Liberty: A Muslim Perspective":

> In short, from the Muslim perspective that is mine, our duty is simply to bear witness in the most courteous way that is most respectful of the inner liberty of our neighbors and their sacredness. We must also be ready at the same time to listen to them in truthfulness. We have to remember, as Muslims, that a *hadith* of our Prophet states: "The believer is unceasingly in search of wisdom; wherever he finds it he grasps it." Another saying adds: "Look for knowledge everywhere, even as far as in China." And finally, it is up to God to judge, for we, as

---

[16] See Abdullahi Ahmed El Naiem, "A Modern Approach to Human Rights in Islam: Foundations and Implications for Africa," in Claude Welch and Ronald Meltzer, eds., *Human Rights and Development in Africa* (Albany: State University of New York Press, 1984), pp. 75-89; "Religious Freedom in Egypt: Under the Shadow of the Islamic *Dhimma* System," Swidler, *Religious Liberty and Human Rights*, pp. 43-62. An-Na'im has translated into English Taha's 1967 fundamental work *The Second Message of Islam* (Syracuse University Press, 1987), but because An-Na'im was also imprisoned for years, the English translation was published only in 1987. See also Abdullahi An-Na'im, "Mahmud Muhammad Taha and the Crisis in Islamic Law Reform: Implications for Interreligious Relations," *Journal of Ecumenical Studies*, 25,1 (Winter, 1988), pp. 1-21,

17

limited human beings, know only in part. Let me quote:
"To each among you We prescribed a Law and an Open
Way. And if God had enforced His Will, He would have
made of you all one people. But His plan is to test you in
what He hath given you. So strive as in a race in all
virtues. The goal of you all is to God. Then will He
inform you of that wherein you differed" (Qur'an, V,
51)....

At the heart of this problem we meet the ticklish
subject of apostasy...the Qur'an argues, warns and advises,
but never resorts to the argument of the sword. That is
because that argument is meaningless in the matter of
faith. In our pluralistic world our modern theologians
must take that into account.

We can never stress too much that religious
liberty is not an act of charity or a tolerant concession
towards misled persons. It is a fundamental right of
everyone. To claim it for myself implies *ipso facto* that I
am disposed to claim it for my neighbor too.[17]

Hasan Askari, formerly Chairperson of the Sociology Department of Muslim University of Aligarh, India, and then a Fellow at the
Center for the Study of Islam and Christian-Muslim Relations, Selly
Oak Colleges, Birmingham, U.K., has long espoused authentic interreligious dialogue, placing at the base of which a deabsolutized understanding of truth:

One who does not allow for alternatives within one's own
religious tradition may not allow for more than one
religious approach.... [But we must] hesitate to absolutise
any of the approaches within one or other plurality as the

---

[17] From a lecture at a *Journal of Ecumenical Studies* sponsored
conference at Temple University, Nov. 3-8, 1985: "Religious Tolerance and
Human Rights within the International Community, within Nations and
within Religions." An earlier version was given at the Second World
Congress on Religious Liberty, Rome, Sept. 3-4, 1984. Published as
"Religious Liberty: A Muslim Perspective," in, Swidler, *Religious Liberty*,
pp. 181, 187.

only true approach.... All religions, and all approaches within each one of them, are relative to the Absolute Truth [God].... The worst of all defiance is to be locked up within one's own tradition and refuse to embrace each and every one, whatever his or her face and creed.[18]

Likewise deeply involved as critical-thinking, committed Muslims in interreligious dialogue not only with Christians but also with Jews—and others—are the Moroccan Khalid Duran (long at the Deutsches Orient Institut at Hamburg, and more recently at Temple University, the American University, the University of California, Irvine, the Foreign Policy Research Institute in Philadelphia, and now Founder and Editor of the quarterly *TransStateIslam*),[19] and the Pakistani/American Riffat Hassan, Chair of the Religious Studies Program, University of Louisville in Kentucky.[20]

Duran has been active for years in Jewish-Christian-Muslim Trialogue, first in England, then in Germany, and now in the United States, where among other things he has served as the Muslim Coordinator of the "International Scholars Jewish-Christian-Muslim Dialogue." His thought and writings are a rich source for dialogic bridge-building. For example, on the complicated issue of Christian Mission/Muslim Dawa, from the Muslim side he insists that "Islamic religion—or 'normative' Islam—provides ample scope for a concept of mission

---

[18] Hasan Askari, "Within and Beyond the Experience of Religious Diversity," John Hick, Hasan Askari, eds. *The Experience of Religious Diversity* (Hants, England: Gower, 1985), pp. 191, 217. See also his article, "The Dialogical Relationship Between Christianity and Islam," *Journal of Ecumenical Studies*, 9,3 (Summer, 1972).

[19] *TransStateIslam* is published in Washington, DC. See also, Khalid Duran, "Muslim Openness to Dialogue," Leonard Swidler, ed., *Toward a Universal Theology of Religion* (Maryknoll, NY: Orbis Books, 1987), pp. 210-217; "Religious Liberty and Human Rights in the Sudan," Swidler, *Religious Liberty*, pp. 61-78.

[20] See, e.g., Riffat Hassan, "Messianism and Islam," *Journal of Ecumenical Studies*, 22, 2 (Spring, 1985), pp. 261-291; "The Basis for a Hindu-Muslim Dialogue and Steps in that Direction from a Muslim Perspective," Swidler, *Religious Liberty*, pp. 125-142.

adjustable to a pluralist society."[21] He centers this claim in the "central theme of Al-Qur'an, namely, humanity's responsibility for this world, its mission as God's vicegerent—humanity as the administrator (Caliph) of the earth. This is a broader sense of mission and a more essential one than that of mere proselytizing." He notes that,

> As such, there is no inherent inability in Islam to conceive of mission as something above and beyond proselytizing. The difficulty lies with an onerous historical legacy that has come to be misunderstood as Islam per se. It would be patently wrong to gloss over this formidable obstacle to pluralism. Muslims need to be made aware of the disparities between their faith and their practice. This will remain difficult as long as education remains the privilege of a few percent of the population, with the standards of religious education, moreover, on the decline.[22]

Duran then moves in the direction of strongly advocating the separation of religion and state in his promotion of what he refers to as "secularism," which he insists is needed "as a means of protecting Muslims against themselves, or, more precisely, of protecting some Muslims against some others, not to speak of secularism as a protection of non-Muslims from Muslims."[23]

Riffat Hassan has been active in the Trialogue in America since 1979, and recently established an ongoing Christian-Muslim Dialogue in her native Pakistan. Hassan's writings also are a rich source of dialogue material with not only Christians and Jews, but also with all religious persons and all those of "good will." This is particularly clear

[21] Khalid Duran, "Muslims and Non-Muslims," in: Leonard Swidler and Paul Mojzes, eds., *Attitudes of Religions and Ideologies Toward the Outsider* (Lewiston, NY: Edwin Mellen Press, 1990), p. 97 ; and in: Leonard Swidler, *Muslims In Dialogue* (Lewiston, NY: Edwin Mellen Press, 1992), p. 103.

[22] Ibid., pp. 103f.

[23] Ibid., p. 108.

in her reflections on Islam and human rights, for which as a general context she claims that

> It is imperative that Muslims rethink their position on all vital issues, since we can no longer afford the luxury of consoling ourselves for our present miseries and misfortunes by an uncritical adulation of a romanticized past. History has brought us to a point where rhetoric will not rescue us from reality and where the discrepancies between Islamic theory and Muslim practice will have to be accounted for.[24]

Hassan then went on to insist that "human rights....are so deeply rooted in our humanness that their denial or violation is tantamount to a negation or degradation of that which makes us human." Human rights, she wrote, "were created, as we were, by God in order that our human potential could be actualized." Because human rights are not a human invention, "I do not look for their origin or essence in books of law or history but in those books of scripture which contain God's eternal message and guidance to humankind."[25] Hassan then spells out at least seventeen specific human rights asserted in the Qur'an.

Riffat Hassan penultimately ends her essay with severe criticism:

> If Muslims were to exercise all the human rights granted to humankind by God, they would create a Paradise on earth and have no need to spend their time and energy dreaming about the "*hur*" promised in the afterlife. Unfortunately, at this time the spectrum before us appears very bleak, as more and more human rights disappear under the pressure of mounting fanaticism and traditionalism in many areas of the Muslim world. I am particularly

---

[24] Riffat Hassan, "On Human Rights and the Qur'anic Perspective," in: Arlene Swidler, ed., *Human Rights in Religious Traditions* (New York: Pilgrim Press, 1982), p. 54; and in: Leonard Swidler, ed., *Muslims In Dialogue* (Lewiston, NY: Edwin Mellen Press, 1992), p. 449.

[25] Ibid., p. 450.

21

concerned about serious violations of human rights
pertaining to the rights of women, the rights of minorities,
the right of the accused to due process of law, and the
right of the Muslim masses to be free of dictatorships.

hope":

However, ultimately she ends with a note of "hope against
hope":

In the end we have what seems to be an irreconcilable
gulf between Qur'anic ideals and the realities of Muslim
living. Can this gulf be bridged? To me, the answer is
immaterial, because those of us who believe that human
rights cannot be abandoned, even when they are being
denied and aborted, will continue to strive and hope and
pray for the securing of these rights—regardless of the
chances of success or failure.[26]

It should be added that Riffat Hassan, besides being deeply
involved in interreligious dialogue, is also one of those rare creatures,
a Muslim feminist. Amidst a life of many demands, she is striving to
finish a major book on women in Islam. On the way to it she has
published a number of essays on the topic.[27]

5. Conclusion: A Commission

Since 1989, the "Annual International Scholars Jewish-
Christian-Muslim Dialogue" has been meeting in the United States,
Europe and the Middle East though the nine scholars from each of the
three traditions come from all over the world. Very productive progress
has been made, including the publishing of this volume. With such
dialogue partners, and others not here mentioned, authentic dialogue on

---

[26] Ibid. p. 463.

[27] See, e.g., Riffat Hassan, "'Jihad Fi Sabil Allah': A Muslim Woman's
Faith Journey from Struggle to Struggle to Struggle," Leonard Grob, Riffat
Hassan and Haim Gordon, eds., *Women's and Men's Liberation - Testimo-
nies of Spirit* (New York: Greenwood Press, 1991), pp. 11-30; "The Issue
of Woman-Man Equality in the Islamic Tradition," ibid., pp. 65-82.

the highest level, and not just prolegomena thereto, between Islam, Judaism and Christianity, and other religions as well, is not only possible—it is actual!

However, important as this scholarly level dialogue is—and it is extremely important, for these scholars are the shapers of the shapers of opinion—the dialogue must also be translated onto the middle and grass-roots levels. That in part is the responsibility of every reader of this essay.

I urge, then, you readers to immediately begin to make use of the work of these pioneer scholars in dialogue, both through their writings, and even more so in person. Begin the work of dialogue with sensitivity to your "other" sister and brother and persevere in it, for it will lead not only to a cessation of hostilities and a resolution of tensions, but it will also lead to a deepening and enriching of your own inner and communal life.

II. THE DIALOGUE DECALOGUE
Ground Rules for Interreligious, Interideological Dialogue

Leonard Swidler

Dialogue is a conversation on a common subject between two or more persons with differing views, the primary purpose of which is for each participant to learn from the other so that s/he can change and grow. This very definition of dialogue embodies the first commandment of dialogue.

In the religious-ideological sphere in the past, we came together to discuss with those differing with us, for example, Catholics with Protestants, either to defeat an opponent, or to learn about an opponent so as to deal more effectively with her or him, or at best to negotiate with him or her. If we faced each other at all, it was in confrontation—sometimes more openly polemically, sometimes more subtly so, but always with the ultimate goal of defeating the other, because we were convinced that we alone had the absolute truth.

But dialogue is *not* debate. In dialogue each partner must listen to the other as openly and sympathetically as s/he can in an attempt to understand the other's position as precisely and, as it were, as much from within, as possible. Such an attitude automatically includes the assumption that at any point we might find the partner's position so persuasive that, if we would act with integrity, we would have to change, and change can be disturbing.

We are here, of course, speaking of a specific kind of dialogue, an interreligious, interideological dialogue. To have such, it is not sufficient that the dialogue partners discuss a religious-ideological subject, that is, the meaning of life and how to live accordingly. Rather, they must come to the dialogue as persons somehow significantly identified with a religious or ideological community. If I were neither a Christian nor a Marxist, for example, I could not participate as a "partner" in Christian-Marxist dialogue, though I might listen in, ask some questions for information, and make some helpful comments.

It is obvious that interreligious, interideological dialogue is something new under the sun. We could not conceive of it, let alone do it in the past. How, then, can we effectively engage in this new thing? The following are some basic ground rules, or "commandments," of interreligious, interideological dialogue that must be observed if dialogue is actually to take place. These are not theoretical rules, or commandments given from "on high," but ones that have been learned from hard experience.

FIRST COMMANDMENT: *The primary purpose of dialogue is to learn, that is, to change and grow in the perception and understanding of reality, and then to act accordingly.* Minimally, the very fact that I learn that my dialogue partner believes "this" rather than "that" proportionally changes my attitude toward her; and a change in my attitude is a significant change in me. We enter into dialogue so that *we* can learn, change, and grow, not so we can force change on the *other*, as one hopes to do in debate—a hope realized in inverse proportion to the frequency and ferocity with which debate is entered into. On the other hand, because in dialogue *each* partner comes with the intention of learning and changing herself, one's partner in fact will also change. Thus the goal of debate, and much more, is accomplished far more effectively by dialogue.

SECOND COMMANDMENT: *Interreligious, interideological dialogue must be a two-sided project—within each religious or ideological community and between religious or ideological communities.* Because of the "corporate" nature of interreligious dialogue, and since the primary goal of dialogue is that each partner learn and change himself, it is also necessary that each participant enter into dialogue not only with his partner across the faith line—the Lutheran with the Anglican, for example—but also with his coreligionists, with his fellow Lutherans, to share with them the fruits of the interreligious dialogue. Only thus can the whole community eventually learn and change, moving toward an ever more perceptive insight into reality.

THIRD COMMANDMENT: *Each participant must come to the dialogue with complete honesty and sincerity.* It should be made clear in what direction the major and minor thrusts of the tradition move, what the future shifts might be, and, if necessary, where the participant has difficulties with her own tradition. No false fronts have any place in dialogue.

Conversely—each participant must assume a similar complete honesty and sincerity in the other partners. Not only will the absence of sincerity prevent dialogue from happening, but the absence of the

Leonard Swidler

assumption of the partner's sincerity will do so as well. In brief: no trust, no dialogue.

FOURTH COMMANDMENT: *In interreligious, interideological dialogue we must not compare our ideals with our partner's practice,* but our ideals with our partner's ideals, our practice with our partner's practice.

FIFTH COMMANDMENT: *Each participant must define himself.* Only the Jew, for example, can define what it means to be a Jew. The rest can only describe what it looks like from the outside. Moreover, because dialogue is a dynamic medium, as each participant learns, he will change and hence continually deepen, expand, and modify his self-definition as a Jew—being careful to remain in constant dialogue with fellow Jews. Thus it is mandatory that each dialogue partner define what it means to be an authentic member of his own tradition.

Conversely—the one interpreted must to recognize herself in the interpretation. This is the golden rule of interreligious hermeneutics, as has been often reiterated by the "apostle of interreligious dialogue," Raimundo Panikkar. For the sake of understanding, each dialogue participant will naturally attempt to express for herself what she thinks is the meaning of the partner's statement; the partner must be able to recognize herself in that expression. The advocate of "a world theology," Wilfred Cantwell Smith, would add that the expression must also be verifiable by critical observers who are not involved.

SIXTH COMMANDMENT: *Each participant must come to the dialogue with no hard-and-fast assumptions as to where the points of disagreement are.* Rather, each partner should not only listen to the other partner with openness and sympathy but also attempt to agree with the dialogue partner as far as is possible while still maintaining integrity with his own tradition; where he absolutely can agree no further without violating his own integrity, precisely there is the real point of disagreement—which most often turns out to be different from the point of disagreement that was falsely assumed ahead of time.

26

SEVENTH COMMANDMENT: *Dialogue can take place only between equals,* or *par cum pari* as Vatican II put it. Both must come to learn from each other. Therefore, if, for example, the Muslim views Hinduism as inferior, or if the Hindu views Islam as inferior, there will be no dialogue. If authentic interreligious, interideological dialogue between Muslims and Hindus is to occur, then both the Muslim and the Hindu must come mainly to learn from each other; only then will it be "equal with equal," *par cum pari.* This rule also indicates that there can be no such thing as a one-way dialogue. For example, Jewish-Christian discussions begun in the 1960's were mainly only prolegomena to interreligious dialogue. Understandably and properly, the Jews came to these exchanges only to teach Christians, although the Christians came mainly to learn. But, if authentic interreligious dialogue between Christians and Jews is to occur, then the Jews must also come mainly to learn; only then will it too be *par cum pari.*

EIGHTH COMMANDMENT: *Dialogue can take place only on the basis of mutual trust.* Although interreligious, interideological dialogue must occur with some kind of "corporate" dimension, that is, the participants must be involved as members of a religious or ideological community—for instance, as Marxists or Taoists—it is also fundamentally true that it is only *persons* who can enter into dialogue. But a dialogue among persons can be built only on personal trust. Hence it is wise not to tackle the most difficult problems in the beginning, but rather to approach first those issues most likely to provide some common ground, thereby establishing the basis of human trust. Then, gradually, as this personal trust deepens and expands, the more thorny matters can be undertaken. Thus, as in learning we move from the known to the unknown, so in dialogue we proceed from commonly held matters—which, given our mutual ignorance resulting from centuries of hostility, will take us quite some time to discover fully—to discuss matters of disagreement.

NINTH COMMANDMENT: *Persons entering into interreligious, interideological dialogue must be at least minimally self-critical of both themselves and their own religious or ideological traditions.* A lack of such self-criticism implies that one's own tradition already has all the correct answers. Such an attitude makes dialogue not only unnecessary, but even impossible, since we enter into dialogue primarily so *we* can learn—which obviously is impossible if our tradition has never made a misstep, if it has all the right answers. To be sure, in interreligious, interideological dialogue one must stand within a religious or ideological tradition with integrity and conviction, but such integrity and conviction must include, not exclude, a healthy self-criticism. Without it there can be no dialogue—and, indeed, no integrity.

TENTH COMMANDMENT: *Each participant eventually must attempt to experience the partner's religion or ideology "from within";* for a religion or ideology is not merely something of the head, but also of the spirit, heart, and "whole being," individual and communal. John Dunne here speaks of "passing over" into another's religious or ideological experience and then coming back enlightened, broadened, and deepened. As Raimundo Panikkar notes, "To know what a religion says, we must understand what it says, but for this we must somehow believe in what it says": for example, "A Christian will never fully understand Hinduism if he is not, in one way or another, converted to Hinduism. Nor will a Hindu ever fully understand Christianity unless he, in one way or another, becomes Christian."

Interreligious, interideological dialogue operates in three areas: the practical, where we collaborate to help humanity; the depth or "spiritual" dimension where we attempt to experience the partner's religion or ideology "from within"; the cognitive, where we seek understanding and truth. Interreligious, interideological dialogue also has three phases. In the first phase we unlearn misinformation about each other and begin to know each other as we truly are. In phase two we begin to discern values in the partner's tradition and wish to appropriate them into our own tradition. For example, in the Buddhist-Christian dialogue Christians might learn a greater appreciation of the meditative tradition, and Buddhists might learn a greater appreciation of the prophetic, social justice tradition—both values traditionally strongly, though not exclusively, associated with the other's community. If we are serious, persistent, and sensitive enough in the dialogue, we may at times enter into phase three. Here we together begin to explore new areas of reality, of meaning, and of truth, of which neither of us had even been aware before. We are brought face to face with this new, as-yet-unknown-to-us dimension of reality only because of questions, insights, probings produced in the dialogue. We may thus dare to say that patiently pursued dialogue can become an instrument of new "revelation," a further "un-veiling" of reality—on which we must then act.

There is something radically different about phase one on the one hand and phases two and three on the other. In the latter we do not simply add on quantitatively another "truth" or value from the partner's tradition. Instead, as we assimilate it within our own religious self-understanding, it will proportionately transform our self-understanding. Since our dialogue partner will be in a similar position, we will then be able to witness authentically to those elements of deep value in our own tradition that our partner's tradition may well be able to assimilate with self-transforming profit. All this of course will have to be done with complete integrity on each side, each partner remaining authentically true to the vital core of his/her own religious tradition. However, in significant ways that vital core will be perceived and experienced differently under the influence of the dialogue, but, if the dialogue is carried on with both integrity and openness, the result will be that, for example, the Jew will be authentically Jewish and the Christian will be authentically Christian, not despite the fact that Judaism and/or Christianity have been profoundly "Buddhized," but because of it. And the same is true of a Judaized and/or Christianized Buddhism. There can be no talk of a syncretism here, for syncretism means amalgamating various elements of different religions into some kind of a (con)fused whole without concern for the integrity of the religions involved—which is not the case with authentic dialogue.

III. INTERNATIONAL SCHOLARS' ANNUAL TRIALOGUE (ISAT)

Leonard Swidler

1. The Origin of ISAT

"No peace among nations without peace among religions, no peace among the religions without dialogue among the religions." Thus starts the February, 1989 address of the Catholic theologian Hans Küng at the UNESCO Conference in Paris on world peace and dialogue among religions. It is precisely this concept that underlies the establishment of the long-term Jewish-Christian-Muslim scholarly dialogue known as the International Scholars' Annual Trialogue (ISAT), which held its first annual conference in the spring of 1989 in Philadelphia, Pennsylvania.

The effects of such a long-term "fundamental research and dialogue" approach to the interrelationship among the three "Semitic" religions are difficult to predict. We do know, however, that the long-term "fundamental research and dialogue" approach to the interrelationship between Protestantism and Catholicism in Germany in the 1950s had a profoundly positive effect on the revolutionary changes that Protestant-Catholic relations have undergone since the early 1960s.[1] One cannot guarantee such positive results in the much more complex Jewish-Christian-Muslims relationship, but one can guarantee that without such a "fundamental research and dialogue" approach in a long-term manner positive developments in their relationship will NOT come about. This will also insure the continued undermining of the world peace process.

ISAT is composed of 27 scholars, nine from each of the three religious traditions, Judaism, Christianity, Islam. The composition of ISAT remains basically the same, though different local participant-observers are usually invited to each annual meeting. Every effort was made to include in ISAT representatives of the major divisions of each of the three religions—women scholars as well as men scholars.

The importance of the same scholars meeting regularly is that only after certain basic understandings have been achieved and personal

---

[1] See Leonard Swidler, *The Ecumenical Vanguard* (Pittsburgh: Duquesne University Press, 1965).

trust has been won can dialogue move beyond the superficial level. That is what is happening in this interreligious "think tank." "Basic research" is being done   ere. As in basic research in the physical sciences, immediate applicability is not the primary focus, but laying the necessary foundation for any future practical developments. The ISAT scholars come (originally) from the United States, England, Israel, Germany, Yugoslavia, Greece, Austria, Morocco, Pakistan, France, Algeria, Spain, Tunisia, Egypt, Turkey.

The sponsoring bodies of ISAT have been the *Journal of Ecumenical Studies (JES)* and the National Conference (NCCJ), the former being responsible for personnel and content and the latter, finances and logistics. The General Coordinator as well as the Christian Coordinator is Prof. Leonard Swidler, Temple University, Philadelphia; the Jewish Coordinator was Prof. David Blumenthal, Emory University, Atlanta; and the Muslim Coordinator is Prof. Khalid Duran, Freie Universität Berlin, and Dr. Peter Laurence was the NCCJ Coordinator.

The *Journal of Ecumenical Studies* is a scholarly quarterly devoted to interreligious, interideological dialogue which was founded by Arlene and Leonard Swidler in 1963—the latter is still its Editor. Its Board of Associate Editors includes Catholics, Protestants, Orthodox Christians, Jews, Muslims, Hindus, Buddhists, and Taoists. Beyond that, scores of scholars around the world of the various religions regularly participate in the work of JES. JES has been judged by the Directors of Ecumenical and Interreligious Institutes around the globe as *"the world's foremost periodical of ecumenical and interreligious affairs."*

The National Conference (NCCJ) was founded in the United States in 1926 to work on all levels to eliminate religious prejudice and promote religious harmony and cooperation, first especially among Jews and Christians, but more recently also among all religions and ideological groups. It has developed over sixty-five major regional organizations in the U.S. and a multi-million dollar annual budget and has close ties with sister organizations throughout the world through the International Council of Christians and Jews (ICCJ)

ISAT met almost every year, usually immediately after New Year's day, develops its own agenda, made assignments for the preparation of what needed to be done for the next meeting, as well as whatever publication work was jointly decided on. ISAT is on the one hand careful not to force external results before they are mature, but on the other hand attempts to do whatever it can to promote Trialogue both through scholarly and more popular publications and through the mass media, particularly in the regions where it meets.

2. Initial Dialogues Test the Waters

If authentic dialogue is to occur—that is, each partner comes to learn from the other—then it is imperative that those who are open to learning from others be the invited dialogue partners. This is all the more so in a dialogue entailing Jews, Christians and Muslims for there are so many barriers among the three that is only the literally "eccentric" members of each tradition who are likely to be able to engage in such a Trialogue today.[2] After the pioneers have laid the groundwork—which doubtless will take years—then the more centrist members of each tradition will feel it is safe to tread the path of Trialogue. We know, for example, that it took decades of dangerous and often repressed and condemned dialogue between Catholic and Protestant pioneers before the breakthrough of the Decree on Ecumenism of Vatican Council II (1962-65) made it safe for the Pope to venture forth on the ecumenical journey.

ISAT's first meeting (generously funded by a Presbyterian layman, J. William Robinson) was for three days in April, 1989, in St. Raphaela Mary Catholic retreat house in Haverford, a suburb of Philadelphia, Pennsylvania, a city whose very name means "Brotherly-Sisterly Love." Because it was vital at the beginning of our project that we (1) began to get to know each other as persons, (2) set an irenic and high scholarly tone, and (3) decide on our own agenda, the three coordinators planned a very "low-key" initial program by distributing three already-published essays, one each by one of our colleagues in each of our traditions, which focused on some aspect of interreligious dialogue to serve as launching pads for our discussions. Assuming that the three papers were read ahead of time by all, commentators from each of the other two traditions were assigned for each paper and ample time for free dialogue was provided.

---

[2] See Leonard Swidler, ed., Muslims in dialogue. *The Evolution of a Dialogue* (Lewiston, NY: Edwin Mellen, 1991).

Though all of us had had a good deal of experience in dialogue, still, given the relative newness of this three-way dialogue for many of us and our widely differing backgrounds, we believed it was wise to stress from the very beginning the need for all of us consciously to strive to be as thoroughly dialogic as possible. We were successful, and an irenic but frank tone was set from the very beginning.

For the second meeting (generously funded, as were most of the subsequent meetings, by the Mormon layman James Sorenson), held in January, 1990, in Atlanta, Georgia, the theme of the assigned papers was "The Understanding of Revelation in the Three Traditions." The third meeting, in Orlando, Florida, took up the theme, "The Dilemmas of Human Dignity and Tradition" and also spent time on exegeses of the Torah, New Testament and Qur'an.

3. Jews-Christians-Muslims Pass Impasse

"We are at an impasse. Each of our traditions, Judaism, Christianity, Islam, has at its core a central 'absolute,' which is non-negotiable and blocks the possibility of genuine dialogue: The Chosen People-Promised Land, The Christ, The Qur'an." Thus the situation was described at the end of the third ISAT and consequently it was decided to make those three "absolutes" the focus of intense research: nine papers were prepared on the respective "absolutes" as found in each tradition's scriptures, history and contemporary thought.

These papers were the basis of the dialogue January, 1992 dialogue at Emory University in Atlanta. By then a deep trust among the participants had developed that allowed them to be self-critical even in front of the "outsiders," and to accept constructive critiques offered by them. "We have long since passed the stage of 'ecumenical politeness,'" remarked Pinchas Lapide, a Jewish participant from Germany-Israel, "and can now proceed to remove both the beam from our own eye and the speck from our brother's or sister's."

The "Chosen People" with its intimate connection to the "Promised Land" has been understood by Jews on one extreme to mean that the Jewish people are uniquely privileged by God and that the Holy Land (stretching from the Nile to the Euphrates, i.e, from Egypt to Iraq) has been eternally committed by God to their complete possession.

Leonard Swidler

More commonly the "Chosen People" concept has been understood to mean that the Jews—now scattered in the "diaspora"—have been
chosen to make known to the "nations" God's ethical laws (Ten
Commandments, etc.). Some Jews even spoke of possessing, that is,
living in, the Holy Land without necessarily having sovereignty.

In modern times the idea of the Chosen People has been quasi-
rejected by some Jews, as reflected in the humorous verse: "How odd
of God to choose the Jews," and even directly repudiated by others, e.g.,
Mordecai Kaplan and the Reconstructionists. Even Zionism is understood by some Jews to mean that the state in the Holy Land should
include fully non-Jews as well as Jews. Clearly the Chosen People-
Promised Land is only a "relative absolute," given to constant reinter-
pretation and negotiation.

Concerning the Christian non-negotiable "absolute," Jesus the
Christ, the variation in interpretation over the centuries has been as
great. The first followers of Jesus experienced him as a great teacher
and spokesperson, or prophet, of God: a "Rabbi" and "Nabi." Some of
his followers also saw him as the "Messiah," that is, the "Anointed One
of God" who would expel the hated occupiers of the Holy Land, re-
establish the Kingdom of Israel, and bring peace throughout the world.
Because of his execution, however, Jesus was not perceived by most
Jews thereafter as the Messiah, but for the Gentile followers the Hebrew
"Messiah" was greatly spiritualized into the Greek *Christos*, "Christ."

The largely metaphorically oriented Semitic thought pattern, and
hence language, of the New Testament was later increasingly understood
by the then mostly Hellenistic followers of Jesus as if it were Greek
abstract metaphysical language—thus in the early Ecumenical Councils
claiming divinity as well as humanity for Jesus.

This meant that Jesus the Christ was "absolute"; all truth and
goodness was to be found in him. Thus, there was no point to dialogue
with non-Christians, since they could communicate no truth or value
which the Christians did not already possess in their founder, Christ.

However, today there are many committed Christian scholars
who are convinced of the rightness of the view of the first followers of
Jesus: Jesus is experienced as a great teacher and model of how to live
an authentic human, indeed, "divine" life; moreover, Jesus was divine
for he was totally open to and permeated by all reality, including
Ultimate Reality, God. However, because Jesus' humanity was filled

with divinity does not mean that divinity did not also permeate other beings, including other religious figures.

Clearly the non-negotiable "absolute," The Christ, has been interpreted not only in the traditional exclusivistically absolute manner but also in early and contemporary Christianity in a "relatively absolute" manner, i.e. as absolutely the best teacher and model of life for Christians who also provides a model for all humans, divinity "enfleshed," without excluding the possibility of other religious figures also being teachers and models of life, also "enfleshing" divinity in themselves.

For traditional Islam (the term means "to submit" to God) its non-negotiable absolute, the Qur'an, is the very word of God dictated verbatim to Mohammed by the angel Gabriel—correcting the previous revelations of God found in the Bible, but distorted there by the Jews and Christians. Thus, not to follow the Qur'an is not to follow God's correct word, not "to submit" to God.

However, in contemporary Islam an increasing number of scholars and educated laity understand the Qur'an as God's message, and therefore absolute, but necessarily communicated to limited humans in a human, and therefore limited, language. Moreover, the Qur'an itself makes clear that God does not expect all people to follow the religion of Islam, that so long as people follow their consciences they will be blessed. Thus Islam's "non-negotiable absolute" likewise is also often understood in a non-absolute way.

Thus, a major conclusion of the intense discussions of this Trialogue was that it is obvious that each of the three "non-negotiable absolutes" have been subject to an immense amount of interpretation and "negotiation" within each tradition. Hence, they do not block dialogue, though they make it difficult at times—but also enriching!

4. The Graz Trialogue

The fifth annual Trialogue was held in January, 1993, in Graz, Austria and was locally sponsored by the Akademie Graz, Afro-Asiatisches Institut Graz, and Pro Oriente-Sektion Graz. We spent two days in closed sessions and four papers were prepared for this dialogue. Three were on the common topic: "How to Conceive and Implement the Good: A Self-Critical Reflection"—Jewish (Professor Arthur Green), Christian (Professor Paul Mojzes) and Muslim (Professor Fathi Osman).

Leonard Swidler

A fourth paper was prepared by Professor Leonard Swidler, entitled, "Towards a Universal Declaration of a Global Ethic."

One session was devoted to hearing about the situation in Bosnia from Professor Paul Mojzes, Dr. Jure Kristo, Professor Smail Balic and Professor Khalid Duran, all from or closely connected with Bosnia. One free day was spent on a tour of Graz. The fourth day was a public day with an extraordinarily sensitive and moving liturgy for peace in the morning—with music, readings from the three traditions and symbolic gestures (reuniting the altar which had been broken into four pieces). The afternoon was devoted to a public Panel Discussion by Professors Pinchas Lapide, Gordon Kaufman and Riffat Hassan, followed by a press conference and a reception by the mayor of Graz.

a) Publicity

Several Austrian newspapers from both Graz and Vienna covered the dialogue over several days. Austrian Radio also held a panel discussion with several ISAT participants, and Austrian Television carried an hour-long discussion between Rivka Horwitz, Paul Mojzes and Khalid Duran. In addition, Dr. Jochen Klicker of Radio RIAS in Berlin was a full-time participant-observer and conducted taped interviews with six ISAT participants, to be aired later; a month later he produced an hour-long discussion on Bosnia with Khalid Duran, as well as several other radio presentations by him on Islam in a dialogical context. A Cairo newspaper reporter caught up with Professor Fathi Osman (originally from Egypt) in Vienna and did a lengthy interview with him, and Mag. Gudrun Harrer of the leading Viennese newspaper *Der Standard* published a full-page overview of the dialogue along with lengthy interviews with Professor Khalid Duran and Professor Abderrahmane Lakhsassi of Morocco.

b) Books

Work of course has been completed on this book of a selection of the papers from the several sessions of the Trialogue as the first of what is foreseen as an ongoing series.[3]

---

[3] It is hoped that this volume will be the first of an ongoing series of volumes resulting from the continuing Trialogue.

c) Spin-offs

On January 12, 1993, four of our members, Professors Swidler, Lapide, Knitter and Duran, conducted a day-long Trialogue Symposion on *"Auf dem Wege zu einem gemeinsamen Weltethos"* ("Toward a Universal Global Ethic") in Munich, Germany sponsored by the "Katholisches Institut für missionstheologische Grundlagenforschung." It was extremely successful both qualitatively and quantitatively; concerning the latter, the hall held 130 places, all of which were sold out ahead of time, and an additional 80 had to be turned away!

There was coverage by the Bavarian press and an extended conversation interview with the four of us was taped by the Bavarian Radio and aired later; Bavarian Television was also present and active, taping for a later large program. The four presentations will also appear together in book form (auf deutsch), edited by Dr. Franz Wolfinger, Director of the Munich Institute. I also took the occasion of being in Germany and accepted invitations to lecture on different dimensions of interreligious dialogue at the universities of Munich, Tübingen and Regensburg. In the second and third weeks of January Professor Khalid Duran also did several lengthy radio shows on Islam through Dr. Jochen Klicker of RIAS.

5. "This Year in Jerusalem!"

We decided on two topics for 1994, namely, "Women in Judaism, Christianity and Islam," and a continuation of the issue "Toward a Universal Declaration of a Global Ethic." The topic of women in our three traditions will continue for more than one year; how it was to be approached was decided by a team consisting of Professors Riffat Hassan, Denise Carmody and Nancy Fuchs-Kreimer.

Plans to have the January, 1994 Trialogue in Los Angeles were far advanced when the revolution in the political situation in the Near East occurred. Quickly plans were changed to hold the 1994 ISAT in Jerusalem. For this, two further topics were added which would be particularly apropos for the new place and situation: "The Relationship Between Religion and Politics: Jewish, Christian and Muslim Views" and "Visions of Peace: Jewish-Christian-Muslim." This latter became the general theme of ISAT in Jerusalem.

37

All agreed that the December 31, 1993-January 5, 1994 Jerusalem ISAT meeting was a unique growth experience for everyone involved. Moreover, many dialogical encounters doubtless will be happening in Israel-Palestine because of ISAT's presence there.

We all had previously thought that a meeting in Jerusalem was many years in the future, but gathering in Jerusalem in the midst of the Peace Process was an extraordinary opportunity to be present when and where the tides of world and religious history were visibly shifting. We were always conscious of this during our short week in Yerushalaim-Jerusalem-Al Quds.

Shortly after September 13, 1993, plans began to be developed to hold the annual trialogue *not* in Los Angeles but in Jerusalem. Great pains were taken to strike a balance among Jewish, Christian, and Muslim, Israeli and Palestinian local involvement in terms of local scholars, local religious and political leaders as well as Jewish, Christian and Muslim (and Mormon) venues. Score upon score of faxes, e-mail messages, and long-distance and international phone calls and hundreds of (hu)man hours went into these preparations. Nine Local Participants were in fact eventually invited to the Trialogue, but the de facto participation was only partial, apparently because of other commitments.

Efforts to meet with religious leaders, Jewish, Christian and Muslim, of the area met with mixed results. The Anglican Bishop in Jerusalem, Rt. Rev. Samir Kafity, in fact met with ISAT twice and addressed us once. A meeting at the Al-Aksa Mosque with Muslim Religious leaders was successfully arranged. A meeting with the local Jewish religious leadership did not materialize.

Up until the last moments various high-level political leaders, both Israeli and Palestinian, were scheduled to meet with ISAT (e.g., Israeli Foreign Minister Shimon Peres, Deputy Foreign Minister Yossi Beillin, Jerusalem Mayor Ehud Ohlmert, PLO Chief Negotiator Faisel Husseini, PLO Spokesperson Hanan Ashwary, Bethlehem Mayor Elias Freij). But unpredictable diplomatic and political developments prevented many of those meetings. We did however, meet with Deputy Mayor Hanna J. Nasser of Bethlehem and two of his colleagues and with several leaders of Mr. Husseini's Arab Studies Society. On the Israeli side we had a brief visit from the former Mayor of Jerusalem Teddy Kollek and a more lengthy and very impressive audience with President Ezer Weizman of Israel.

The most impressive encounter with a local Jewish institution and its members was the day-long visit with the Shalom Hartman Institute. We received a passionately delivered address by the founder David Hartman, which was followed by an intense dialogue.

The visit (by the *Goyim*—on Shabbat afternoon) to the Roman Catholic sponsored ecumenical research and study center at Tantur (between Jerusalem and Bethlehem), with a lengthy discussion with its Rector Father Thomas Stransky, was extremely enlightening.

Almost by accident the existence of a Palestinian Christian and Muslim dialogue research center, "Al-Liqa," was discovered by Leonard Swidler in his visit with Bethlehem Lutheran Minister Mitri Raheb. A meeting of ISAT with Al-Liqa took place at their center on the edge of Bethlehem, with a presentation being given by the Director Dr. Geries Khoury. Among other things, it was learned that Al-Liqa has been involved for several years in Jewish-Christian-Muslim dialogue.

On the last evening, a reception, panel presentation (on "Visions of Peace") and discussion, followed by a dinner, was held with the Rainbow Group, an interreligious dialogue association in its 35th year of existence.

A lunch, dinner and two ISAT sessions were held at the extraordinarily beautiful Jerusalem Center of Brigham Young University. It was at this dinner that the former mayor of Jerusalem for 27 years Teddy Kollek spoke, as did also ISAT Supporter James Sorenson. The day ended with a splendid concert by the Tel Aviv Campus Symphony Orchestra, with the Tchaikovsky piano concerto with a fabulous young Galilean Arab soloist as the *pièce de résistance*.

Ultimately four scholarly dialogue topics were prepared for the Jerusalem ISAT, namely, "Women in the Three Traditions" (Denise Carmody, Nancy Fuchs-Kreimer, Rivka Horwitz, Riffat Hassan, Sona Khan), "The Relationship Between Religion and Politics" (Paul Mendes-Flohr, Leonard Swidler, Khalid Duran), "Visions of Peace: Jewish-Christian-Muslim" (Avi Ravitsky, John Cobb, Jr., Fathi Osman) and "Declaration of a Global Ethic." In fact, at the last moment the latter topic was dropped and the second-last was reduced to a single panel presentation rather than the originally planned four sessions—all because the schedule became too crowded.

Media coverage was fairly extensive, subject to the vagaries of last-minute breaking political developments. Thorough Austrian newspaper coverage was assured by the constant presence of the Arabist reporter for the Viennese daily *Der Standard* and the Viennese weekly *Die Furche*, Gudrun Harrer.

The end of the Jerusalem ISAT came with Middle East peace slowly, painfully, but most felt surely, on the way, and with most, if not all, ISAT International Participants and Staff, as well as Local Participants, exhausted but exhilarated.

6. Renewal and Dialogue-Oriented Muslim Organization Launched

For Muslims, and indeed for non-Muslims as well, who feel the need for an open-minded, committed, learned Muslim scholar of Islam for a lecture or to be a dialogue partner, a breakthrough occurred in the fall of 1996 in London: The official establishment of an international organization of renewal and dialogue-oriented Muslim thinkers and scholars, the Ibn Khaldun Society. The address is: Professor Khalid Duran, 1718 M Street NW, Suite 244, Washington, DC 20036-4504. E-mail: iis@ix.netcom.com.

These Muslim scholars are all deeply involved in a modern renewal of Islam, including interreligious dialogue. It is to this organization that Christians, Jews, and Muslims hopefully will turn when looking for Muslim lecturers and dialogue partners, and not to the so-called "fundamentalists," the Islamists, of the Islamic world.

7. The Future

It is clear that ISAT has begun to attain the necessary "critical mass" for creative "chain-reactions" to start to occur: Perhaps most importantly, the thinking of the nearly thirty ISAT scholars regularly involved as well as the many Local Participants—all of whom are opinion shapers in their respective faith and scholarly communities—is being deepened and transformed in dialogical directions. The first ISAT publication in English is now a reality and a German version is in the offing. The positive impact on the local communities where ISAT was held has been growing to the point where in 1993 the creative influence on Graz and beyond throughout much of Austria in January, 1993, was dramatic. The January 1994 Jerusalem dialogue produced still further scholarly progress, while contributing in a modest way to the continuation to the peace process in the Near East.

In brief, the creative cross-pollination one hopes for in interreligious dialogue is beginning to happen in, through and around ISAT, and will doubtless occur in greater quantity and quality in the foreseeable future.

IV. DO WE ALL WORSHIP THE SAME GOD?

John Hick

1. It Seems We All Worship One God

As Jews, Christians, and Muslims we all believe—do we not?—that it is true in some important sense that we all worship the same, because the only, God.

Certainly, our scriptures encourage us to think this, at least in that each later holy book assumes that the God of whom it speaks is that previously made known in earlier revelations. Thus we read in the Qur'an that a Muslim is to say to Jews and Christians, as people of the Book, "We believe what has been sent down to us, and we believe what has been sent down to you. Our God and your God is one, and to Him we submit" (28:46, Ahmed Ali translation). We also read: "We have sent revelations to you as We sent revelations to Noah and the prophets (who came) after him; and We sent revelations to Abraham and Ishmael and Isaac and Jacob and their offspring, and to Jesus and Job...and to Moses God spoke directly" (4:163-4). Clearly, if it was the Allah of the Qur'an who inspired the Hebrew prophets and spoke directly to Moses, and who was later inspiring Jesus, then to worship the God of these earlier revelations is to worship the Allah of the Qur'an.

Again, the New Testament is full of references to the Torah and assumes throughout that the God whose coming reign Jesus proclaimed is the God of Abraham, Isaac and Jacob. Jesus himself was a devout Jew, and during his lifetime some of his fellow Jews speculated that he was one of their ancient prophets returned to life: "'Who do men say that I am?' And they told him, 'John the Baptist; and others say, Elijah; and others one of the prophets'" (Mark 8:27). Again, in preaching Jesus as the messiah, the early church presented him as the fulfillment of the expectations of the Jewish scriptures. Thus according to Acts, Peter, preaching in Jerusalem shortly after Jesus' death, declared that "The God of Abraham and of Isaac and of Jacob, the God of our fathers, glorified his servant Jesus, whom you delivered up and denied in the presence of Pilate" (Acts 3:13-14). Clearly then, according to the New Testament, the God whom Jesus called his heavenly Father was also the God of whom the Torah had previously spoken.

The Torah itself does not of course speak of Yahweh as being also the God of the later New Testament and the still later Qur'an. But it is a very natural Jewish view, in the light of Jesus' manifest Jewishness, and of Islam's continuation of a strict monotheism within the Semitic tradition, that Christians and Muslims are, at least in intention, worshipping the same God whom the Jews have always worshipped.

Let us, then, adopt as our initial position, which we are however prepared to modify or complicate if and as required, that we all—Jews, Christians and Muslims—worship the same God.

2. And Yet It Seems We Worship Different Gods

Having said that, however, we must immediately begin the complicating process. For within the conception of God found in each of our three traditions there are both a universal aspect, relating God to the whole world and the entire human race, and a more particular aspect relating God in a special way to a particular historical group or individual. The universal aspect is common to Judaism, Christianity and Islam, whilst the particular aspect is distinctively different in each case. The term "ethical monotheism" points to the former. Each tradition speaks of God as the sole creator of heaven and earth, indeed by implication as the creator of everything other than God; and clearly there can only be one such being. Thus the Jewish and Christian scriptures begin by affirming that "In the beginning God created the heavens and the earth" (Genesis 1:1) and the Qur'an likewise declares that "Your Lord is God, who created the heavens and the earth in six spans" (10:3).

This one and only God, the supreme being, the Lord of all, is also understood within each tradition to have a moral nature encompassing both the more demanding attributes of justice, righteous wrath, absolute claim, and the more tender and giving qualities of grace, love, mercy, forgiveness. Thus according to the Hebrew scriptures Yahweh "judges the world with righteousness" (Psalm 9:8) and yet is "merciful and gracious, slow to anger and abounding in steadfast love" (Psalm 103:8). And according to the New Testament "the wrath of God is revealed from heaven against all ungodliness and wickedness" (Romans 1:8), and yet at the same time "God is love" (I John 4:8) and "If we confess our sins, he is faithful and just, and will forgive our sins and cleanse us from all unrighteousness" (I John 1:9). And according to the Qur'an "The Lord is quick in retribution, but He is also oft forgiving, most merciful" (7: 167). Thus in their universal aspect, as forms of

43

ethical monotheism, these three intertwined traditions proclaim God as creator of the universe, self-revealed to humanity as our just judge who is at the same time loving, gracious and merciful. Thus far it can indeed readily be said that we are all worshipping the same God.

But when we proceed from this universal aspect to the historically particular aspects the picture becomes more complicated, and it ceases to be evident that we are all speaking about the same God. For the particular forms in which the universal deity is experienced within the events of human history are so different as to create a presumption of three Gods.

Thus the God of Judaism, in his particular aspect as the Yahweh of the Hebrew Bible, is distinctively the God of the Jews, standing in an unique relationship to his chosen people, who are linked to him in a special covenant. The prophet Amos relays the word of the lord, "You only have I known of all the families of the earth" (Amos 3:2). The Yahweh of the Torah is also, to be sure, aware of other nations. But he generally subordinates them, within his concern, to the children of Israel. Thus he encourages the Israelites to slaughter the original inhabitants of Canaan in order to make it their own, and later uses the Assyrians to chastise his people when they had turned away from him, and later again he has them taken into exile in Babylon. For the special covenant relationship with God is not only a great honor and blessing but also a great trial and responsibility—the divine word given to Amos continues, "therefore I will punish you for all your iniquities." But Israel is still at the center of Yahweh's attention. He is integral to the history of the Jews, as they in turn are integral to the biography of Yahweh. He cannot be extracted from this context of Jewish history. He could not, for example, have switched his sphere of operation from Palestine to China without so changing his concrete character as to become, in effect, a different deity.

He is thus a particular divine personality with a certain distinctive provenance: he is deeply involved in the affairs of the ancient Near East, but has no real relationship to the rest of the human race living in China, India, Russia, Europe, Africa, Australia and the Americas. The universal deity of ethical monotheism thus seems in the Hebrew scriptures to have taken on a particular, limited, local form as the Yahweh of Israel.

44

Again, the God of Christianity in his particular aspect as the God of the New Testament, and as further defined by the ecumenical Councils, is a triune Being related to humanity through one particular individual who is God the Son incarnate. Modern New Testament scholarship has made it extremely doubtful whether this belief in divine incarnation can be attributed to Jesus himself. But we are concerned here with Christianity as a vast long-lived historical reality; and by the early fourth century (at the Council of Nicaea, 325 C.E.) the church had established Jesus' identity as the second Person of a divine Trinity living a human life. And clearly the Trinity, consisting of God the Father, God the Son, and God the Holy Spirit, is not identical with Yahweh as described in the Jewish scriptures and tradition. One obvious difference is that between a pure monotheism and a modified trinitarian form of monotheism; and another is that between a divine concern centered upon the children of Israel and one that embraces all humanity, and even stigmatizes the Israelites as those among whom God became incarnate but who willfully rejected him.

And yet again, the Allah of Islam, in his particular aspect as interacting with the Muslim community in seventh century C.E. Arabia, is different from the Yahweh of Israel and from the Holy Trinity of Christianity. The Qur'anic revelations often occurred in response to specific issues arising in the life of the prophet or of the early Muslim community. Like Yahweh, Allah gives commandments to a particular community, aids them in battle, and uses them as his chosen servants. He is as strongly linked to the prophet Muhammad and the Muslim community in Mecca and Medina as is the Christian God to the "Christ event" in first century Palestine or Yahweh to the events of biblical history. Thus the God of Islam, as a concrete divine figure who speaks in the Qur'an, is distinct from the God of Christianity, in that Allah is not a Trinity and did not become incarnate in Jesus of Nazareth; and different also, though to a lesser degree, from Yahweh in that the qur'anic Allah's focus of interest is in Arabia rather than Palestine, and that the Jews have a secondary rather than a central place in his concern.

Thus when we think of God, not in God's universal aspect as the creator of the universe and the gracious Lord of all humankind, but as a concrete divine personality intervening in human history and interacting with particular individuals and groups, we find that the

45

scriptures of our three faiths depict three distinct divine personalities. One of these is the God of a group of Semitic tribes whom he adopts as his specially chosen or treasured people; another is a complex Trinity, one aspect of whom becomes incarnate on earth and founds a new religion; whilst another enters into a special relationship with a prophet in Arabia, through whom he creates the community of those who submit their lives to Allah. Thus the personal profiles and stories of Yahweh, the Holy Trinity, and Allah, although overlapping, are sufficiently different for it to be difficult to say that those who worship them are all worshipping identically the same God.

But whilst the three scriptural deities are concretely described in unique terms, yet each description also includes a universal element. Thus in the Hebrew scriptures we read that "thou art the God, thou alone, of all the kingdoms of the earth" (2 Kings 19:15); and rabbinic Judaism concluded that "the righteous of all nations have a share in the world to come" (Talmud: Sanhedrin, 13). Within Christianity it is possible to hold that the divine Logos who or which became incarnate as Jesus of Nazareth is also at work in other ways within the other religions of the world. And in Islam there is the qur'anic concept of the Jews and Christians as people of the Book, and also the idea that all sincere monotheists are Muslims in the basic sense of those who submit themselves to God. And so it is possible in each case to see lying behind these concrete historical divine personalities the infinite depth of the Godhead transcending the particular relationship to humanity recorded in each scripture and indeed, according to the deeper thinkers of each tradition, transcending altogether the range of our finite human understanding.

At the same time, however, the historical particularity of each tradition provides a basis for the assumption of its unique superiority among the religions of the world. The Jewish concept of the chosen people, in so far as it is taken seriously, must make Jews feel that they have a specially important role within God's providence. This role is a burden and responsibility as well as a privilege; but on both counts it singles them out as living in an unique relationship with God. The Christian belief in Jesus as God the Son incarnate entails that Christianity was, uniquely, founded by God in person. It would seem to follow that Christianity must have a privileged status among the religions of the world, and indeed that it must be the religion that God intends for the whole human race. And the Muslim claim that Muhammad was the seal of the prophets, and the Qur'an the final revelation, completing and perfecting the earlier ones, gives to Islam the sense of superseding Judaism and Christianity and being God's appointed religion for all humanity.

To some extent these claims to unique superiority can be modified or de-emphasized by the more ecumenically-minded within each tradition. Thus a Jew can say that every people is in its own different way chosen by God, and has its own special vocation within the divine plan. A Christian can say that whilst God is self-revealed to Christians by becoming personally incarnate, God is also self-revealed in other lesser ways within other religious traditions. And a Muslim can speak of the eternal heavenly Book of which the Arabic Qur'an is a human reflection, other sacred scriptures being different reflections created for the benefit of other communities. We must note, however, that each of these ways of ameliorating the overt absolutism of one's own tradition conceals a residual covert absolutism. We are all God's chosen peoples; but still Israel is chosen for the central and most important role. God is known within all the great traditions; but still only in Christ has God become directly and personally present on earth. We all live in response to genuine divine revelations; but still only the Muslim Umma is living in response to God's final and definitive revelation. Thus these modifications are more of the nature of concessions to ecumenical politeness than unreserved acceptances of the others' equal status before God.

3. Possible Solutions to the Apparent Contradiction

With these various reminders and discriminations in hand, let us return to our original question: Do we all worship the same God? As we have seen, the difficulty in answering this question arises from the historical particularities of the three traditions rather than from their common ethical monotheism. Let us first try out some fairly simple ways of holding that, despite these different particularities, we do all worship the same God.

One obvious possibility is to say that we worship the same God but call that God by different names. (Thus Joseph Campbell once said, "There you have the three great Western religions, Judaism, Christianity, and Islam—and because the three of them have three different names for the same biblical God, they can't get on together").[1] But the difficulty facing this suggestion is that it is not only the names but also the descriptions which go with them that are different. We cannot claim that the three scriptures describe recognizably the same concrete divine being but refer to that being by different names—as I might be called John by some, Professor Hick by some others, and the Reverend John Hick by yet others; for the story of my life is a single story which includes the three contexts in which I am called by these three different names. But the qur'anic Allah is not the subject of the same story of divine-human interaction as the Christian Trinity; nor does the Trinity, with its second Person becoming incarnate, figure in the Torah and Talmud. Thus with the different names there go—as we have already noted—significantly different descriptive stories.

Could we perhaps, however, as a second possibility, combine the three stories into a single more complex narrative of divine activity on earth? Could we say that the one God was first self-manifested within Jewish history for some two thousand years; and then became incarnate as Jesus of Nazareth, thereby revealing a previously hidden trinitarian nature; and then some six centuries later reverted to the original unitarian nature as the Allah of the Qur'an, now denying that he had ever become incarnate? This is, surely, not an option that can be seriously contemplated from within any of our three traditions.

But, as a third attempt, we should note that it is sometimes possible to refer successfully to one and the same entity by means of quite different descriptions, and even to do so without being aware that these descriptions have the same referent. A well-known example is that of the evening star and the morning star, which are described and identified differently, one as appearing at dusk and the other at dawn, and which were long assumed to be two different stars, known to the ancient Greeks as Hesperus and Phosphorus respectively. We now know them both to be the planet that we call Venus. Could Yahweh, and the heavenly Father, and Allah, likewise be the same being, mistakenly thought to be three? Again, to adapt another well-known example, the

---

[1] Joseph Campbell, *The Power of Myth* (New York and London: Doubleday, 1988), p. 21.

same person, namely Sir Walter Scott, is truly described as the author of Waverley, as the greatest Scottish novelist, and as the sheriff-depute of Selkirkshire in 1800.

Could not the same God, then, be differently described by Jews, Christians, and Muslims as a result of their encountering that God in different historical situations? The difficulty here is that varying descriptions of the same entity must be mutually compatible. It must be possible for them to apply to the same being—as for the author of Waverley to also have been the greatest Scottish novelist and the sheriff-depute of Selkirkshire in 1800. But this is not analogously the case with our different descriptions of God.

The qur'anic account explicitly contradicts the Christian account of God as a Trinity, one member of whom became incarnate as Jesus of Nazareth. Again, the understanding of God in the Torah implicitly, and the continuing rabbinic understanding of God explicitly, conflicts with the Christian trinitarian and incarnational concept. The divergence between the Torah's and the Qur'an's descriptions of God is much less extensive and might permit a theory that the same God had moved his focus of interest and sphere of operation from Palestine to Arabia, and from the Jews to the Arabs, in the seventh century C.E. However any such theory would be firmly, and surely rightly, rejected by post-biblical Judaism as imperialistically supercessionist.

And so it does not seem at all sufficient simply to say that identically the same God is being named and described differently. The differences between these describable divine personalities go too deep for that to be plausible. Nor, as a final attempt at a simple and easy solution, can any of us accept a polytheism, even a limited triadic polytheism, according to which there exist a Jewish God, a Christian God, and a Muslim God. For we are united in believing that there is but one God, who is the creator and ultimate ruler of all things. We all affirm *La-ilaha-ill'allah*—there is no God but God.

The next possibility, then, is for us each to revert to a traditionally confessional position from which we claim that our description of God is the true description and the others are mistaken in so far as they differ from it. On this absolutist basis a Jew will hold that Christianity is profoundly in error in claiming that God (i.e., God the Son) became incarnate and summoned both Jews and Gentiles to accept him as their divine lord and savior; and that Islam is in error, though perhaps less

49

profoundly so, in claiming that God spoke to Muhammad in a way that entails a switch of the focus of divine concern from the Jews to the Arabs, from Palestine to Arabia, from Jerusalem to Mecca. On this same absolutist basis a Christian will hold that both Jews and Muslims are profoundly in error in turning their backs on God's redeeming presence on earth in Jesus Christ. And a Muslim, again on this absolutist basis, will hold that Christians are profoundly in error in their belief that Jesus was God's only-begotten Son; and that the Jews are also in error, though less profoundly so, in failing to acknowledge God's final revelation in the Qur'an.

These confessional claims are not only possible, but represent the attitude—whether or not explicitly articulated—of the large majority within each of our three traditions. And indeed if we each take what our scriptures and traditions say in a straight-forward and literal way, this kind of absolutism seems unavoidable. Our own tradition, whichever it is, must be right and the others wrong on any central matters on which they differ; and our own tradition must accordingly be superior to the others in virtue of its greater access to the truth and its more direct relationship to God. This implication of our traditional belief-systems should be frankly acknowledged rather than merely tactfully overlooked if we are ever to move beyond the static situation of rival absolutisms. For it is discomfort with these absolute claims that forces us to ask important further questions.

In speaking of this discomfort I can only report my own experience. When as a Christian I look at my Jewish and Muslim colleagues—who have become Jewish and Muslim friends—in these meetings, having interacted with you now for several years, I have to say that you do not seem to me as you ought to seem if the traditional absolutism of my own tradition is valid. For if it is valid, it follows that you have a lesser access to vital truth and live in a less direct relationship with God than myself. But I do not find that I can honestly believe that this is the case.

However, I realize on further reflection that this "not seeming as you ought to seem" does not necessarily follow from the Christian absolutist premise; for it could well be that you are exceptionally good products of your traditions and I an exceptionally bad product of mine, so that the manifest integrity of your faith, and your evident dedication to God's service, is only impressive relatively to my own deficient standpoint. But then when I look more widely at the many Jews, Christians and Muslims whom I know I still do not find that the generality of Christians are more truly religious, or more honest and truthful, or more loving and compassionate, or more thoughtful for others, than are the generality of Muslims or Jews. And I ask myself, Is this what I should expect if Christ is the unique savior of humankind and Christianity? Is the stream of life in which his influence is most powerfully felt religiously superior to other traditions?

I therefore look next at the long histories of our three faith-communities, at their scriptures and literatures, their saints and sinners, the societies and cultures that they have inspired; and again I do not find that one stands out as manifestly superior, morally and spiritually, to the others. Each is a complex historical mixture of good and evil, each with its strong points and its weak points, its shining peaks and its grey doldrums. But if I try to quantify these immensely varied goods and evils, spread as they are across the centuries, so as to produce three numerical conclusions, I find that the complexities and incommensurabilities make this impossible in practice. Further, each of these traditions has, so far as we can tell, been more or less equally fruitful in saintliness, producing extraordinary men and women whose spirit and lives make God more real to the rest of us.

These are of course both empirical (in the sense of observational) judgments. *A priori* each tradition has presumed a superior access to truth and a uniquely close relationship to God, resulting in a morally superior culture and history and in the production of more and/or better saints. Otherwise what would be the concrete value of divine revelation; what human difference would it make? However, empirically these *a priori* claims cannot be at all easily sustained, and indeed in my view cannot be sustained at all. In saying this I am of course making a statement in an area of virtually infinite complexity, in which no one can know all the facts, and concerning which endless discussion will always be possible. But rather than needing to prove that my own over-all global impression is correct, I suggest that the onus of proof falls upon anyone who wishes to maintain that some one tradition (namely, their own) is observably morally and spiritually superior to the others.

But perhaps someone will respond that these comparative questions are out of order. Perhaps our three traditions are simply different and incommensurable. Perhaps there are no inter-traditional criteria, but by Christian criteria Christianity is superior, by Jewish criteria Judaism, and by Muslim criteria Islam? This is at first glance an attractive idea. However it does not seem so attractive if we distinguish between, on the one hand, basic moral principles, such as valuing and caring for others as much as for oneself, and on the other hand, specific community norms, such as not eating pork, or monogamy, or fasting during Ramadan. On this latter level it will of course follow that those who do not observe our particular code of practice must be judged to be falling short.

But on the level of basic moral principles I suggest that there is sufficient convergence of ethical insight for common assessments to be possible. Each of our three traditions calls us to treat others as we would wish to be treated ourselves. Jesus taught, "As ye would that men should do to you, do ye also to them likewise" (Luke 6:31); the Talmud teaches, "What is hateful to yourself do not do to your fellow man. That is the whole of the Torah" (Babylonian Talmud, Shabbath 31a); and Muhammad taught that "No man is a true believer unless he desires for his brother that which he desires for himself" (Hadith: Muslim, chapter on iman, 71-2; Ibn Madja, Introduction, 9; Al-Darimi, chapter on riqaq; Hambal 3, 1976). Again, each tradition calls us to be just, honest, and truthful, and to care for those—primarily recognized in earlier societies as the widows and orphans—who cannot care for themselves.

It accordingly seems to me possible, from a Christian point of view, to make some comparative judgments that could be assented to by Muslims and Jews. Thus I would put to the historical credit of Judaism, for example, its being the birthplace of ethical monotheism in the West, and its production of an enormous wealth of significant individuals who have contributed notably to virtually every aspect of Western civilization; and to its discredit, for example, the contemporary misuse of power, now that it has power, in relation to the Palestinians. I would put to the historical credit of Christianity, for example, its civilizing of pagan Europe and its being the birthplace of modern science; and to its discredit, for example, its motivating and validating of vicious antisemitism, and of the destructive colonial exploitation of what today we call the Third World. And I would put to the historical credit of Islam, for example, its positive and constructive influence in millions of lives and its great cultural contribution to a considerable segment of the world;

and to its discredit, for example, the continued practice of hideously inhumane forms of punishment in some Islamic countries.

Of course not all Christians would concur with these judgments concerning the debit side of their own tradition; nor would all Muslims and Jews concur concerning the debit sides of their's. But I fancy nevertheless that many thoughtful Christians, Muslims and Jews are in fact in broad agreement on such matters. When we think of the fruits of religion in promoting human welfare, seen in terms of the universal human values of justice, peace and happiness, I suspect that we all operate on essentially the same fundamental moral insights. This, at any rate, is the thesis that I propose for discussion.

Essentially the same seems to me to be true when we consider what are often called spiritual criteria, meaning the criteria by which we may recognize saintliness. Is it the case that by Christian criteria Christian saints are superior, by Jewish criteria Jewish saints, and by Muslim criteria Muslim saints? I do not think so. I am not of course thinking, in the Christian case, of the tests for canonization used by the Roman church. By these criteria it is true by definition that all saints are Christians. Nor am I thinking of saints as a separate species of human-ity; saintliness is a matter of degree. I am thinking of those all too rare individuals who are manifestly much more advanced than the rest of us in the transformation from natural self-centeredness to a new orientation centered in the transcendent reality that we in our three traditions call God. I know a small number of people in whom I can see very clearly the fruits of this transformation, and I know by report a larger number of others. These are spread over the Christian, Jewish, Muslim, Hindu, Buddhist and Sikh communities. And it is my strong intuitive conviction that if they were brought together each would feel a deep affinity with the others, despite the fact that they adhere to different religions, think in terms of different theological and philosophical systems, and engage in different religious practices; and despite the fact that some are contemplatives and others political activists. Again, I cannot prove this; and yet I think it likely that many of you share the same intuition.

4. A Preferred Solution

If you have been sympathetic to what I have thus far been saying, you will experience a discomfort analogous to my own with the

53

assumption that one's tradition must be morally and spiritually superior to all others. However, this discomfort will exist alongside a continuous awareness that this is the tradition into which I was born and which has formed and nourished me, so that I am inextricably a part of it and it a part of me; and I cannot imagine myself being transplanted into any other tradition. But, further, what we have also recognized in our interactions and discussions is that not only do I, as a Christian, feel this intrinsicality to the Christian tradition, but I know that you as Jews and you as Muslims feel a like intrinsic relation to your own tradition; and you in turn each know this of the rest of us. Where, then, do we go from here; and where do we arrive in response to our original question: Whether we all worship the same God?

Here I can only offer a suggestion, draw a picture, spell out a possibility, and wait to see whether you also find that it makes good sense.

If then we hold, with the universal aspect of our three faiths, that there is only one God, who is the source of all other existence and the ultimate lord of the universe, and if we also hold that the particular God-figures of our three traditions are, as concrete historical realities, significantly different, does it not follow that these three divine personalities cannot each be simply identical with the one universal God? They may be authentic manifestations, "faces," forms, expressions, of that one God, or ways in which the one God appears to human beings from different points of view or within different human contexts, but they cannot all be purely and simply identical with the one God. And so we have either to revert to the residual absolutism of our own faith, or draw a distinction of some kind between the one universal God and our three particular manifestations of that God. Such a distinction seems to me unavoidable once we take serious account of religious realities beyond the borders of our own tradition.

The simplest and most satisfactory way to draw this distinction is I suggest between, on the one hand, God *a se*, in God's eternal self-existent being, "before" and independently of creation, and on the other hand God *in relatione* to God's creation, and thus as thought and encountered by human beings. This is the familiar distinction, classically drawn by Immanuel Kant, between something as it is in itself, a *Ding an sich*, and that same thing as humanly perceived, with all that the human mind contributes to the process of perception.

In using this basic distinction we do not of course need to adopt Kant's own particular account of the way in which the mind organizes the impacts of the environment through an innate system of categories, bringing it to consciousness as the three dimensional world of objects of which we are aware. We are concerned only with his more basic thesis that awareness of our environment is not a purely passive registering of it in consciousness but an active process of selecting, ordering, and interpreting. We know from many sources that the world as we are aware of it represents our distinctively human selective simplification out of a virtually infinitely richer and more complex reality that would utterly bewilder and overwhelm us if we were immediately conscious of it.

Our perceptual machinery is attuned only to a minute proportion of the total range of information flowing through and around us: for example, to electromagnetic waves between sixteen and thirty-two millionths of an inch out of a spectrum extending from cosmic rays as short as ten thousand millionths of an inch to radio waves as long as eighteen miles. And after this physical filtering has taken place there is a constructive activity of the mind whereby we order the world by means of a system of concepts which endow it with forms of meaning in terms of which we can behave appropriately within it.

For example, when I see a fork on the table I see what is there as a fork, an instrument to aid eating, this seeing-as having as its dispositional aspect my being in a state of readiness to behave in ways appropriate (as it seems to me) to that thing's being a fork. But a stone age person transported here in a time machine would not see what is there as a fork, for he or she would not have the concept of a fork with which to experience in this way. A large part of the field of meaning in terms of which we experience our everyday environment is thus culturally formed. In other words, we ourselves partially construct the meaningful world which we inhabit. All this is, I think, so widely agreed today, as a result not only of the philosophical analyses of Kant and others, but also of an accumulation of work in cognitive psychology and the sociology of knowledge, that we can safely proceed to ask if it offers any useful hints for the epistemology of religion.

Can we apply the distinction between a reality as it is in itself, and that reality as humanly perceived in terms both of the universal "shape" of the human mind, and of its culture-specific conceptual

55

John Hick

systems, to our awareness of God? It seems to me that we can, and that this will enable us to understand the relationship between our three traditions. (It can also, in an extended form, enable us to understand the relationship between religions more generally, but that is not our immediate concern here.) We shall then say that we are aware of God, not *an sich*—that would be equivalent to perceiving the world as it is independently of a perceiver—but as God is thought and experienced through the conceptual "lens" of our own tradition. For each tradition functions as a kind of mental "lens"—consisting of concepts, stories (both historical and mythical), religious practices, artistic styles, forms of life—through which we perceive the divine. And because there is a plurality of such "lenses" there is a plurality of ways in which God is concretely thought and experienced.

This suggests that each concrete historical divine personality— Yahweh, the Heavenly Father, the Qur'anic Allah—is a joint product of the universal divine presence and a particular historically formed mode of constructive religious imagination. That there is an element of human imaginative projection in religion has surely been undeniable since the work of Feuerbach in the nineteenth century, reinforced by the more recent discoveries of the ethnologists, anthropologists, and historians of religion in correlating concepts of God with cultural circumstances, which rest in turn upon a complex of geographical, climatic, economic and political factors.

For example, ancient settled agricultural societies tended to worship female deities, whilst pastoral herd-keeping societies tended to worship male deities. The sociobiologist Edward O. Wilson says, "The God of monotheistic religions is always male; this strong patriarchal tendency has several cultural sources. Pastoral societies are highly mobile, tightly organized, and often militant, all features that tip the balance toward male authority. It is also significant that herding, the main economic basis, is primarily the responsibility of men."[2] A range of other instances were assembled by the great pioneer in this field, Max

---

[2] Edward O. Wilson, *Of Human Nature* (Cambridge, MA: Harvard University Press, 1978), p. 190.

56

Weber.[3] The principle that he and others have uncovered means that, for example, the female divine personalities worshipped by the pre-Aryan inhabitants of Harappa in India, and the male divine personalities worshipped by the pre-Islamic nomadic tribes of Arabia, owed their gender to the basic economic and cultural patterns of these different human communities. Of course from a naturalistic, or reductionist, point of view they were all created solely by the human imagination. But even from a religious point of view we have to accept that they were partially so created. And it seems evident to me that this general principle applies also to the "high" religions of Judaism, Christianity and Islam. Each different awareness of the divine includes an element of creative human imagination guided by concrete historical circumstances.

This means in turn that the biblical Yahweh was formed at the interface between the transcendent universal God and the particular mentality and circumstances of the people of Israel—later taking on a more universal character, whilst however retaining continuity with his tribal past, in the Judaism of the rabbis. With the birth of Christianity and its splitting away from Judaism this divine personality can be said to have divided into two, one form developing into the Adonai of rabbinic Judaism and the other into the heavenly Father—later elaborated into the Holy Trinity—of Christianity, with both universal characteristics and a particular historical linkage to Jesus of Nazareth and the Christian church. Later again the divine presence that had formed in interaction with the Jewish people took yet another "name and form" as the Allah of the Qur'an, again with both a particular historical linkage to the prophet Muhammad and the life of seventh century C.E. Arabia, and universal characteristics which became increasingly prominent as Islam developed into a world faith.

This model of one ultimate divine Reality, God in Godself, and a plurality of human communal awarenesses of that divine Reality, does justice, as it seems to me, to the two perceptions on which we want to insist. One is the sufficiency and beauty and life-giving and life-transforming power of our own tradition at its best, with its unique remembered history, way of life, manner of prayer, cherished literature,

---

[3] Max Weber, *Sociology of Religion* (Boston: Beacon Press, 1963 - original 1922).

its saints and scholars, its architecture, music and other artistic creations, such that we rightly cling to it and seek to live within it and to contribute to its ongoing life. The other perception that most, perhaps all, of us want to insist upon is our acceptance of the equal right, and indeed necessity, for our colleagues to view their own tradition in precisely the same way. Further, this recognition is not merely a matter of politeness, concealing a belief that God as thought and encountered by another faith-community is less authentic than God as known by us. By that route we only make a circular return to the traditional superiority-claim, discomfort with which caused us to look further.

I believe that it is an authentic religious intuition that requires us to move beyond politeness to a deeper acceptance of the validity—and so far as we can tell the equal validity—of the other two Abrahamic traditions. To unfold the implications of this move must involve extensive new thinking. I have been pointing to one possible direction for such thinking. But I do not suggest that this is the only possible way. If there is another that seems more adequate, may we please have it set before us?

If we do adopt some such pluralistic model, will it not follow that we should each try to influence our own community towards a de-emphasizing and eventual elimination of its absolute claim over against other traditions—the claim to be in a uniquely important sense God's chosen people; the claim that Christianity alone was founded by God in person when he became incarnate as Jesus Christ; the claim that Islam alone is a response to God's final and unsurpassable revelation? It is not appropriate, in my view, for any of us to presume to tell our colleagues of other faiths how to try to influence the development of their own tradition so that it can contribute to the hoped for world community of the twenty-first century, a world community without which there will be world chaos and destruction. As a Christian I can make suggestions within my own community, and what I and a number of other Christian theologians have collaborated in suggesting is that we should regard the idea of divine incarnation as a metaphorical or mythic concept, so that the revelation through Jesus can be understood as being of the same kind as the revelations through Moses and Muhammad.[4]

I know of course that this kind of revisionary work is much easier in some circumstances than in others. Within Christianity it is easier for someone like myself who is a Protestant, rather than a Catholic, and who has been working in a secular university rather than a church seminary setting; though even in such maximally favorable circumstances one has to expect to be a target of fundamentalist wrath and unceasing conservative criticism, and to be excluded from any official influence within one's own church. Among Muslims revision is clearly easier for those working in the West rather than in most Muslim countries today. And among Jews there must be comparable distinctions between easier and most difficult settings. It is thus to be expected that different people will be able to proceed at different paces in publicly thinking through the implications of the insight that one's own tradition is not the one and only "true religion."

However the world needs this developing pluralistic outlook, not only because it is intellectually realistic but also because it can defuse the religious absolutism which has validated and intensified virtually every international conflict in every age. The modern weaponry that we saw in use in the recent Gulf war, and on an even more frightening scale at Hiroshima and Nagasaki, have produced a world which can no longer afford such intra-human conflicts. Hans Küng has written that "There will be no peace among the peoples of this world without peace among the world religions."[5] I would add that there will be no true peace among the world religions without the recognition by each that the others are different but equally valid responses to the ultimate divine Reality that we call God.

---

[4] See e.g., John Hick, ed., *The Myth of God Incarnate* (London: SCM Press, and Philadelphia: Westminster Press, 1977).

[5] Hans Küng, *Christianity and the World Religions* (New York: Doubleday, 1986), p. 443.

V. THE ABRAHAMIC RELIGIOUS TRADITIONS: MAKERS OF PEACE OR CONTRIBUTORS TO HUMAN ANNIHILATION?[1]

Gordon D. Kaufman

The dropping of the atomic bomb on Hiroshima on 6 August, 1945, brought humanity into a radically new historical situation. Technological advances had now placed into human hands new powers of destruction so massive that the accepted conceptions of warfare as an instrument of national political policy were rendered obsolete for the great powers. Nevertheless, huge stockpiles of increasingly powerful nuclear weapons were built up in the arms race, and we now have on the ready nuclear explosives which could set off the most horrifyingly destructive war humankind has ever seen. Though today it seems less likely than it did ten years ago that we are about to destroy ourselves directly in a nuclear war, we are coming to see that the rapidly growing ecological crisis confronts us with much the same ultimate consequence.

How should the Abrahamic religious traditions respond to this frightening late twentieth century global situation? What can they say to it or about it? Clearly, this sort of predicament was not envisaged anywhere in the Bible or by subsequent Christian, Jewish or Muslim writers up to 1945. In the eschatology of the Abrahamic religions the end of history is pictured quite differently than we today actually face it: it was undergirded by faith in an active creator and governor of history, one who from the beginning was working out purposes for human beings which were certain to be realized as history moved to its consummation. The end of history, God's climactic act, was to be a consummation that the faithful could look forward to with hope, for it would be the moment when God's final triumph over all evil powers was accomplished. In contrast, the end of history which we in the late twentieth century must contemplate—an end brought about by nuclear holocaust or ecological collapse—must be conceived primarily not as God's doing but as ours. Moreover, it is difficult to think of it as part

---

[1] Some materials for portions of this article were drawn from the following: (a) Chs. 1 and 2 of *Theology for a Nuclear Age*, by Gordon D. Kaufman (1985), used by permission of Westminster/John Knox Press, and of Manchester University Press; (b) "Religious Diversity and Religious Truth," in *God, Truth and Reality*, ed. by Arvind Sharma (1993), used by permission of The Macmillan Press Ltd.

of a grand plan bringing about the salvation of humanity; it is, rather, the extinction—the total obliteration—of human life on earth.

Our religious traditions did not contemplate human powers and responsibilities of anything like the scope and magnitude which we must today consider: humankind was never believed to have the power utterly to destroy itself; that power lay with God alone. But in their focusing in this way on God's activity in the world, these religions (at least in their traditional forms) obscure what is central and novel in the potential event that now confronts us, namely, that it will be we human beings who will be responsible if this catastrophe occurs; this event confronts us primarily as an act of human doing rather than of divine will, and both our actions and our hopes with respect to it, therefore, must be directed toward the transformation of our human attitudes and ideas, our institutions and policies. Our traditional images of God's providential care guaranteeing ultimate human fulfillment have become not only somewhat outmoded in today's world; they have become misleading and dangerous in certain important respects because they tend to distract us from looking squarely at our own responsibilities in these matters. Instead of helping to make peace in today's world, therefore, in some respects they contribute directly to the enormous problems humanity today faces.

New ways of thinking in many spheres of life are desperately needed in our time. We now realize, as earlier generations apparently did not, that the earth has quite limited resources; if we do not move quickly to contain the human population explosion (on the one hand) and toward radical conservation of energy, water, minerals, arable land and so forth (on the other), human life as we know it can no longer be sustained. We are poisoning ourselves in many ways, some known to us, many unknown: the atmosphere, especially surrounding our cities, has become polluted and is dangerous to breathe; fish can no longer live in many of our rivers and lakes; the food that we eat apparently contains cancer-causing agents; "acid rain" falls on our forests and kills the trees. It is clear that we humans dare no longer think in terms simply of meeting our immediate short-range needs, whether as individuals or as societies, and that we dare no longer follow uncritically traditional practices or traditional religious teachings with respect to these matters; if we do not take account of the long-range consequences of our present practices—however correct or important these practices may have

61

Gordon D. Kaufman

seemed in the past—the ecological crisis in which we now live will deepen beyond repair.

New thinking is also required politically. It is no longer possible or appropriate for nation-states or ethnic enclaves to regard their most fundamental task to be the defence, protection and enhancement of the way of life of their people. That has always been the first duty of politics, and the doctrines of national sovereignty and of the right to self-determination of each people have been its modern expression. According to these conceptions national strength shows itself most fully in the capacity to destroy a threatening enemy, and so-called "ethnic cleansing" may sometimes seem appropriate. We are now in a situation, however, in which destruction of a supposed enemy can no longer be the ultimate method of national or ethnic defence. We continue, nevertheless, to be engaged in arms races and enormously bitter local wars around the globe; and the possibility of nuclear catastrophe remains an outstanding symbol and warning that with our overwhelming technological power we may in fact be on the way to bringing human history to its close. It is obvious that, before it is too late, we must learn to develop a politics of the reduction of tension—of peacemaking and of interdependence—rather than of ethnic self-protection and national sovereignty, but no one seems to know how to make effective moves in this direction.

In all of this the symbolism of our Abrahamic religious traditions has in certain respects been more a hindrance than a help. As many have argued, this symbolism has been partially responsible for our ecological blindness; and it too easily lends itself to the reinforcement and legitimation of our parochial political and ethnic objectives, as we can see in many struggles today. Each side in these local wars appears to believe that it is God's battle that they are fighting, and they are fully justified, therefore, in doing whatever is required not only to protect themselves but, if necessary, to torture and destroy the enemy. Unfortunately, in our traditions religious and cosmic sanction to legitimate our own policy objectives is readily at hand; and, as we all know, it has been frequently invoked in the past and it continues to contribute to the ferocity and inhumanity with which today's wars are fought. Believers find extra strength and courage for the great battle they are fighting because of their confidence that God will bring them victory, no matter how powerful are the forces in opposition; moreover, whatever God is

62

believed to command must be obeyed, no matter how cruel or destructive to those other humans which we regard as God's enemies. The power, faithfulness and majesty of God, when it can be invoked in support of one's political or military cause, or one's way of life, is among the strongest motivations known to humankind.

Whatever justification there may have been for such ways of thinking in the past, we can see that in face of the magnitude of technological power now being exercised by human beings, immersing ourselves in such ideas effectively deepens our problems rather than helping to resolve them. These ideas have often nourished and authorized massive historical evils, as we are all aware: many sorts of imperialism and colonialism, slavery, unrestricted exploitation of the earth's resources, racism and sexism, persecution of those thought of as heretics or infidels, even attempts at genocide. We have today come to a turn in human affairs, however, in which such "misunderstandings" or "mistakes" (as we may view these matters in hindsight) are no longer tolerable. We must, therefore, critically examine our religious symbols and ideas, and attempt to reconstruct them in ways that will more likely assure, so far as we can see, that they will help us address the deepest human problems we now face, not further complicate them. When we employ the symbol "God" today, it must be in a much more carefully restricted form than most Christians, Jews, and Muslims have been willing heretofore to acknowledge. It is important that we come to see all our religious symbolism against the background of the ultimate *mystery* of human life. This is, I strongly believe, a principal demand laid upon all of us who today realize we now live face to face with the possibility that we humans may be in the act of annihilating ourselves.

At its deepest level, we must confess, life confronts us as mystery—and this is particularly true now at the end of this century. We humans are faced with many questions about ourselves and our world: Are there some forms or modes of life which are more "authentically" human than others? Is it really the case, as we have been taught in our religious traditions, that the central problems, or malformations, or diseases of human existence or the human spirit are essentially religious in character, and that their solution, therefore, is to be found basically in religious faith and practice? What is a truly "good" life in today's world? Can certain religious or philosophical or moral or scientific traditions give us ultimate answers to these sorts of questions, or are all

Gordon D. Kaufman

of these in various ways both helpful and misleading, leaving us in a problematic relativism? Should the world, and human existence within it, be understood most fundamentally with reference to "God" or "Allah," to "material energies," to "life," to some other central focus? Or should we banish all such questions from our minds and live out our existence, so far as possible, simply in terms of the day to day problems that confront us? We do not know, and we can see no way in which we will ever be able to find, fully satisfactory answers to these questions. This inscrutable mystery—or these many mysteries—of life increasingly provide the deepest context of our existence today.

The various religious traditions around the world provide their adherents with visions of the whole of reality; that is, they present us with interpretations of this ultimate mystery within which human life transpires—interpretations which have proved sufficiently meaningful and intelligible to enable most human beings in the past to come to some significant understanding of themselves in relation to the enigmatic context within which their lives have proceeded, and which were sufficiently appealing to motivate women and men to attempt to live fruitfully and meaningfully within that context. As we all know, many such visions of the ultimate reality with which we humans have to do, and of the meaning of life, have appeared in the course of human history. But the enormous muddle into which we humans have gotten ourselves in the twentieth century makes clear that none have really succeeded in dissolving the ultimate mystery within which life moves on.

Our various religious traditions have not, unfortunately, been candid about this, especially when they claimed to present a kind of definitive Truth about life, that which alone can bring true salvation from our deepest ills. Although claims of this sort have often enabled religious groups to attract faithful—indeed fanatical!—devotees by downplaying in this way the profound mystery within which we all live, in so doing they have in fact falsified our actual human condition of living in face of mystery; and they have all too frequently become thereby (as I have been suggesting) dangerous threats to human life and flourishing rather than trustworthy guides. Today such attitudes and practices only worsen the global problems with which we must now come to terms. The only possible check against the monumental deceits which our human religiosity is capable of working on us and on our desire for

64

certainty in a terrifying world—is a constant reminding of ourselves that it is indeed *mystery* with which we humans ultimately have to do; and therefore we dare not claim certitude about the right and the true, the good and the real, but must acknowledge that in these things we always proceed in a kind of trust or faith, as we move forward through life into the uncertain future before us. Precisely because of the mystery, we must give a much more prominent place in our religious visions of reality to forthright acknowledgement of our ultimate *unknowing* with respect to the deepest questions of life and death; precisely because of the mystery, we must engage in relentless critical questioning of our faiths, their symbols, and the practices they have inspired in the past; precisely because of the mystery, we must undertake disciplined but imaginative construction of more adequate religious visions to guide life, visions to which we can, because of their acknowledgement of the ultimacy of the mystery within which we live, afford to give ourselves in trust and faith.

Although the various patterns of religious understanding, and the diverse notions of religious truth among us Christians, Jews, and Muslims, are intelligible and persuasive in their own terms, on some fundamental issues they often stand (as we all know) in great tension, even contradiction, with each other. In my view we make a serious mistake today if we continue simply to follow the approach which has been characteristic of our religious communities in the past, according to which we attempt to evaluate the religious views of others simply and directly in terms prescribed by our own (rival) pattern of meanings and criteria: this is no longer appropriate since it fails to take into account the fact that (in light of the mystery) our own religious views, and our criteria of judgment, are likely quite as parochial as those others which we are seeking to assess. Do these facts drive us, then, into a complete skepticism about all religious truth, or into a relativism which prevents our making any judgments at all? I do not think so. What they do demand is that we reconsider our inherited ways of thinking about religious truth in light of the issues we have just now been noting.

In place of the absolutistic conceptions of truth which we have inherited from our several religious pasts, I want to propose a dialogical and thus a pluralistic understanding. Experiences from everyday conversation, particularly the free and spontaneous conversation that can occur among equals such as friends, can provide a model for developing such

65

Gordon D. Kaufman

a notion of truth. Our traditional conceptions of religious truth appear
to be based on teacher/student or guru/disciple patterns of relationship,
patterns in which truth is something *known* to one of the parties—i.e., is
essentially a *possession* of one of the parties—and is then communicated
to, passed over to, the other party who receives and accepts it. A
unidirectional relationship or movement of this sort characterizes much
traditional religious thinking and practice with respect to truth—consider
the special authority given sacred texts by readers and interpreters, and
especially by many religious communities; the religious importance of
prophets to whom God is believed to have revealed divine truth; the
authority of most religious teachers in relation to their disciples; the
importance of the activity of preaching to audiences (large or small),
audiences which remain basically hearers, recipients of the word; the
authority given to traditional teachings and practices. In all these
instances truth is treated as though it were a kind of *property*, something
that is owned by one party, and thus is not directly available to others,
but which can be passed on or given over to others if the owner so
chooses. If we move away from this property-model of truth, however,
to a model based on the experience of free and open conversation, a
quite different conception comes into view.

In sharp contrast to many formal religious "dialogues," in which
all the participants have specific agendas in mind which they wish to
pursue in representing properly their respective communities and traditions, a typical conversation among friends often proceeds quite sponta-
neously. Though in each remark the speaker is attempting to "say something" that is fitting at that moment—and in that respect has something
"true" in mind—the "truth" which may emerge in the course of the
conversation cannot be understood simply in terms of these individual
speeches taken up one by one, as though each stood on its own feet. For
the conversation often develops "a life of its own" (as we say), and it
may move in directions no one anticipated and lead to new insights and
ideas which none of the participants had previously considered. Thus
conversation is itself sometimes the matrix of significant creativity in
human life. An intervention by speaker B moves the conversation in a
way speaker A had not intended; and a succeeding intervention by C
moves it on a slightly different tack, not anticipated by either A or B,
so that when A responds again, it will be with a comment not directly
continuous with his/her earlier remark, but which takes account of what

66

B and C unexpectedly said. Thus the path of the conversation as a whole, though continuous, is not a direct working out of the original intention A was attempting to express. (Here the difference between our conversation-model and most interreligious dialogues—where formal papers are prepared ahead of time and then published afterwards, often without significant alteration of the text—is obviously quite marked.)

This conversational model, by leading us to focus on the way truth *comes into being* rather than on its existence as a *possession* that belongs to someone, can assist us in our reflection on religious truth. From this point of view it does not seem particularly illuminating to regard truth as a possession of some sort, even a possession belonging in common to a community. Rather, truth is perceived as a process of becoming, a reality which *emerges* (quite unexpectedly) in the course of the conversation—a reality which, if the conversation goes forward, may continue to break in upon the participants. It is a reality which will harden and die-away, however, if the participants in the conversation attempt to freeze it into legalistic definitions and formulas which thereafter are regarded as authoritative bits of knowledge, to be respected and revered and learned but not to be criticized and creatively transformed in further conversation. I call this a "pluralistic" or "dialogical" conception of truth, because here—instead of taking truth to be a characteristic of certain words or propositions or texts which can be learned and passed on (more or less unchanged) to others—it is identified as a living reality which emerges within and is a function of an ongoing living interchange among a number of different voices.

Perhaps we can see more clearly just what is involved here if we contrast a conversation with a lecture. In its very form a lecture expresses an essentially monolithic conception of truth: it suggests that truth is the sort of thing which can be presented quite adequately by a single voice in continuous ongoing monologue, and which can be brought to a satisfactory conclusion at a particular point in time. The model of conversation suggests, in rather sharp contrast, that many voices, representing quite different sorts of experience and points of view, are required even to begin to articulate truth; and, indeed, that truth demands a kind of open-endedness into an indefinite future. In conversation every voice knows that it is not complete in itself, that its contribution is in response to, and therefore depends upon, the voice(s) that came before, and that other voices coming after will develop

67

further, modify, criticize, qualify what has just been said. Free-flowing conversation presupposes a consciousness of being but one participant in a larger developing yet open-ended pattern of a number of voices, each having its own integrity, none being reducible to any of the others; and it presupposes a willingness to be but one voice in this developing flow of words and ideas, with no desire to control the entire movement (as in a lecture or other monologue). When truth is conceived in these pluralistic and dialogical terms, no single voice can lay claim to it, for each understands that it is only in the ongoing conversation as a whole that truth is brought into being. In this model truth is never final or complete or unchanging: it develops and is transformed in unpredictable ways as the conversation proceeds.

I want to suggest now that a pluralistic understanding of religious truth, based on the model of what can occur in serious conversation, is much better fitted to our needs in the contemporary world than the ordinary monolithic conceptions which most of the religious traditions take for granted; for this is a model which demands that all participants in the discussion of the profound mysteries of human existence—that is, each of the different religious traditions of humankind—should be encouraged to interact with each other on basically equal terms: all must recognize that they, along with the others, are in search for truth; none should any longer claim, moreover, that they alone possess final religious insight or understanding, that they have, in effect, definitely overcome the ultimate mystery of human life; each wishes, of course, to contribute whatever it can from the riches of its own past to the ongoing conversation, and will be listened to respectfully and attentively; and all expect to learn from the others, through appropriating with appreciation what they have to offer, and through opening themselves willingly to probing questions and sharp criticism. Each participant in this conversation of religious traditions posits the others as substantive contributors to our collective pursuit of (religious) truth, and thus is open in principle to contributions from those others—instead of these several voices each presuming that they are fully capable of expressing (by themselves) all that needs to be said about life and about death. If we were to move into processes of free and open conversation of this sort with each other on the most profound religious issues—and were prepared also to re-orient our practices and teachings accordingly—our several religious traditions would contribute quite significantly to peace-making in today's very divided world.

Traditional hierarchical and authoritarian patterns of religious understanding and reflection—and the absolutistic claims about religious truth which they have fostered—seriously compromise the understanding that (as I have suggested here) in our religious stories and symbols, in our religious doctrines and religious reflection, we are dealing with matters of profound, ultimately unfathomable, mystery. It is presumptuousness of the highest order, therefore (in my opinion), for any individuals or groups to make absolutistic claims to knowledge on such matters. The concept of mystery levels all human cognitive elites and all religious hierarchies with respect to these ultimate questions of life and death, and thus calls into question all absolutistic claims. The most desirable overall context, therefore, for dealing with the profound religious and theological issues that so trouble us today—issues which are proving destructively divisive in today's world—is unrestricted interchange among all interested parties. The best image for conceiving how the religions interested in peace-making should today proceed is not that of exclusive protectionism with respect to what is taught in their sacred texts and traditions (however important these may be) but is, rather, to be drawn from free-flowing, open and unfettered conversation.

It should not surprise us to discover that the efforts made from time to time (in many religious traditions), to freeze truth into unalterable authoritative monolithic forms have always failed. The relentless forward movement of history into open and unexpected futures repeatedly discloses how fully the ultimate mysteries of life and death elude our every attempt to capture or control them in our words, in our particular styles of reflection or meditation, in our special ritualistic practices; it reminds us again and again, in short, that it is simply as finite human beings—with our own particular limitations of vision, insight and understanding, and our own propensities to prejudice and self-interested falsification—that we carry on all our meditation, reflection, worship, and other religious activities.

For this reason, in today's world claims to infallibility or absoluteness with respect to our religious, social, and philosophical convictions—either by individuals or groups—are no longer appropriate or responsible. In light of the enormity of the problems humanity as a whole today faces, involving many questions seldom (if ever) taken up

69

Gordon D. Kaufman

in earlier periods, it is important that we learn to keep our religious views as open and flexible as possible. For only thus will we be enabled to engage fully and properly the complex problems—religious as well as socio-political and ecological—which today are posed for humanity. Only thus do we have some chance of coming to grips in a fruitful and redemptive way with the profound mysteries with which life today confronts us.

VI. HUMAN DIGNITY AND THE CHRISTIAN TRADITION

John B. Cobb, Jr.

Introduction

The basic issue this topic raises for me is that of universality and particularity. So far as I know, all the religions either arising in what Karl Jaspers called the axial time (800-200 B.C.E.), or deeply shaped by insights developed during that period, have strong universal elements. Central to these are ideas of what we today call human dignity. Jaspers included Judaism as an axial religion, and I think rightly so. Christianity and Islam arose out of Judaism and continued in their different ways its universalistic teaching of human dignity.

But of course all of the axial traditions also had many teachings of a particularistic sort. Some of these were not consciously so, but instead unconsciously reflected the particular circumstances and culture in which they arose. Others were quite consciously particularistic, dealing with the importance of particular practices, particular events, and particular communities. These teachings have given rise in all the axial traditions to tensions with the implications of the universalistic teaching of human dignity. I take it that these tensions are the topic of our Jewish-Christian-Muslim dialogue.

The formulation of our topic suggests to me that we are not deriving our notions of human dignity primarily from our several traditions. Instead we are taking it from contemporary discourse that itself has a more universalistic ring. To be quite specific, we are taking it from a consensus that is rooted in the European Enlightenment and which, to a remarkable extent, has become universal, at least among the cultural elites of the world. It is embodied in the United Nations 1948 Universal Declaration of Human Rights.

We are assuming that all of us in this dialogue subscribe to the doctrine of human dignity, not merely as one doctrine among others but as a norm in terms of which other ideas can be judged. We assume that in this respect we are not untypical of an important segment of our several communities. If we continue to subscribe to teachings whose effects appear to be in tension with human dignity, we require special justification for doing so. In the concluding sections of these reflections, I want to raise questions about these tacit assumptions.

John B. Cobb, Jr.

1. What Is the Enlightenment?

If I am correct about our topic, then it becomes important to say how I view the European Enlightenment. I see it as an attempt to discover or invent a new religion, or a substitute for religion, that would be purely universal, free from all particularities. Since its interest in religion was practical and ethical, it was not the subtleties of religious experience that interested it, but the grounds for moral action in the world. One approach was to search for a common and primal essence in all religions and to liberate this from the distorting accretions of cultural history and self-interested priestcraft. Another was to derive the needed teachings from reason, without regard to whether they have been embodied in traditional religions. In either case, everything in these religious traditions that is in tension with this universalistic teaching is to be set aside.

Whereas traditional religions appealed to some form of heteronomous authority, the Enlightenment appealed to the authority of individual conscience and reason. The discovery of religious or moral truth did not require supernatural revelation, extraordinary experience attained by special disciplines, or arduous intellectual activities. The needed truth is present in, or available to, common sense, and common sense is understood literally as a sense that is common to all. The task is to strip away cultural overlays and superstitions, so that the truth will appear. Thus the Enlightenment attributes dignity to each human being, first, as his or her own authority in matters of moral and religious belief.

The Enlightenment affirms human dignity in a second way. When common sense is given free reign, not only do individuals recognize their own dignity, but they see that all other individuals also have such dignity. In Kant's famous and important phrase, no human being should ever be treated only as a means. All human individuals are ends in themselves. That implies, of course, that human beings as human beings have rights, and much of the most creative work of Enlightenment thinkers has been spelling out these rights.

All of us, I think, are children of the Enlightenment. Certainly I am. We insist upon our own rights, and, to whatever extent we are moral, we insist that the rights of others be respected too. We believe that these rights derive simply from being human and do not depend on ethnicity or gender or social status or religious beliefs, or even moral character. This is the clearest way in which we affirm human dignity. And, at least in most of these formulations, we do not appeal directly to our traditions. Instead, we work to get the support of our communities of faith for these universal principles.

2. The Relationship of the Enlightenment to Christianity

The second question that follows from my understanding of our topic is how Christianity is in fact related to this Enlightenment faith. My answer is that the relation is very close: Christianity was the context in which it arose and one of its major sources; it was, indeed, *the* major source, albeit this was not intended or recognized.

I interpret the Enlightenment as arising from the Biblical and classical traditions under the impact of the great success of the natural sciences, especially physics. Of course, the history was complex. And I am assuming, contrary to the Enlightenment's own assumptions, that the particularities of history were determinative both of the occurrence of the Enlightenment and of its beliefs.

For me, this assumption does not necessarily deny the universalistic claims of the Enlightenment. The analogy with physics can be used to support this possibility. One may argue that gravity is a universal force that abides by definite laws. The discovery of this, of course, was possible only under very specific circumstances, but what is discovered is a universal truth available to people in very different historical circumstances. The situation with respect to human dignity and human rights might be similar.

The confidence in reason, I think, was largely the outgrowth of the success of physics. Whereas during most of European history people looked back to the Bible and the classics as coming from a time when there was greater wisdom than at present, the advance of physics both expressed confidence in the ability of people now to gain new knowledge and demonstrated that this confidence was justified. Past authority in the natural sciences gave way to present use of reason in interpreting the data. Why should reason not also enable people to understand themselves and their societies better?

When people trusted their conscience and their reason, what they found were some basic convictions that had been nurtured by Christianity. I do not mean here that they were not nurtured in other

73

traditions. I mean only that in fact those first engaged in constructing Enlightenment beliefs were socialized in Christendom.

For many of them these beliefs included the existence of a creator and moral judge. But clearest of all was the importance of morality and its basic structure. This basic structure required that other humans be treated with respect, i.e., at least implicitly, that dignity be attributed to them. The importance of belief in a divine Creator-Judge lay in the pressure it placed on individuals to conform to what they knew to be right. That it is right to act in accord with the dignity of others and oneself was known independently of any belief in God. Morality based on the dignity of all human beings was autonomous.

Christianity not only contributed the structure of belief that was discovered in "common sense," it also played a large role in spreading Enlightenment beliefs around the world. First, during the eighteenth and nineteenth centuries, it was deeply affected by the Enlightenment, internalizing many of its teachings. Second, when it engaged in the great 19th-century enterprise of foreign missions, its message expressed this internalization, and its policies were deeply informed by it. For the most part those in Africa and Asia who became Christians through that missionary movement became Christians of this Enlightenment sort. Equally important, many who did not become Christians still assimilated the Enlightenment aspects of what the missionaries taught.

3. Christian Tradition and Human Dignity

My third question is: What are some of the major elements in the Christian tradition that have socialized Christians into taking for granted that all human beings have dignity? Again, I want to make it very clear that I am not claiming anything distinctive about these teachings. Most are common to the Abrahamic faiths and derive in fact from the Jewish scriptures. However, I shall discuss them as they have functioned for Christians.

The first is the doctrine of the *imago Dei*. Stated in this technical form, of course, it did not become part of the common sense of Christendom. But the idea that human beings are created by God purposefully, with a special relationship to God, and with special privileges in relation to other creatures, took deep hold on the consciousness of Christendom. *All* human beings are created in the image of God. *None* are mere animals. Even those who most emphasized the terrible effects of sin on human beings retained the sense that all have importance to God and in themselves.

The second element is the commandment to love our neighbors as ourselves. Of course, it would in principle be possible to interpret "neighbors" in a restrictive way. But Jesus' explanation of who our neighbors are, made this impossible for Christians. Our neighbors are other people regardless of their ethnicity or religious faith or social class. *All* are to be loved. Such love either responds to an actual dignity in those who are loved, or it attributes dignity to them.

Third, Jesus' teaching accents the implication that what is important is how we treat the neighbor. In his parable of the last judgment, the questions asked of those who are being judged have to do only with this. In the Sermon on the Mount, also, what is accented is the universality of love and moral responsibility as well as its radicality.

Fourth, in the theological interpretation of Jesus' coming and fate, it is emphasized that Jesus came because of God's love for the whole world and that Jesus' died for all. It is true that for quite special reasons some have taught that Jesus' died only for the elect, but this has never been the dominant rhetoric.

Fifth, the New Testament uses parental language about God's relation to human beings. God is depicted as the Father of all people, and all human beings are children of God.

Sixth, the Church Fathers borrowed heavily from Greek philosophy. Perhaps the most important borrowing was the Platonic and Stoic doctrine of the human soul. This doctrine also supported the view that every human being has a peculiar worth and dignity that cannot be measured by outward conditions.

This is, of course, not an exhaustive or scholarly account of the sources in Christianity that support the Enlightenment position. However, I hope that simply reminding ourselves of these central and repeatedly emphasized features of the tradition will suffice to explain how self-evident the dignity of human beings had become in Christendom by the time of the Enlightenment. Repetition of the doctrines themselves was no longer needed to support what everyone already knew. Indeed, no argument was required. It sufficed simply to point out what was evident to all.

75

4. Christian Violation of Human Dignity

My fourth question is as follows: If Christian teaching of universal human dignity was so central and so thoroughgoing, why has Christian practice so often violated the dignity both of Christians and of others? I will try to answer this question under two headings: sin and doctrine.

The role of sin in Christian history is self-evident to Christians and non-Christians alike. Christians have no disposition to minimize it. Indeed, the Christian doctrine of original sin leads us to expect that sin will play an enormous role in human history, and that the church and its members are in no way exempt. It may be that the doctrine of original sin should be treated under the heading of those doctrines that have led to the violation of human dignity. But that is a complex question, and I will not in fact go into it.

At any rate, Christians know that our behavior is constantly falling short of what our own teachings require of us. We confess this in every service of worship. The emphasis on undeserved forgiveness plays an utterly central role in our corporate life. Hence, when we are reminded of our failures to respect the dignity of others, we feel no need to defend ourselves by denial. We simply acknowledge our sinfulness, ask for forgiveness, and undertake to improve.

This sinfulness is too often understood moralistically as a conscious choice of doing what we know we should not do. But Christian thought generally criticizes this as profoundly inadequate. Our sinfulness is much more deeply rooted than that. We debate among ourselves just how that is to be understood, but in general it is associated with an egocentricity to which our separate identity inclines and even virtually compels us. We love ourselves more than we love our neighbors and hence repeatedly use our neighbors more as means to our ends than as ends in themselves.

Further. to whatever extent we overcome the distortions of egocentricity, this is usually by identification of ourselves with a group. We surrender our individual interests in favor of group interests. We divide the world into "us" and "them." Our very devotion and sacrifice to the cause or group heightens the opposition to the other. Appeals to the universal dignity of human beings often seem quite ineffective against this strong identification with particular groups. Hence Christians incline to attribute much of the evil we have inflicted on the world to the kind of corporate sin to which original sin gives rise.

Unfortunately for those Christians who want to hold to traditional teaching, these explanations, however true they may be, are only partial. Traditional teaching itself has exacerbated the problem. It is often the most devout Christians, the ones who try hardest to conform to the teaching of their church, who are most destructive of the dignity of others. This fact compels theologians who have internalized Enlightenment values to become radically critical of the tradition. In what ways have Christian teachings, central to the tradition, supported and encouraged the violation of human dignity?

First, there is a profound shift within the New Testament itself, from the view that loving the neighbor means feeding the hungry, clothing the naked, and visiting the prisoner to the view that first and foremost it means sharing the good news of God's gift of salvation in Jesus Christ. Obviously, those who made this move did not think of it as denying human dignity. It is precisely because of the intrinsic importance of every human being that the greatest good is to be shared with all.

Nevertheless, the shift has horrendous consequences. Whereas the hungry want food, the naked want clothes, and the prisoners want visitors, most people do not want to hear the gospel. The decision that the gospel is something *they* desperately need is made by *us* Christians. Our recognition of their dignity does not include profound respect for their own judgments as to what they need. We Christians know better.

Formally speaking, this is not a uniquely Christian problem. Most people think they know what some other people really need in some areas better than these other people know themselves. It is difficult to conceive of bringing up children without this assumption on the part of parents. Our whole educational system assumes that society knows better than those being educated what they need to know. Most arguments assume such beliefs on both sides. During the Nazi era most of us thought we knew what the German people really needed better than they did themselves. In my experience, the Buddhists for whom I have greatest respect believe that they know what I need much better than I do. I would not want a society in which all of this disappeared.

Nevertheless, the Christian problem is not simply analogous to these others. In general these others express judgments about the relativities of history, judgments without which no society can survive. On the other hand, Christians have usually claimed that what we offer has *absolute* importance. This has often taken it out of the sphere of historical relativity and open discussion.

The problem is compounded among Christians by the fact that many who did not think they wanted to hear the gospel find in it, when they do hear it, just what Christians have claimed. They are converted by it, and, as converts, they are likely to be especially confident in the value and validity of insisting that others listen. Since Christianity is composed of converts and their descendants, this continual reinforcement has played a large role in perpetuating the judgment that we know what is truly good for others and that, therefore, truly to respect their dignity is often to violate their express wishes.

Second, the understanding of what is promised in the gospel has often been separated from the actual effects in the course of personal life and human history. When this happens, then even when the obvious effects are destructive, there is faith that the true and ultimate consequences are positive. The Platonic doctrine of the soul lent itself to this interpretation of the gospel, since one could sharply distinguish the salvation of the soul from any observable effects. One could even contrast them, suggesting that misery in this life will be more than compensated in the other.

The extreme implication of this separation of salvation from actual existence in the world was the justification of torture. There are all kinds of theological reasons to oppose torture and to deny its efficacy for salvation, but this did not prevent its extensive use in certain periods. It is hard not to believe that this was primarily an expression of sin rather than sincere faith, but there is strong evidence that many Christians sincerely tortured bodies for the sake of saving souls.

If this aberration were the only expression of this teaching, I would ignore it in this general survey. But obviously this is not the case. Consider the defense of slavery as for the sake of bringing benighted Africans to the gospel so that their souls could be saved even if their bodies were in chains. Or consider the official practice of making Jewish life miserable so as to encourage conversion or to force Jews to function as a negative witness to Christ. The examples can be multiplied.

Third, the universal tendency to divide the world between "us" and "them" is heightened by Christian doctrine. Christianity began by overcoming existing divisions between Jew and Gentile, Greek and barbarian, slave and free. But its very success in creating a new community led to doctrines about that community that created new and even more intense divisions.

Christians believed, with some exaggeration but also considerable justification, that the church was something radically new. The community they experienced there crossed all natural and social boundaries. Especially when the church was small and subject to persecution, there was an intensity in its fellowship that was discontinuous with what its members had experienced elsewhere. Further, this community was open to all, so that it did not have the exclusivity of ethnic and social communities in the world. To invite others to join appeared to be a way of recognizing their dignity, not denying it. And many who were invited were grateful.

This experience of a new kind of community led to the belief that it was truly of God and not of the world. Thus it was not understood sociologically but rather supernaturally. As in the case of the gospel, the supernaturalist interpretation removed it from the ambiguities of history. As the actual quality of community declined, the supernatural claims for what transpired within it became more pronounced. The belief that originally made some sense, that the salvation found within the community was unique and uniquely valuable, became an objective doctrine that there was no salvation outside the church. This encouraged an arrogance on the part of the church that led to justification of all sorts of policies designed to strengthen the church at the expense of the dignity of members and outsiders alike.

I will add a fourth topic. From the earliest days it was discovered that differences of belief, even quite subtle ones, could be highly disruptive of the community. The emphasis, especially by Paul, on the completely free character of God's gift, could lead to believers deciding that personal morality was no longer important. On the other hand, those who saw that this was wrong were sometimes persuaded that a complex pattern of behavior and ceremonial observance was needed. The accurate formulation of the gospel was crucial for community survival. Precisely because the new community was not constituted by natural or social ties, it had to be united by a common faith. Hence, from very early on, "faith" was not only the trust in God through which believers received God's gift, but also the beliefs that could be the shared basis of the community. In other words, doctrine was crucial.

Because of this, the church developed complex ways of settling issues that arose within it. It gave authority to leaders within the congregations, the bishops, and when these did not agree with one another, it assembled them in great international councils. The hope was that these would achieve consensus which would then put an end to the quarrelling among the churches. To some extent this worked, but not all could share in the agreements. Hence the result of such councils was often the excommunication and exile of those who would not fall into line. Obviously the actual course of events was very complex, with political power struggles becoming deeply mixed with doctrinal ones, different councils coming to conflicting conclusions, and further councils needing to decide which earlier councils to follow. Instead of uniting the church, the councils ultimately divided it. It is only because of the Muslim context in areas where Nestorianism and Monophysitism prevailed, that we are not much more aware of those divisions.

Each branch of the church, nevertheless, was united around particular answers to the disputed questions. Once these answers were established, believers were not entitled to raise them again or to offer opposing answers. "Right doctrine" was now imposed from above on penalty of severe punishment: usually excommunication from the church, but later, civil punishment as well. Orthodoxy became an essential element in the life of the church.

Orthodoxy in this sense meant that the dignity of individual believers was restricted or denied. Their own experience and honest reflection were suppressed by heteronomous power. To be a Christian meant to subordinate oneself to such authorities. It was not even necessary to understand what one was commanded to believe. The real requirement was acceptance of ecclesiastical authority and obedience.

The actual history is far more complex than this. The church has always allowed a good deal of free discussion and debate. There is always room to discuss what official teachings mean, and in that discussion remarkable developments can occur. The case of the doctrine that there is no salvation outside the church is of particular interest, since those who now assert what that doctrine originally intended are subject to excommunication by the Roman Catholic Church. As churches multiplied, so that the decision as to which one to join became truly free, the weight of authority in matters of belief greatly declined. Nevertheless, for many people, being a Christian is understood to involve surrender of one's freedom to think freely for oneself and acceptance of heteronomous authority.

Once again there is nothing exhaustive about this list. My concern has been to consider features of Christian teaching that have been very important to the tradition and that can be easily seen to have led to practices that are destructive of human dignity. I hope you will agree that the ones I have mentioned belong in such a list.

There are two places at which I believe that we now know how to change our doctrines so as to avoid the negative effects. One change is easy and, I believe, has already occurred in large measure. I have spoken of the separation of salvation from actual life and its consequences in torture, enslavement, and persecution. I think the church has repented of this doctrine, and has done so on the basis of renewal of its own deeper sources.

The second is far less widely accepted. This entails the removal of supernaturalism from Christian teaching. That is not the removal of belief in God but rather rejecting the view that the mode of divine activity in the world is supernatural. We can and must speak of the presence and work of God in the church, but we need not represent that as discontinuous with the presence and work of God in the world. It has its special characteristics that need to be described, but that is true of the work of God in other communities of faith as well. Similarly, one may continue to believe that there is life after death. But the supernaturalist belief that such life is discontinuous with life here and now can and should be rejected. If life here and now is a measure of the gift of God in salvation, then the absolutization of the salvation offered in Christ disappears. Salvation is restored to the relativities of history.

These moves will greatly reduce the tension between Christian teaching and human dignity, but they alone do not resolve all problems, for many of the tensions are close to the heart of the faith. The task of truly freeing Christianity from these threats to human dignity remains formidable. Commitment to human dignity and goodwill may motivate these efforts, but there is no simple way of eliminating the tensions.

81

John B. Cobb, Jr.

5. Problems with the Enlightenment View

If the Christian tradition contains within it elements that are inherently threatening to human dignity, should we simply abandon it in favor of Enlightenment values or totally subordinate it to them. I do not think so. I see six fundamental problems with the Enlightenment taken as a solution to the dilemmas of human religion.

First, the Enlightenment provides no basis for its own teaching. Its remarkable success in becoming universal can be claimed to show that no basis is needed, that in fact there is a universal common sense that supports its affirmation of human dignity and human rights. But I do not believe this to be true. I do believe that there are elements of all the great religions that do support human dignity and that it has been possible to draw on them. I also believe that global Westernization has carried with it Enlightenment values, so that the Universal Declaration of Human Rights could win the day chiefly among a Westernized elite.

But now there is a healthy reaction to the Europeanization of the globe that accompanied colonialization and still accompanies its new economic forms. Asian religions and cultures, for example, are no longer on the defensive. They will formulate matters of "human dignity" in their own way, and the implications of these formulations will be quite different.

Equally important, the Christian context that made human dignity self-evident has eroded. The cutting edge of philosophy for two centuries has worked more against this self-evidence than for it. Neither positivism nor deconstruction provides it any support. The implications of Nietzsche and Heidegger will not be expressed in a "Universal Declaration of Human Rights." In general the move has been to cultural relativism at a level that undercuts any notion of universal common sense.

Second, Enlightenment teachings are too vague to provide adequate guidance. Consider the increasingly important question of the right to die. Can the common sense commitment to human dignity help? Of course, it can provide a favorable context for discussion, excluding merely callous positions. But any of the historic religious traditions can do that equally well. Common sense tells us both that it is good for people to be able to make choices and that life is to be protected. To relate these two considerations to the issue at hand requires a probing of anthropological, and ultimately of theological, questions that the Enlightenment sought to avoid.

This is but an illustration of the fact that the real issues we face are not settled by appeals to common moral values alone. They involve judgments at other levels also. In the case of the abortion issue, we have to ask what a human being is, whether being human is an either/or matter, and if so, when the fertilized ovum becomes human. Traditional religious teachings do not carry us far toward satisfactory resolution, but at least they recognize the complexity of such problems and the multiple levels of discourse needed to work them through. The Enlightenment simplification does not help.

Third, the Enlightenment has taught us to think far too individualistically. It attributes dignity to the individual as individual. The rights it discusses are the rights of individuals. Much has been gained by this move. But the price in traditional community has also been enormous.

The Enlightenment arose in a context in which strong community pressures could be taken for granted. It affirmed that there were limits to what the community could do to its individual members for the sake of its perceived interests. For example, individuals must be allowed to believe what seems true to them and to express those beliefs. Even if it is easier for the community to function when all believe alike, it is wrong for the community to suppress honest thinking. Which of us will not agree? Yet which of us has dealt fully with the problems that arise when there are no limits to such diversity?

When, on grounds of Enlightenment individualism, we develop an economics than ignores the interests of community altogether, aiming only at increased production and consumer sovereignty, when communities around the world are collapsing and the resulting alienation of young people causes a profound breakdown in the order needed for healthy personal life, then an ethics that continues to emphasize only individual dignity and rights becomes counterproductive. What these alienated youth need is not the acknowledgment of their dignity and the observance of their rights. It is belonging to a community with values that can give them moral character. The interest of traditional religions, including Christianity, in human community becomes far more pertinent and helpful than Enlightenment individualism.

John B. Cobb, Jr.

Fourth, the Enlightenment anthropology is erroneous, and it has led to poor policies and programs. It depicts us primarily as individuals who are members of the human race. As such we have certain capacities and certain rights. The task of society is to give us the freedom to actualize those capacities and exercise those rights. The differences among us are superficial in comparison with what we share. Our respect for one another's dignity is based on this commonality.

The truth is that we are far more historical or traditional beings that this. The past is internal to our very being. And this past is a highly selected segment of the total human past, a different segment for different peoples. We are not primarily human beings who have superficial differentiations according to the cultures in which we live. We are deeply constituted by those cultures in such a way that what we have in common with those constituted by other cultures has to be discovered. But that does not mean that there is no reason to acknowledge the dignity of the others. What is different from us need not be less valuable. Indeed, its difference may constitute its greatest interest and potential to contribute to us. With all its failures, Christianity provides a more realistic and hopeful basis for approaching the real issues of intercultural life today than does the Enlightenment way of affirming human dignity.

Fifth, the abstraction from the concreteness of culture and tradition has been accompanied by an abstraction from the concreteness of social structures and classes and their effects in shaping human life. The rights on which the Enlightenment focused were the rights that could be exercised by male members of the bourgeoisie. They were largely meaningless to most women and to those men who were forced to labor long hours under inhumane conditions. Of course, Enlightenment concerns could be extended to include the conditions of work. But they excluded analysis of the disempowerment of women and the poor that was involved in the social and economic system engendered and celebrated by the Enlightenment.

This criticism can easily be exaggerated and has been exaggerated by Marxists. The extension of the right to free speech and the right to vote has provided instruments that have enabled workers to improve their lot. Denial of these rights in the Marxist experiments to date has been disastrous. Women suffragists made their gains based on fundamental Enlightenment principles. Nevertheless, the abstractness remains. The critique of Enlightenment theology by black theologians, by Latin

84

American theologians, and by feminists has been devastating. Of course, this critique is in the interest of "human dignity," but the image of that dignity and what is elicited from it in practice are quite changed. The liberation theologians have found far richer resources in Christian tradition than in Enlightenment writers.

Sixth, the Enlightenment affirmation of human dignity has functioned with great consistency to contrast human beings and the rest of the natural world. Human beings are to be treated as ends, never only as means. But all other creatures are properly treated as means only. That means that they are to be used with no concern for their interests. It is no wonder that the exploitation of the planet has been celebrated in Enlightenment thinking as the final triumph of the human spirit.

The Christian record in this same regard is dismal. Of all the world's religions, it is probably the worst. Christian teaching, especially in the West, had long encouraged the subduing of the earth. The Enlightenment in this respect was all too Christian. Nevertheless, Christianity was more mixed. There was some emphasis on a more organic way of thinking, and the dualism of human beings and the natural world was not quite as sharp. The Enlightenment purified Christianity of all of this confusion and inconsistency, and in the process it did us no favor.

Here, too, Christianity holds more promise despite its guilty responsibility. Christianity is capable of repentance in a way the Enlightenment is not, and in fact such repentance is now occurring. Christianity can repent partly because the need and possibility of repentance are built into its fundamental theology. It can repent also because it recognizes the essential limitations of all human efforts to formulate the truth. And it can repent, finally, because there are in its traditions bases for another way of approaching the whole matter. This complexity and confusion within traditions, so objectionable to the Enlightenment mind, is a major part of their resilience, their ability to change as needed, and therefore, their strength.

6. Beyond the Enlightenment to Dialogue

To some extent we have had within liberal Protestantism an actual experiment in giving primacy to Enlightenment values and adjusting the tradition to that. The clearest example is to be found in

Unitarianism. Through much of its history it has been held together by its commitment to the Enlightenment view of human dignity and human rights. This has led Unitarians to be in the forefront of many admirable causes, where other Protestant denominations lagged behind or never joined at all.

On the other hand, it has been peculiarly difficult for the Unitarians, at least their left-wing to which I am primarily referring, to establish community. Their members are largely recruited from denominations in which the mix of Enlightenment values and traditional views is far more confused. They come with strong revulsion to authoritarian use of tradition and the continuation of pre-Enlightenment symbolism and practices. Many come to the Unitarians more in protest against what they have found elsewhere than with a willingness to subordinate their private interests for the sake of building up a strong community.

Unitarians do not refuse to make use of traditional material, but they select it according to its support of Enlightenment values. The more consistent ones do not favor traditional Christian sources over others; so they do not tie themselves to any one tradition. No historic symbolism unites them.

Today the situation is changing. The widespread critique of the Enlightenment has caused them to re-think their relation to it. Many of them have rejected its rationalism in favor of more psychological and mystical sensibilities. And the Unitarians are leading the whole church in affirming the value and importance of the natural environment. Hence what is now going on is a new experiment. My reference above was to the one that is being abandoned. In the new experiment the rhetoric of human dignity is giving way to the language of "creation spirituality." But it is far too early to say where that will lead.

If the Unitarians have experimented with the acceptance of the Enlightenment in replacement for any authority in Christian tradition, liberal Protestantism has experimented with a dialectical relation. It has tried to remove from Christianity everything that works against human dignity, but it has done this in the name of Christ. It has claimed, with some legitimacy, that the values of the Enlightenment are Christian values, and that adherence to these values is what is required by faithfulness to Christ today. At the same time, it affirms the need to maintain the tradition in order to undergird and support these values.

Liberal Christianity has been more successful in sustaining community than have the Unitarians, but the problem affects them, too. Strong community requires strong rootedness in shared tradition. Liberals are too distanced from the tradition, too objectifying of it, to generate and strengthen that rootedness. To unify immersion in the tradition with its critical transformation requires a level of theological imagination and rigor that the influence of the Enlightenment has discouraged. As a result liberal Christianity often has the feel of a half-way house between full-fledged Christianity and the Enlightenment.

A post-liberal Christianity is now emerging that radically rejects Enlightenment universalism. It calls for full re-immersion in the tradition, its language, and its symbols. But it does so with one very important difference. Post-liberal Christians recognize that Christianity is one cultural-linguistic system alongside others. They live and let live. They do not seek to teach others or to learn from them. They simply live out their particular set of meanings in community with other Christians calling one another to faithfulness.

My own view is that this is an inherently unstable program. Christian teaching is universalistic. To accept the linguistic and symbolic system as the basis for life together inevitably introduces those universalistic implications. In my view there is danger that many of the gains that have been made in the correction and redirection of aspects of the tradition will be lost in this form of post-liberal Christianity. Hence I deplore the enthusiasm with which it is greeted.

My own biases are probably largely clear from what I have written. We do need a post-liberal Christianity that relativizes the Enlightenment. It was an important epoch of Western history and of Christian history as well. Even its claims to universality have positive value. But we now see that it was in many respects shallow and mis-leading. We need to assimilate its gains in a wider context. Our tradition provides resources for this creative transformation. As it engages in this transformation, it needs to listen carefully to the voices of outsiders, especially those whose dignity it has repeatedly offended. It can learn from them, not only what it must avoid in future, but also ways in which they have dealt more successfully with similar problems. Hence, interreligious dialogues such as this one are of the greatest importance.

VII. THE QUR'AN AND THE "OTHER"

Abderrahmane Lakhsassi

O People of the Book! Let us come upon a formula which is common between us—that we shall not serve anyone but God, that we shall associate none with Him. (Qur'an, 3:64)

On this *aya* (verse) Fazlur Rahman comments as follows:

> This invitation, probably issued at a time when Muhammad thought not all was yet lost among the three self-proclaimed monotheistic communities, must have appeared specious to Christians. It has remained unheeded. But I believe something can still be worked out by way of positive cooperation, provided the Muslims hearken more to the Qur'an than to the historic formulations of Islam and provided that recent pioneering efforts continue to yield a Christian doctrine more compatible with universal monotheism and egalitarianism. (*Major Themes of the Qur'an* (Chicago: Bibliotheca Islamica, 1980), p. 170)

1. Framing the Problem

Exploring these "historic formulations of Islam" which have bothered Fazlur Rahman and other modernist Muslims since the last century is my purpose here. It is a truism to say that Muslims' view of the Qur'an and its message depended throughout history on the socio-historical context which serves as the background for its explanation. Muslims were indeed more liberal toward other faiths and beliefs as well as toward their own coreligionists at a time when Islamic society espoused a liberal world view than in times of crises. One need only to remember the Mu'tazilite relative open-mindedness in the ninth century and contrast it with the Sunni reaction that followed it in the tenth-eleventh centuries to appreciate the various ups and downs of Islamic societies on this issue of religious tolerance. Whereas the former defended the salvation of sincere *dhimmis* (non-Muslims living under

Muslim rule), the former attacked them on this precise point.[1] This took place in the Muslim East, but the same scenario could equally be said to have happened in the Muslim West—for instance in Cordova during the tenth century and the Almohad reaction that followed.

Of course this reaction touched not only *dhimmis*, as it is often reported, but concerned all those who put reason first in tackling religious as well as secular issues. *Falasifah* (Hellenistic philosophers) as well as certain liberal theologians (*Mutakallimun*) can be recalled here. As the previous tolerant atmosphere of ninth century was beneficial to them, they suffered equally from the same orthodox reaction of which the *dhimmis* were victims. Concerning the Abbasids of Baghdad, the Shi'ite Muslim Ameer Ali writes: "A rescript was issued placing rationalism under the ban, and proclaiming the re-establishment of the old doctrines in the fullest rigor. The Rationalists were expelled from public offices, and lectures on science and philosophy were interdicted. *Kazi [Qadi]* Abku Duwad and his son, prominent Mutazilites, were thrown into prison, and their property was confiscated. But Mutzwakkil's persecution was not confined to the Rationalists."[2] Indeed, the People of the Book suffered too.

Fortunately, later on a voice well respected in orthodox milieux felt the necessity of reminding the faithful Muslims to avoid fanatic attitudes. Ghazali (d. 505/1111) was indeed among those who professed the belonging *in voto* of any sincere Christian or Jew to Islam, and concluded with such a liberal injunction as the following: "Broaden God's mercy, the Most High, and do not measure divine things with

---

[1] Louis Gardet, *Les Hommes de l' Islam* (Paris, Hachette, 1977), wrote: "La réaction sunnite des X-XIè s. devait reprocher aux Mu'taziltes d'accorder le salut éternel aux "protégés" de bonne foi; et Jurjani, au XVè siècle, s'en fera l'écho. Des Mu'tazilites s'en défendirent. Le *Kitab al-intisar* de Khayyat rapporte que Thumama, l'un des représentants du Mu'tazilism baghdadien au IXè siècle, condamnait à l'enfer éternel Juifs et Chrétiens; et s'il rencontrait l'un d'eux qui n'est point impie, il disait: 'il n'est point juif [ou chrétien]'. Ce fut la thèse dominate au cours de siècles." (p.98)

[2] Sayed Ameer Ali, *A Short History of the Saracens* (London: Macmillan and Co. 1900), pp. 288-9.

narrow measures of the establishment."[3] Historically, however, it was indeed the official Establishment that shaped the divine message and became the measure of things.

2. The Historical Background

> "What do you say about Jesus?"
> "We say about Jesus that which our Prophet has told us (may blessings and peace be upon him): Jesus is the servant and messenger of God, the spirit and word of God whom God entrusted to the Virgin Mary."

This conversation took place in the very beginning of Islam between a group of Muslim refugees and the Christian king of Ethiopia. After hearing the reply, the latter who picked up a stick from the ground said: "I swear, the difference between what we believe about Jesus, Son of Mary, and what you have said does not exceed the width of this stick."[4]

Relations between Christians and Muslims in the subsequent years did not take this conversation as a starting point, however. What determined the status of Christians under Muslim rule during the Prophet's time and that of his successors is rather a political treaty between him and the Nestorian Christian community of Najran in the Yaman.

> Arab historians have preserved the text of this treaty which served as a model for future agreements with the "People of the Book," that is, with Christians and Jews. This text is certainly not wholly authentic, but it may retain some of the original conditions. The community

---

[3] *Faysal al-tafriqah bayna al-islam wa l-zandaqah* [Distinguishing Principle Between Islam and Unbelief] (Cairo, 1319/1901), p.75. Text given by R. Casper at the end of his article "Le statut des non-musulmans de'après Ghazali," in *IBLA* (Tunis), 2 (1968), p. 313. See also Louis Gardet, *Hommes de l'Islam*, p. 98.

[4] Cited by R. Marston Speight, *God is One, the Way of Islam* (New York: Friendship Press, [1989] 3rd printing 1990), p.1.

was placed under Muslim protection in return for the payment of an annual tribute of two thousand garments of a specific value. In the event of war it was to provide thirty coats of mail, thirty camels, and thirty horses. It would give board and lodging to the Prophet's envoys for up to a month. The people of Najran had only to refrain from the practice of usury. In return for this they were indemnified against any attack on their persons, property or religion. Bishops and priests would not be removed from their sees, or monks from their monasteries.[5]

The treaty of Najran was used and applied during the Prophet's time and later. When open conflict broke out between the rising Muslim community and the Jewish tribes in Medina, a new agreement was reached with the Jews. The latter were forced to surrender to the Muslim community half of their agricultural produce while keeping their own land. But it was believed that the second Caliph, 'Umar Ibn l-Khattab, whom A. Guillaume calls the Saint Paul of Islam, expelled in 14-15/635-36 all the People of the Book from Arabia. 'Umar's starting point was the doctrine that only Islam and no other religion should ever be accepted in the Arabian peninsula. "According to the author of the prophet's biography, it was claimed that the prophet on his death-bed had said that two religions should not coexist in Arabia. Abu Bakr, who of all men would have been sure to know the truth, did nothing to carry out the alleged dying command of Muhammad, and Umar said that he had never heard a word of it; but when he was assured that Muhammad had indeed uttered these words he proceeded to expel Jews and Christian from the Hijaz."[6]

---

[5] Maxime Rodinson, *Mohammed*, first published in French 1961; English trans. by Anne Carter, 1971, Penguin Press, 1977, p. 271.

[6] A. Guillaume, *Islam* (first published 1954), Pelican Book, 1977, p. 96. About 'Umar's sternness see page 49; the author reported also (p.54) the story of the Prophet playing with his women who stopped chatting loudly and freely when 'Umar' entered: "Umar, said the Prophet to him, if the devil himself were to meet you in the street he would dodge into a side alley!" On this issue Philip Hitti, *History of the Arabs* (New York: Macmillan [1st ed. 1937] 1984, p. 169) wrote: "The second cardinal point in 'Umar's policy was to organize the Arabians, now all Moslems, into a

91

The so-called pact of Umar that fixed the status of *dhimmis* in the Islamic City and remained in effect until the 19th century (Khat-i-Hamyun, 1856) was not, according to Louis Gardet, the work of the second caliph, as usually believed. Rather the Umayyad Umar ibn Abdel-Aziz, known as 'Umar II (98-102/707-720) was responsible for fixing the terms under which Jews and Christians were to live in the City. There is no question that this new pact is more severe than the Najran treaty. For one thing, the earlier pact avoided humiliating the People of the Book, whereas 'Umar's pact forced the *dhimmis* to wear special clothes which would distinguish them socially. Thus a limitation was placed on their citizenship which was nevertheless recognized.[7]

We should not, however, overemphasize this religious segregation and oppression. Rather, we must take into account the relative tolerance that distinguished the Muslim community of the classical age from many societies of the same era. In spite of the limitation of their field of action from which the *dhimmis* no doubt suffered, it is an undeniable fact, as Guillaume put it, that "Jewish and Christian writers of the time express their satisfaction at the milder rule of the Arabs and thank God for their deliverance from the tyranny of Byzantium."[8]

3. Past Qur'an Commentaries

These historical attitudes towards the People of the Book were simultaneously reflected in the way Qur'anic verses concerning Jews and Christians were explained and interpreted. Various readings given

---

complete religio-military commonwealth with its members keeping themselves pure and unmixed—a sort of martial aristocracy—and denying the privilege of citizenship to all non-Arabians."

[7] For 'Umar II see Louis Gardet, *La Cité musulmane*, pp. 345-6. "Dans le pacte de Najran, il était précisé que ses bénéficiaires chrétiens 'ne seraient pas humilies'. Le pacte de 'Umar au contraire fixe aux protégés un statut d'humiliation. Il les marque de la rouelle, bleue pour les Chrétiens, jaune pour les Juifs, brune pour les Mazdéens, leur assigne résidence en des quartiers fermés chaque soir par des chaines, et impose maintes limites à leur citoyenneté qui reste cependant reconnue." Gardet, *Les Hommes de l'Islam*, p. 100.

[8] Guillaume, *Islam*, p. 80.

in different times to verses 3: 106/110 for instance mirrored the changes of attitudes due to social pressure and historical events in various periods. Commentators depending on the socio-historical issues of their time projected different views in explaining them. As Fazlur Rahman put it, "It is quite true to say that whatever views Muslims have wanted to project and advocate have taken the form of Qur'an commentaries."[9] Thus readings of the divine book offered by religious scholars (*fuqaha'*) can be taken as one of the most interesting means for taking the pulse of Muslims' history and society.

If for a modern liberal intellectual such as Rahman the Qur'an insists that "no community may lay claims to be uniquely guided and elected" (Qur'an 2:105/111, 107/113, and 114/120),[10] it is worth noting that the Islamic exegetical tradition stresses the other side where it is said that among human communities the Muslim one is exclusively "the best." From Tabari to Sayyid Qutb, this idea was maintained throughout, though with different emphases. How this was achieved and with what conceptual tools it was done is not an easy process to unveil. To trying to carry out this difficult task, we will pay special attention to two basic notions that contributed significantly to such a *tour de force*: the notions of *ijma'* (consensus) and that of *naskh* (abrogation) as they are related to our topic. Whereas the latter is indeed a Qur'anic notion (2:100/106; 22:51/52), the former is not. Both, however, belong to historical necessity felt by the *fuqaha'* in their struggle to solve particular socio-historical problems of the Ummah (community). Today both notions are also questioned from all sides—e.g., Fazlur Rahman for *ijma'* and Mahmud Taha for abrogation.[11]

---

[9] Fazlur Rahman, *Islam*, (Chicago: University of Chicago Press [1966], 1979, p.41.

[10] Fazlur Rahman, *Major Themes in the Qur'an* (Chicago: Bibliotheca Islamica, 1980), p. 165.

[11] As Abdullahi Ahmed An-Na'im put it in his introduction to the English translation of M.M. Taha's *The Second Message of Islam*, "What is revolutionary in his [Taha's] thinking, however, is the notion that abrogation process (*naskh*) was in fact a postponement and not final and conclusive repeal." (p.21) "This shift is made possible through examining the rationale of abrogation (*naskh*) in the sense of selecting which texts of the Qur'an and Sunnah are to be made legally binding, as opposed to

93

In this paper we will try, as a useful exercise that can cast light on our concern here, to explore these readings of God's Book on one particular issue—precisely that of the Muslim community being "the best," as stated in 3:106/110, leaving the rest of Fazlur Rahman's wishes mentioned in the passage cited at the beginning of this paper to Christian and Jewish friends to fulfill.

Let's now examine exegetical texts by M. Tabari (d. 310/ 923), F. Razi (d. 604/1208), Baydawi (d. 716/1316), M. Abduh (d. 1905), and S. Qutb (executed in 1966)—being the most representative of those who embarked in this painstaking exercise. The whole *aya* (3:106/110) states in Muhammad Marmaduke Pickhall's rendering as follows:[12] "Ye are the best community that hath been raised up for mankind. Ye enjoin right conduct and forbid indecency; and ye believe in Allah. And if the People of the Scripture had believed it had been better for them. Some of them are believers; but most of them are evil-livers."

a) Tabari and the Idealization of the Madinan Community

Let us remark first that Tabari is writing right after the Mutawakkil's edict (235/850) when the wave of Sunni old doctrines have been re-established after a phase of liberalism led by the Mu'tazilah school of theology. Tabari's *Jami' al bayan* as one of the very first written commentaries of the Qur'an,[13] gives three different interpreta-

---

being merely morally persuasive." (p.24)

[12] Blachère's French rendering (*Le Coran* [Paris: Maisonneuve et Larose, 1966], p. 90) reads as follows: "Vous êtes la meilleure communauté qu'on ait fait surgir pour les Hommes; vous ordonnez le Convenable, interdisez le Blâmable et croyez en Allah. Si les Détenteurs de l'Ecriture avaient cru, cela eût été mieux pour eux. Parmi eux, il est des Croyants, mais la plupart sont des Perves." He adds as a commentary that the Sh'ites substitute here as in verse 100 the term *a'immatin* for *ummatin* in *khayra ummatin*, "the best community"; the meaning then would be: You are [O Ali's followers!] the best Imams, etc.

[13] Al-Tabari, *Jami' al-bayan* (Beirut: Dar al-Fikr, 1408/1988), 30 vols., see vol. IV, pp. 43-6. Before Tabari there was what was called "interpretation of arbitrary opinion" (*tafsir bi'l-ra'y*). As a reaction to this, Qur'anic commentary (*'ilm at-tafsir*) was developed in order to make some order in dealing with the explanation the divine book. For the main principles guiding this new science then, see Fazlur Rahman, *Islam*, p. 41.

tions to this sura: 1) The sura concerns those first Muslims who emigrated with Muhammad from Mecca to Medina, and particularly the Prophet's companions. 2) It means that if you accomplish the conditions stated, i.e., if you command the belief in God and his prophet and the following of His Law, and if you forbid associating any other deity with God and distrusting His prophets and all that He forbids, then you are the community that was brought to people during your time. 3) The third interpretation also concerns the first elements of the Muslim community: You are "the best community" because you are the most numerous people that responded positively to Islam—so states Tabari.

What can we conclude from these three main interpretations? First, that the author of *Jami' al-bayan* does not include in the "best Community" the majority of Muslims in the Prophet Muhammad's time, let alone the community as a whole. Even the last two interpretations do not extend the community's beneficence to other generations of Muslims. Both exclude from this election the Muslim community of Tabari's era, for instance. All of them restrict the *aya* to some or the majority of the first Muslims. All exclude the Muslim community as a whole and particularly any other generation than that of Muhammad's.

To this sura, however, Tabari gives a last interpretation which goes beyond the historical context of the revelation to touch the community's essence. This explanation might appear to contradict the three first ones since it specifies the permanence of "the beneficence" as an inherent and intrinsic quality of the community. "You came into existence as the best community, that is, you were so in the Preserved Tablet," says Tabari. The creation of this community as being "the best" is not therefore something in the past—that which is not any longer in the present, but rather a permanent quality. Yet this does not necessarily mean that the historical community composed of the following generations are touched by this quality. The restriction of this positive feature to the first Muslims can be, in Tabari's mind, written in the Preserved Tablet without necessarily influencing the whole community.

b) Razi and the Problem of Ijma' and Jihad
Unlike Zamakhshari (467-538/1075-1144), for instance, whose

comments on this part of the sura are very succinct,[14] Razi goes into great detail to elaborate on every aspect of it. Starting his explanation of this verse by stating that, "this community will gain happiness, perfection, and divine grace in the hereafter because, on earth, it was the best," he then goes on to distinguish four topics in the sura's first part. Thus, being "the best" community is taken for granted and serves for Razi as a premise in building the rest of his argumentation.[15]

Unlike Tabari, however, Razi maintains that the past tense expressed by *kana* means that the community is no longer "the best." On the contrary, Muslims, for him, were and still are the guided and elected people as a community. The past tense of the verb "to be" is mainly used to place emphasis on the fact that it is indeed so—mainly because of what follows, i.e. "because you forbid evil and command good and believe in God." Moreover, "if the People of the Book believed the way the Muslims do, they would benefit from the same qualifications as you did, i.e., being 'the best' community."

For Razi, the addressees are naturally the Prophet's companions (those who were present during the revelation) but the text is meant to speak to all members of the community in the same way and form as the formulation of fasting for instance. Being the best community then concerns the whole Islamic Ummah—not only the first Muslims or the first Muslim community. Therefore, the Islamic community in Razi's time is included and does have a share in this beneficence. This is what "that had been raised up for mankind" (*ukhrijat li-l-nas*) means, i.e., it appeared to people until it was known and distinguished from other communities. The Muslim community is consequently the best among communities in all periods of history because it does what other communities do not do: forbidding evil and commanding good. As this is done by later generations of Muslims and not only the first, the beneficence covers them all.

---

[14] Al-Zamakhshari, *Al-Kashshaf 'an haqa'iq al-tanzil wa 'uyun al-aqawil* (Beirut: Dar al-Fikr, 1397/1977), 4 vols., vol. 1, pp. 454-5.

[15] Al-Razi, *Tafsir l-Fakhr al-Razi (Mafatih al-ghayb)* (Beirut: Dar al-Fikr, 1410/1990), 32 vols., vol. 8, pp. 193-9.

i) Razi and *Ijma' al-ummah*

Here Razi is not afraid to recall another Qur'anic passage that attributes positive points to people other than Muslims and confronting it with sura 3:106/110. With the idea that the consensus (*ijma'*) of this community can serve as a proof, he unconditionally agrees. He then argues the case as follows: God said: "And of Moses' folk there is a community who lead with truth and establish justice therewith" (7:159). Addressing Muslims, God said after that: "You are the best community." This way of putting things and mentioning Muslims as being the best after qualifying other groups with the same positive features implies that people mentioned by this *aya* are better than the people of Moses "who lead with truth and establish justice therewith." If, then, the latter are better than the former, continues Razi, it becomes necessary that the Muslim community guide and do justice only in the light of truth... Therefore this community judges only in the light of truth and its consensus becomes an argument of truth. Moreover, argues Razi, "The definite article of 'the evil' and 'the good' shows that it is *all* evil that they forbid and *all* good that they command; thus, their consensus becomes true and sincere, therefore an argument of proof."

There are two fundamental issues to discuss in relation to Razi's way of interpreting. The first concerns the process of abrogation (*naskh*) and the second the problem of consensus (*ijma'*). Let us start with the last issue. We have in what precedes a typical example of employing rational arguments in tracing the notion of consensus back to the Qur'an itself. Razi, with his arsenal of philosophical argumentation introduced in orthodox circles to counter-attack the liberal thought of the philosophers as well as other theologians, is conceptually equipped and chronologically well situated after Ghazail to do so. We know, however, that the concept of *ijma'* of the Islamic community is not Qur'anic and that it was Shafi'i (d. 204/820) who first introduced it "so that, if necessary, the consensus of scholars of a particular school of law could be overridden."[16] To support his doctrine, "the father of Islamic Jurisprudence" based it on the famous hadith: "My community would

---

[16] R.M. Savory, "Law and traditional society," in R.M. Savory, ed., *Introduction to Islamic Civilization* (New York: Cambridge University Press, 1976), p.57.

not agree on an error," which for us today sounds like it belongs more to a period when the community was threatened by internal strife and eventual disintegration than to the Prophet himself. Besides this famous Tradition, the Qur'anic verse, "We have made you a median community" (2:137/143), is often quoted by Islamic orthodoxy to support the general consensus (Baydawi for instance).

Although in practice the principle of *ijma'* was applied only within certain and narrow boundaries at the time of Shafi'i, "by the beginning of the tenth century A.D., jurists of all schools felt that all essential questions had been thoroughly discussed and final answers to all problems reached. The consensus of the Islamic community, once arrived at, was considered infallible and was unlikely to be amended by a succeeding generation of scholars."[17]

Throughout Muslim history it was a dominant belief that the general consensus, *ijma'* must come immediately after the *sunna* (Traditions) and the Qur'an, and before the *qiyas* (reasoning by analogy) as a principle of Muslim orthodox faith and law. As it was claimed that Islamic law is based on divine authority, any one who defied it was branded as an innovator (*mubtadi'*) which means a heretic. All orthodox schools of jurisprudence accepted it and only the now vanished Zahiri school rejected it. Like the latter, the Wahhabis, accepted only the consensus of the Prophet's companions. The Shi'a and the Ibadiyyah of course do not admit *ijma'*.

Discussing the science of the principles of Jurisprudence *'ilm usul al-fiqh*) and its four basic kinds of evidence (Qur'an, *sunna*, consensus, and analogy), Ibn Khaldun (d. 1406) says about the third principle, *ijma'*, that it "is justified by the fact that the men around Muhammad had agreed to disapprove of those who held opinions different from theirs. In addition, there is the established infallibility of the Muslim nation (as a whole) (*al-'ismah al-thabitah li'l-ummah*)."[18] Yet, even Ibn Khaldun admits that "some scholars differed on the matters of general consensus and analogy." But since "this is exceptional" as he

---

[17] Ibid., p. 57.

[18] Cf. F. Rosenthal, trans. and ed., *The Muqaddimah: An Introduction to History*, (Bollingen Series XLIII) (Princeton: Princeton University Press [1958] 1967), 3 vols., vol. 3, p. 25.

says, he does not consider worthwhile to go into detail about these exceptions. This shows one basic point concerning the Islamic doctrine of *ijma'*: There has never been complete agreement as to the validity of a consensus arrived at by a body of *ulama'* (recognized teachers of Islam) belonging to one generation and its binding force upon other generations. Though most scholars would say all future generations are bound by the consensus arrived at by the previous one, there are nonetheless some religious authorities who, according to Fazlur Rahman, think that the *ijma'* can be changed. As he put it, "there is no consensus on the doctrine of consensus."

Moreover, Rahman here makes another important point, that is, although an agreement about a decision may be arrived at by a group of religious scholars and in this way practically represent a consensus of the community, there is nevertheless nothing which makes it irreversible. Moreover, according to some jurists, apart from the concord about the existence of the five pillars in Islam and that the basic and first one among them is profession of divine unicity, there is even no complete agreement or consensus on the details of the other four.[19]

There is yet another lesson to draw from Razi's argumentation. The process of abrogation (*naskh*) not only touches some injunctions inside the Islamic message but goes outside Islam to affect other faiths.[20] The orthodox Islamic attitude towards Judaism and Christianity is

---

[19] About the consensus in modern Islamic society Fazlur Rahman (*Islam*, p. 262) writes: "When the assembly enacts a certain law, that law may be right or wrong (for no individual or group is inerrant), but in so far as it reflects the will of the Community, it will be both Islamic and democratic; i.e. it will represent the consensus (*ijma'*) of the Community. But this is a consensus that can always be changed, since it is always potentially possible for a minority to become a majority opinion through the process of debate."

[20] While there is no mention of *ijma'* in the Qur'an, the term *naskh* is definitely Qur'anic. "Never sent We a messenger or a prophet before thee but when He recited (the message) Satan proposed (opposition) in respect of that which he recited thereof. But Allah abolisheth (*fa-vansakhu*) that which Satan proposeth. Then Allah establisheth His revelations. Allah is Knower, Wise"; (22:51/52); Also, "Nothing of Our revelation (even a single verse) do We abrogate (*ma nansakhu*) or cause be forgotten, but We bring (in place) one better or the like thereof. Knowest thou not that Allah is Able to do all things?" (2:100/106).

99

controlled by the same process. Razi's use of abrogation in favor of his own community and in detriment of others is of course to be expected. If Ibn Khaldun who had the ambition of writing about human civilization up to his era ignored religious sciences of peoples other than the Muslims, it is mainly because, as Al-Azmeh put it, "the religion of Islam—and, by implication, all the sciences that give it support and articulation—stands to other religions of the book as the Koran stands to other holy books and as the prophecy of Muhammad stands to the prophecies of his predecessors."[21]

ii) Razi and the Notion of *Jihad*

Unlike contemporary Muslims who—in face of the intimidating worldwide campaign that Islam is the religion of the sword and that *jihad* is the cornerstone of that faith[22]—try to relativize and distinguish different meanings and levels of *jihad*, Razi has no problem in making the religious war the most important characteristic which sets Islam apart from other religions. Three levels are usually distinguished in the term *jihad* by Muslim scholars: the personal, the social, and the political. Leaving aside the first called *al-jihad al-akbar* ("the greatest struggle") as well as the third meaning,[23] Razi was mainly concerned with the social dimension of the notion of *jihad* in Islam. That is the struggle of integrating human and divine values into Islamic society.

---

[21] Aziz Al-Azmeh, *Ibn Khaldun* (London & New York: Routledge [1st ed., 1982], 1990), p. 104.

[22] According to M. Shaltut, previous rector of Al-Azhar (*al-Qur'an wa-l-qital* [Beirut: Dar al-Fath, 1983], p.8), only six verses in the Qur'an mention the term *harb* (war), while the word peace is evoked in more than thirty-three verses. See Mohamed Talbi, "Le Message de paix des religions," paper given at the International Symposium on Peace-Justice-Development: The Contribution of Religions to a Peace Order in the Middle East; 25-27 Sept. 1991, St. Augustin/Bonn, Germany.

[23] That is, the struggle to oppose injustice and oppression when necessary by force. A good example illustrating this third meaning of *jihad* would be the Algerian revolution against the French in modern times, as was the resistance against the Crusaders in the medieval period.

Why does "enjoining right, prohibiting wrong and believing in God" make Islam the best since most communities do the same? asks Razi, answering through the scholar al-Qaffal: "this community is distinguished from previous ones by the *jihad* in commanding good and forbidding evil. The *jihad* is then the best form of worship, and since it is stronger in our law than in that of any other community, it makes the Muslim community the best community".[24] Razi continues, according to al-Qaffal: "no just person is to deny the benefit to religion of combat since most people customarily like their own religion. Out of fear of being killed they progressively move from darkness to light."

About precedence of "commanding good and forbidding evil" to "believing in God," Razi's answers: Believing in God is some- thing common among many communities. What makes this community the best is something else, i.e., *al-amr bi-l-ma'ruf wa nahy 'an l-munkar.*[25]

c) Baydawi and the Recapitulation and Abridgement of Ideas
'Abdallah ibn 'Umar al-Baydawl (d. 716/1316) mainly reiterates

---

[24] Then Ibn Abbas is quoted in explaining this verse.

[25] As to *ta'muruna bi-lma'ruf...bi-llah,* Razi goes into detail to answer three questions. For Abu Bakr Ibn 'Arabi (468-543/1076-1151), this *aya* is a proof that commanding the good and forbidding evil is a religious duty imposed on at least a sufficient number of Muslims (*fard kifayah*) who should fulfill it. It may become *fard al-'ayn* (to which every Muslim is bound) if the person is known for having an efficient view (*Ahkam al-qur'an* (Beirut: Dar al-Fikr, n.d.), 1, p. 292).

As to the rest of the *aya,* Razi thinks that if the People of the Book entered Islam, they would have leadership, which for him is what mainly prevented them from abandoning their religion. For Razi, People of the Book are of two groups: believers, and those who despite their belief are *fasiqqun* in their own religion. Among the first are Abdallah b. Sallam and a group of Jews, and Al-Najashi (Negus) and a group of Christians who are among the believers. These were of course Jews and Christians converted to Islam. Of the second type, Razi thinks that they have no power to harm Muslims. They can only hurt them with their tongue, by insulting Muhammad or Jesus, or by showing their unbelief (such as, Azir son of God, Jesus son of God and the trinity), or by altering biblical texts, or "throwing doubt among people," or spreading fear in the weak among Muslims.

ideas developed by previous commentators on this point.[26] One is that the *jihad* is a duty imposed on the community (*fard al-kifayah*) but not on every individual Muslim (*fad al-ayn*). He also insists, like Razi but unlike Tabari, that the beneficence of the Muslim community is not restricted to the first Muslims in spite of the use of past tense at the beginning of the sura. For him the presence of *kana'* by no means signifies that "being the best" stopped applying to the Islamic community of his time. To argue his point, he gives the example of *inna 'llaha kana ghafuran rahiman* (Lo! Allah is Forgiving, Merciful—33:24) which uses the same past tense to express an eternal truth. This is then an everlasting quality that characterizes the *Ummah* since we were so in God's knowledge or in the Preserved Tablet (*al-lawh al-mahfuz*) or among the previous nations. A second point that this verse implies is that continued consensus is a proof (*al-ijma'hujjah*) of the continued beneficence because, as we have seen with Razi, the Muslim community agrees in commanding all good and forbidding all evil.

There is nothing particularly new in this thirteenth-century commentary; it sums up ideas previously developed and stresses philological aspects in the wake of Zamakhshari, from, however, a non-Mu'tazite standpoint. It is usually said that Baydawi's *Anwar at-tanzil wa asrar at-ta' wil* is one of the best Qur'an commentaries. Needless to say, this was no surprise in a historical period that started to look for abridged and ready-made knowledge. One has to wait until the last century when the Islamic societies were forced to wake up from their long stagnation by the advance of Western expeditions at the door of their bedroom. Then the Book is viewed afresh once again and Muhammad Abduh starts talking about the opening the door of *ijtihad*.

d) Abduh and Defensive Islam

The so-called Manar school represented by Muhammad Abduh and Rashid Rida is known for certain new positions in reinterpreting the divine message. It would be useful here initially to resurrect its basic

---

[26] Al-Baydawi, *Anwar al-tanzil wa asrar al-ta'wil*, (with *Tafsir al-ialalayn* of Al-Suyuti and al-Mahalli) (Cairo, 3rd ed., n.d.), vol. 1, pp. 176-7.

objectives as stated by Abduh himself: (1) the reform of the Muslim religion by bringing it back to its original condition, (2) the renovation of the Arabic language, and (3) the recognition of the rights of the people.[27] Of these three points in Abduh's program only the first interests us here. One of the fundamental points treated by both thinkers is that of tolerance, reflected in Rida's opposition to the doctors' *ijma'* concerning the death penalty for apostasy. On the other hand, Abduh's refusal to admit that those who did not have a chance to hear the message of Islam would be damned is very significant. Rather he thinks that their fate would depend on divine mercy. Both positions reflect the new historical context wherein Muslims are forced to live and their awareness of their known position in a world where a pluralistic view is not only more realistic but also desperately desirable.[28]

In dealing with our verse 3:106/110, Abduh reminds us of the context in which this verse was revealed to the Prophet of Islam.[29] After ordering the believers to become brothers and warning them not to split and combat each other, God said that "you are the best community." For Abduh, the beneficence of this community and its merit over other communities reside in these three things: commanding good, forbidding evil, and believing in God the most High. As far as the use of the past tense is concerned, Abduh gave three different explanations:

1) It can mean that the action is complete, i.e., you are the best community in existence now because most communities are corrupted. They ignore commanding good and forbidding evil, and they do not profess the right belief which encourages these things.

2) It can also mean that the action is incomplete, in which case the *aya* means that Islamic community is, in God's knowledge or in past communities as reported in their Books, the best community. i.e., you were in your past life as a community the best one.

A few remarks are to be made at this stage. Abduh's first idea that Christian Western societies are corrupted because they are material-

[27] *Short Encyclopedia of Islam*, see "Muhammad Abduh."

[28] See J. Jomier *Le Commentaire coranique du Manar* (Paris, 1954), chapter ix.

[29] M. Abduh - R. Rida, *Tafsir al-Manar*, pp. 372-5.

istic in outlook is not incompatible with the fact that the Manar school is fascinated by the West's scientific and political achievements. Second, it should be recalled that, on the one hand, Zamakhshari does not elaborate much on this sura, and that, on the other hand, his idea is incorporated in Abduh's second explanation already taken up by Baydawi.

3) There is still a third possible explanation mentioned by Abduh: The verb "to be" in the past tense (*kana*) means here becoming, i.e., "you have become" the best community. But this explanation, he says, is the weakest. Indeed, there is no surprise in Abduh's rejection of this last possibility. The state of Islamic societies, harassed from all sides by European colonial aggressions from the 19th century on, cannot fit with such an interpretation. Moreover, for Abduh this beneficence is not extended to those of the community who are Muslims only by name, not even to those who perform the five religious duties, unless they command good, forbid evil, and adhere to the way of God while avoiding religious divisions.

It is worth noting at this point that Islamic proselytism is an idea very dear to the Manar school. R. Rida wanted to spread reformist viewpoint in the Muslim world to protect Islam from Western assault. Using a similar idea mentioned in a previous verse of the same sura ("And there may spring from you a nation who invite to goodness, and enjoin right conduct and forbid indecency. Such are they who are successful" (3:100/104), the Manar school develops the ideal society for spreading what they consider to be the true Islam.[30]

This *aya* concerns those to whom it was addressed first, i.e., the Prophet and his companions in which all the aforementioned conditions are true. That believing in God came last is explained by the fact that the first two conditions—commanding good and forbidding evil—is customarily praiseworthy among all people, be they believers or unbelievers. Moreover, these two qualities are a safeguard for believing in God.

In brief, says Abduh, the Qur'an clarifies the state of all communities in terms of their beliefs, their customs and their deeds and weighs them with a precision never seen in any book, be it a scientist's or a historian's. "If we gather all that was said in the Qur'an about the

---

[30] J. Jomier, *Le Commentaire*, p. 333.

People of the Book and others, and expose it to their scientists, philosophers, and historians, they would admit that it is true."

Such a conclusion should not surprise us if we keep in mind one of the principle doctrines of the Reformist school: That Islam is the source of Western Renaissance. Now that Europe has discovered scientific knowledge, why, asks R. Rida, did Western Christians not embrace Islam, which, according to Abduh, is more rational and closer to reality than Christianity?

e) Qutb and the Duty of Leadership

Sayyid Qutb was born one year after Abduh's death in 1905. If the latter is the founder of Islamic Reformism (*Salafiyyah*), the former is considered to be one of the most important ideologues of today's Islamism. It was correctly said that *Salafiyyah* is fascinated by the West and wants to modernize Islam, whereas Islamism is deceived by it and wants to Islamize modernity. The Islamicists' picture of the Western culture is as oversimplified and caricatured as is the Western image of Muslims and their faith presented by the media. To appreciate S. Qutb's conception of Islam, it is necessary to remind us here of his perception of Western civilization itself. Introducing the English translation of the last volume of his Qur'anic commentary, the author's brother summarizes this perception:

> The non-Muslims, on the other hand, confront humanity with a host of philosophical, social, political and economic doctrines which banish religion from practical life and at best restrict it to a tiny corner of man's conscience so that it may become purely a relationship between the individual and his Lord that has no bearing whatsoever on society and its active life, or, at worst, fight it tooth and nail and bar its existence. As a result, human life is full of many sorts of political, social and economic injustice which know no limits. It witnesses various types of intellectual and moral perversions unknown in history. The advocates of such perversion and deviation try nevertheless to dress their erring ways in a scientific garment and they hold to them as if they were truth itself or the ideal sought after. This they do despite all that they

105

suffer in consequence of nervous and psychological diseases—worry and restlessness, madness and suicide, alcoholism, drug addiction and crime.[31]

This is the background against which S. Qutb presents his image of Islam and how it should be understood. "His driving objective was that the Muslims of today should be able to live and practice true Islam in the same way as the early Islamic generations. They would then rescue themselves and would be able to show all mankind the road to salvation." (p. xiii) Thus S. Qutb's mission is not restricted to the Muslim part of humanity like that of Abduh who tried to catch up with the modern Western world. Rather he extends his objectives to cover the whole humanity that is now, in his opinion, in distress.

It is significant enough that one of the suras quoted and discussed in this introduction is exactly that which is our concern here: 3:106/110. The image of Islam Muslims present today, says M. Qutb,

is nothing more than the indistinguishable negative of the true image of Islam as it was practiced by the early Islamic generations, who perfectly fulfilled Allah's own description of them: "You are truly the best nation that has ever been raised up for mankind: You enjoin the doing of what is right and forbid the doing of what is

---

[31] Sayyid Qutb, *In the Shade of the Qur'an*, intro. by Muhammad Qutb (London: MWH London Pub., 1979, 1981), xii. Yusuf Ali also emphasizes Islam's mission to humanity. Yusuf Ali on verse 3:110:

The logical conclusion to the evolution of religious history is a non-sectarian, non-racial, non-doctrinal, universal religion, which Islam claims to be: For Islam is just submission to the Will of God. This implies (1) Faith, (2) doing right, being an example to others to do right, and having the power to see that the right prevails, (3) eschewing wrong, being an example to others to do eschew wrong, and having the power to see that wrong and injustice are defeated. Islam therefore lives, not for itself, but for mankind. The People of the Book, if only they had faith, would be Muslims, for they have been prepared for Islam. Unfortunately there is Unfaith, but it can never harm those who carry the banner of Faith and Right, which must always be victorious (*The Holy Qur'an* [Beirut: Dar al-Arabia, 1968], p. 151, note 434).

wrong and you believe in Allah." Hence they were able to write that incomparable page in human history. They established truth and justice on earth and raised for mankind an inimitable civilization which builds up its structure in the material and spiritual worlds at the same time. It is a civilization which unites the two worlds and achieves harmony between body and soul, religion and politics, faith and science, the present life and the hereafter, the practical and the ideal. (p.xii)

Commenting on the same verse in *Fi zilali l-qur'an* (In the Shade of the Qur'an),[32] S. Qutb says that it means: a community with a special role, a special position and a special account. This, in his opinion, is what the Muslim community today must realize in order to take leadership in the world since it is the best. To provide the true belief, the true conception, the true order, the true social behavior, the true knowledge and science are its basic duties. It is its duty always to be in the leadership position and know what this role requires: First to protect life from evil and corruption and acquire the necessary force to command good and forbid evil...It is the best community not for any other reason than protecting human life from corruption and promoting good deeds, with of course belief in God which, in S. Qutb's opinion, sets the boundaries of these two things. Consequently, belief in God is the necessary criterion for true values and authentic knowledge of good and evil. Reforming society alone is, therefore, not enough. Belief in God must also permeate those who do the job. The Muslim community fulfills its true existence only if it commands good and forbids evil. Otherwise it does not exist and it is also not Islamic.

Then Qutb goes on to reinforce his argument from the Prophet's *sunna*. The first Prophetic Tradition (*hadith*) mentioned is: "Any one among you who sees evil has to combat it with his hand; if he cannot he shall use his tongue, and if he cannot he shall do it with

---

[32] Sayyid Qutb, *Fi zilal al-qur'an* (Cairo: Dar Ihya' al-kutub al-'arabiyyah, 3rd ed., 1961), vol. iv, pp. 30-4.

his heart."[33] Then the five other Traditions with the same theme are cited, all of them, says S.Qutb, proving the authenticity of this attitude for Islamic society as well as the necessity of instilling this particular attitude. The attitude commanded by these hadiths contain important elements of orientation as well as important pedagogical and method-ological aspects.[34]

4. Contemporary Reformist Interpretations

The main problem with religions—at least with Islam, which is our main concern here—is that they equate faith with the cultural form taken historically by that same faith. All Muslim reformists start with this epistemological distinction in order to look again under the fog of the historical accumulation of interpretations. Fazlur Rahman's new and liberal reading proceeds from the same starting point and operates with equal methodological means today. In dissociating the institutional shape assumed throughout its history from the Qur'anic text, he strives to save what can be saved in the divine words in an age preoccupied with human rights, individual dignity and tolerance without which life today would be impossible for everyone.

a) Rahman's Theory of Qur'anic Rejection of Election
In his *Major Themes of the Qur'an*, Fazlur Rahman opposes the idea of exclusiveness claimed by most Qur'an commentators from Tabari to S. Qutb. According to him, the movement of the argumenta-tion in the Qur'an shows its basic anti-election outlook: "When God

---

[33] On this Hadith, see A. Lakhsaassi, "Société et religion dans la poésie berbère Honneur et *hudud* Allah chez Lhajj Belaid," in *Poésie chantée dans le Maghreb des campagnes, des villes, de l'exil,* une collection d'études reunie par Marie Virolle-Soulbes et Claude Lefebure (CNRSEHESS) avec le soutien de la MSH (Paris: 1992).

[34] For the rest of the *aya*, S. Qutb maintains that it is better for the People of the Book to believe in this world to avoid division and false conceptions on which their society is based. Like all societal systems not founded on an all embracing belief, on a complete explanation of life, and on a purpose of human existence and man's position in this universe, theirs is the same. It is also better for them in the afterlife because it makes them avoid what is waiting the non-believers...

tested Abraham by some words and he [Abraham] fulfilled them, God said [to Abraham], I am going to make you a leader of men. What about my progeny? asked Abraham; He [God] replied, My promise does not extend to the unjust ones." (2:124) Should then Muslims or any other religious group be unjust, they would not be given God's engagement.

To bring his point home Rahman quotes other Qur'anic passages which clearly undermine the idea that a people as a people could have a special favor in God's eyes. For him the continuous reminding statements of the Qur'an on this point just after having referred to the biblical prophets and their people weaken this idea of election: "That is a community that is by-gone: to them belongs what they earned and to you [Muslims!] will belong what you will earn, and you will not be asked for what they had done" (2:128/134, 135/141).

After rejecting what he calls the "mystique of election" Rahman, always on the basis of Qur'anic passages intelligently selected, argues for the existence of universal goodness. For him the Qur'an is consistent on this point and logically consequent with itself in admitting that good people are also found in communities other than the Islamic one: "Those who believe [Muslims], the Jews, the Christians, and the Sabaeans—whosoever believe in God and the Last Day and do good deeds—they shall have their reward from their Lord, shall have nothing to fear, nor shall they come to grief." (2:59/62; cf. 5:73/69)

If the Qur'an is here logically consequent in its general universalist outlook, so is Rahman in tackling this problem in Islamic commentary literature. The two verses just quoted were given of course other interpretations by Qur'an scholars than one offered here by the author of *Major Themes of the Qur'an.* "The vast majority of Muslim commentators exercise themselves fruitlessly to avoid having to admit the obvious meaning: that those—from any section of humankind—who believe in God and the Last Day and do good deeds are saved."[35] Even

---

[35] "They either say that by Jews, Christians, and Sabaeans here are meant those who have actually become 'Muslims'—which interpretation is clearly belied by the fact that 'Muslims' constitute only the first of the four groups of 'those who believe'—or that they were those good Jews, Christians, and Sabaeans who lived before the advent of the Prophet Muhammad—which is an even worse tour de force" (Fazlur Rahman, *Major*

109

when answering to unacceptable claims of the preceding monotheists that the hereafter belongs exclusively to the Jews and Christians, argues Rahman, the Qur'an says: "On the contrary, whosoever surrenders himself to God while he does good deeds as well, he shall find his reward with his Lord, shall have no fear, nor shall he come to grief" (2:106/112).

It should be mentioned here what a modern Qur'an translator and commentator such as Yusuf Ali says about the verse 5:[72] 73/69 where the same idea is reiterated: "As God's Message is one, Islam recognizes true faith in other forms, provided that it be sincere, supported by reason, and backed up by righteous conduct." On the verse 2:59/62 however, he has no comments to add. Rather he goes into a long speculation about Sabaeans and who they are. Is this another and subtle way to avoid admitting the evidence?[36]

If the Qur'an strongly rejects the election of any people as such to the detriment of others and recognizes goodness among at least Jews, Christians and Sabaeans because of their belief in one God and the Day of Judgment, then surely, in good logic, the Muslim community can only be one community among others. To the problem of a multi-community world, the Qur'anic text put forward a clear and definite response in Rahman's opinion:

> And We have sent down to you the Book in truth, confirming the Book that existed already before it and protecting it... For each one of you [several communities] We have appointed a Law and a Way of Conduct [while the essence of religion is identical]. If God had so willed, He would have made all of you one community, but [He has not done so] that He may test you in what He has given you; so compete in goodness. To God shall you all return and He will tell you [the Truth] about what you have been disputing. (5:52-3/48)

Themes, p. 166). For Rahman's major ideas exposed here, unless otherwise specified, see chapter viii and appendix ii in this book.

[36] Yusuf Ali, *The Holy Qur'an*, p. 33.

Quoting two other passages (2:143/148; 2:172/177) on the change of direction of prayer from Jerusalem to Mecca, Rahman maintains that the Qur'an then emphasizes something rather fundamental: being virtuous and competing in good works, not the *qibla* in itself. Having different religious systems and communities in competition with each other underlines nothing more than the divine wisdom behind this plan.[37] From verse 5:[52-3]/48 another important conclusion is drawn: the recognition of the three separate communities: Jews, Christians, and Muslims. This explains why the Meccan terms "sects" and "parties" (*ahzab* and *shiya*), used for the earlier communities, have been dropped after the *Hijra* to Madina where they have been replaced with the term community (*ummah*) or the collectives term "the People of the Book" (*ahl al-kitab*). Now each community is not only admitted to exist independently from the other two but also recognized to possess its own laws and particular rules of conduct (*minhaj*). "Far from seeing refuge in Abraham in order to validate the Muslim community, the Qur'an now recognizes in some fashion the validity of the Jewish and the Christian communities."

Does that mean that the Muslim community has no particularity from the Qur'anic standpoint? It would be absurd of course to argue for such a claim. The Qur'an does maintain that it is still the "ideal" or "best" community (*khaya ummatin*) and members of the two other communities are invited to join as sura 3:106/110 shows. Moreover the Islamic community is the "Median community (*Ummat wasat*)" *par excellence* (2:137/143) which avoids extremes in everything. Elsewhere (5:22/19) this invitation is made even more obvious: "O People of the Book! Our Messenger has come to you now, making matters clear to you, after a long interval between messengers, lest you should say:

---

[37] "The metaphor of competitive race, I believe," writes Dr. Ernest Hamilton in an insightful article, "is central to the Qur'anic invitation to dialogue with the Jews and Christians and is of crucial importance in our understanding of the Qur'anic perspective on the meaning and method of interfaith dialogue." ("The Olympics of 'good works': Exploitation of a Qur'anic metaphor," *The Muslim World*, LXXXI, 1 (1990), pp. 72-81. For the Qur'anic conception of dialogue with the People of the Book, see also Ernest Hamilton, "The Qur'anic Dialogue with Jews and Christians," *The Chicago Theological Seminary Register*, LXXX, 3 (1990), pp. 24-38.

'There has not come to us any bearer of good tidings nor a warner'; now a bearer of good tidings and a warner has come."

One thing is certain, however. Qualified as being "the best community produced for mankind" does not in itself produce election. The Islamic *Ummah* is given "no assurance whatever that it will be automatically God's darling unless, when it gets power on the earth, it establishes prayers, provides welfare for the poor, commands good, and prohibits evil (22:42/41, etc.). In 47: 40/38, the Muslims are warned that "if you turn backs [upon this teaching], God will substitute another people for you who will not be like you" (9:[39]/38).

Any religious reformer, particularly when he professes strict monotheism, has to answer the question of religious diversity. If God is one and the three religions refer to the same being who spoke to humanity on three occasions by sending it the same message, why do our understandings of God diverge? Ernest Hamilton's thesis to solve this theological issue in the Qur'an is that there are different prophetic "readings" of the same Core covenant (*mithaq*). The Torah, the Gospel, and the Qur'an are only a few examples. "The differences in the terms and obligations among various prophetic codes *qur'ans*) are, therefore, natural and are to be accepted."[38] At the historical level, however, being acutely aware of this diversity, Muhammad hoped to be joined by others in his own understanding of this Core message. How naive his attitude was can be measured by the ultimate social and political developments. His efforts have issued historically in almost the opposite

---

[38] According to Ernest Hamilton, two covenants not mutually exclusive are to be found in the Qur'an: the "intrinsic" covenant and the "voluntary" or the "Core" covenant:

> God sent all communities the same covenant, that is the Core covenant, so that one community may not claim to be the sole heir to God's truth of claim to have received better guidance from God than another community (41; 43; 42; 13; 3:73). The concepts of the "chosen people" (5:18; 62:6), of the exclusive possession of divine revelation (3: 72-4; 4: 54; 57: 29) or of "complete," therefore superior, revelation (2: 120; 2: 136; 3: 73) are clearly denounced in the Qur'an as incompatible with God's compassion and justice (62: 6; 57:29)." ("The Qur'anic Concept of the Covenant," *Bouhout* (Revue de la Faculté des lettres et des Sciences Humaines III - Mohammedia - Morocco), #2-3 (1990), p. 15.

result. Not only have the three religious traditions engaged in a long and non-stop apologetic and polemical dispute, but also Islam itself came to be divided into many a sect. In spite of his warning to the Muslims not to split into factions, later on a hadith attributed to Muhammad reports that he had said that Islam will be separated into 73 sects.[39]

If the Qur'an in Rahman's interpretation uses only goodness in deeds to judge not only individuals but also communities, it is useless to inquire, at least in principle, whether there is any comparison between the election of the Jewish people in Judeo-Christian tradition and the privileged position of the Arabs in Islam. Though stated in Arabic with Arabs as the first addressees, the Qur'anic message was not for the latter only. Moreover, it is not true that Scriptures of pre-Muhammad prophets were only each for his community, "nor that when Islam was later linked with Abraham (which happened in Mecca, not Medina), the Qur'an gave up Moses to the Jews and Jesus to the Christians as their properties because of Jewish (and Christian) opposition."[40] For Louis Gardet[41] there is not a total similitude but rather an analogy between the two Semite people in both traditions. In our sense it would be more meaningful to talk about the Arabic language as having a privileged status in Islam than about Arabs as such. And here gain we are talking once more about the Qur'an as an Absolute.

b) Consequences of the Election Theory

There is no question but that to maintain systematically the idea of election and exclusivity cannot be—sooner or later, directly or indirectly—without dramatic consequences for each religious tradition. This is true not only on a socio-historical level, as we have seen with the impact of Mutawakkil's edict (235/850), but also as far as our understanding of human religious experience itself is concerned. Today,

---

[39] On this issue Rahman writes: "Muslims are warned not to split up into parties. It is at this point that the religion of Muhammad is described as 'straight' and 'upright,' the religion of the *hanif* (i.e. of an upright monotheist who does not follow divisive forces) and is linked and identified with the religion of Abraham."

[40] Fazlur Rahman, *Major Themes*, p. 133.

[41] Louis Gardet, *Hommes de l'Islam*, p. 60.

113

there is at least one voice among Muslim intellectuals who has kept disapproving such narrow-mindedness not only in Islam but in all religious systems. Mohammed Arkoun continues to denounce—come hell or high water—what he considers to be at the root of this doctrine of exclusion in the three Abrahamic faiths.

> Traditionalistic theologies have been developed as cultural systems of exclusion, refusal strategies of all that is foreign to the Community (Church, Ummah). Thus epistemological obstacles which render unthinkable all problems liberated today by critical thought have been erected. Until today, Jewish, Christian and Islamic thought avoided problemitizing the phenomenon of revelation outside their own surrounding walls.[42]

Suffice it here as an example to quote one of the most prominent thinkers in Islamic history to illustrate Muslims' attitude towards other religious traditions. Tackling the problem of positive and traditional disciplines as opposed to intellectual and rational ones, Ibn Khaldun wrote:

> These traditional sciences are all restricted to Islam and the Muslims, even though every religious group has to have something of the sort. (The traditional sciences of Islam) are remotely comparable to (those of other religious groups), in that they are sciences of a religious law revealed by God to the lawgiver who transmits it. But as to the particulars, (Islam) is different from all other religious groups, because it abrogates them (*nasikhatun laha*). All the pre-Islamic sciences concerned with religious groups are to be discarded, and their discussion is forbidden."[43]

---

[42] Mohammed Arkoun, *La pensée arabe*, (Que sais-je?) (Paris: P.U.F., 1975), p. 120.

[43] Rosenthal, *The Muqaddimah*. Cf. vol. II, p. 438.

As we can notice once more, the notion of *naskh* has been used here to dismiss any study of other religious heritages and the uniqueness of Muslims' faith has been put forth as an argument to shut the door at the face of other faiths. If at another period of Islamic history a scholar such as Ibn Hazm or even Ghazali was interested in other religious traditions however, it is unfortunately more for polemical and apologetic purposes than for anything else. Needless to say at this point that this is true of all other theologies be they Christian or Jewish.

The consequences of this orthodox and often ultra-orthodox outlook are tremendous. To measure how much human knowledge has suffered from such an attitude, we will not hesitate to quote once more the fourteenth century thinker and his *Muqaddimah*:

> The religious law has forbidden the study of all revealed scriptures except the Qur'an. Muhammad said: "Consider the People of the Book neither as truthful nor as untruthful." Just say: "We believe in what was revealed to us and revealed to you. Our God and your God are one." (29:46-45) And when the Prophet saw a leaf of the Torah in Umar's hand, he got so angry that his anger showed in his face. Then, he said: "Did I not bring it to you white and clean? By God, if Moses were alive, he would have no choice but to follow me".[44]

Thus is summarized succinctly the official orthodox belief in the Muslim world up to now—closely related to another issue concerning the Revealed Books: *tahrif* (Scriptural alteration).

c) Consequences of the Tahrif Theory
From the beginning, Muslim tradition has maintained the doc-

---

[44] Ibid, vol. II, pp. 438-9. The same Ibn Khaldun concludes his discussion on Christian sects with such a typical orthodox discourse as follows: "We do not think that we should blacken the pages of this book with discussion of their dogmas of unbelief. In general, they are well known. All of them are unbelief. This is clearly stated in the noble Qur'an. (To) discuss or argue those things with them is not up to us. It is (for them to choose between) conversion to Islam, payment of the poll tax, or death." (Rosenthal, *The Muqaddimah*, vol. 1, p. 480).

trine of *tahrif* about Christian and Jewish Scriptures since the Qur'an speaks about the Torah being altered, (for the verb *harrafa*, see 2:75, 78, 159, 174; 3:78; 4: 46; 5: 13, 41; 6:91). The *tahrif* doctrine is also a double edged weapon. Like the election theory, sooner or later it can turn against those who make too much use of it. This is precisely what happened in Islam right from its birth when the Prophet himself was charged by his opponents of doing the same dirty job. This is reflected in the Qur'an itself where Muhammad denies substituting one revelation for another (10:16/15). The term used is rather *tabdil,* meaning also change and alteration. Later on with the unavoidable split of Islam into orthodox and unorthodox factions, this doctrine has been in turn employed since then until now by the latter against the former. In the medieval times, Ibn Hazm (d. 456/1054) reported that the Imamite Shi'ah maintained that "the Qur'an was corrupted by adding that which was not in it, by removing a great number (of verses) from it and altering a great number (of verses) in it"[45] It is interesting to note that one of their accusations concerns a term in the verse under study here, i.e., sura 3/110: *kuntum khayra ummatin* (You are the best community) for the Imamite Shi'ah reads *a'immatin* (imams) instead of *ummatin* (community).[46]

This is not a theological dispute belonging only to medieval times, however. As late as the nineteenth century, writes Kohlberg:

> We find a staunch defender of the *tahrif* theory in the person of Husayn b. Muhammad Taqi an-Nuri at-Tabarsi (d. 1320/1905), who devotes a whole book to this question. In the three introductory sections he attempts to prove that since the Bible and the Gospels were corrupted, it is not impossible that the same fate should have befallen the Qur'an.[47]

---

[45] Quoted by E. Kohlberg, "Some Notes on the Imamite Attitude to the Qur'an" in S. M. Stern, A. Hourani and V. Brown, eds., *Islamic Philosophy and the Classical Tradition* (Oxford: B. Cassirer, 1972), p. 209.

[46] Ibid., p. 212. See also note 12 above on Blachère.

[47] Ibid, p. 218.

Hopefully, there is at least one Muslim thinker who stood against the *tahrif* doctrine by rejecting the orthodox interpretation of certain Qur'anic passages. Curiously that thinker is the same Ibn Khaldun we just quoted above. In lucid moments of his scholarly career, by using basic common sense, he could stand up and question Islamic tradition on that problem. As we have just seen him in his orthodox mood, it is only fair to quote him here as he stands almost alone to our knowledge on the issue of *tahrif*: "The statement concerning the alteration (of the Torah by the Jews) is unacceptable to the thorough scholars and cannot be understood in its plain meaning, since custom prevents people who have a (revealed) religion from dealing with their divine scripture in such a manner."[48] As to the problem of the Christian belief in the Trinity, his attitude is as well contradictory as on the Jewish Scripture. In his *History*, he explains this belief by what he calls the superficial reading of the New Testament by the Christians.[49]

5. Conclusion

In discussing the idea of the Absolute in the Qur'an and particularly that of the Islamic Ummah being the best community, I have chosen only Sunni commentators mainly because of the limitation of space in such a paper. For the same reason that it would take us too far in such a work as this one, I have also left aside a thorough discussion of another related sura (2:137/143) which states that the Muslim community is a median one (*ummat wasat*). Without investigating the Shi'ah commentaries on both verses as well as the Sunni's on 2:137/143, it would not be possible for us to present here a more comprehensive perspective on the subject.[50]

---

[48] Rosenthal, *The Muqaddimah*, vol. 1, p. 20.

[49] See Al-Azmeh, *Ibn khaldun*, p. 131.

[50] This is done, at a general level, by Mahmoud Ayoub, "The Speaking Qur'an and the Silent Qur'an: A Study of the Principles and Development of Imami Shi'i *Tafsir*," in *Approaches to the History of the Interpretation of the Qur'an*, ed. by Andrew Rippin (Oxford: Clarendon Press, 1988), pp. 177-98. See also the recent work of Jane Dammen McAuliffe, *Qur'anic Christians: An Analysis of Classical and Modern Exegesis* (New York:

Yet we can still draw some basic conclusions from what has been done here so far. First, that the Qur'anic text, though believed to be a divine scripture, is an open book that has been interpreted according to different socio-historical contexts and times. As Jane MacAuliffe put it, "While the Qur'an is morphologically immutable, it is semantically alive. The invariant structure of the pronounced text perdures but the signification conveyed lives anew through generation after generation of painstaking commentary."[51] Our investigation of the six commentators from Tabari (fourth/tenth century) to S. Qutb (fourteenth/twentieth century) and Fazlur-Rahman (fifteenth/twentieth century) has clearly demonstrated this flexibility. Though every new commentator takes into account his predecessors' work and almost engages himself in a dialogue with them, it is nevertheless true that he at the same time employs a sort of epistemological break in the sense of going back to the original text with a fresh look from the new socio-historical context he is standing.

This is the second point that can be drawn from our study. It is a promising one that can leave the door open for more open-minded-ness toward the "Other" and with more liberty for everyone. This, we hope, will allow other commentators yet to come to give up completely both theories, "election" as well as *tahrif*, the unfortunate consequences of which we have seen. To play with such double edged doctrines is playing with fire; the wielder of the doctrine can hurt the other but does not realize that, sooner or later, he also can get hurt. If we understand that much, it is already a large step down on our common road. Yet, as long as the three monotheistic religions—and why not all religions?— evade conceptualizing the phenomenon of revelation as such, and not only inside each tradition, the necessary large qualitative step will not be accomplished. Such a move might in turn require a complete change of our conceptual tools in approaching religion as such.

Cambridge University Press, 1991, who examines ten commentators, among both Sunnis (6) and Shi'is (4), from Tabari to Tabataba'i (d. 1403/1982). Her concern is, however, their interpretation of seven verses on Christians.

[51] MacAuliffe, *Qur'anic Christians*, p. 291.

VIII. JUDAISM AND "THE GOOD"

Arthur Green

Our Torah begins with goodness. God the Creator speaks the world into existence. Once each day, as being in its infinite variety continues to unfold, God sees that it is good. Six times the narrative of Creation is punctuated with the expression *va yar' elohim ki tov* ("God saw that it was good"), though this phrase is missing from the second day, when God separated the waters above the firmament from those below. Division is not goodness. More notably, the phrase does not appear after the creation of human beings. God "saw that it was good" after He created the animals on the sixth day, but after the emergence of humans we are only given the summary statement: "God looked upon all that He had made, and behold it was very good." That word "very"—*me'od*—added only here, is debated by the rabbis. Some reverse the consonants and read it as *'adam*—"God looked up all that He had made, and behold man was good." But others somewhat shockingly read it as though it were another word similar in sound: *mot* or "death." "God looked upon all that He had made, and behold *death* was good."[1]

The latter is, to put it mildly, hardly a "typically Jewish" or rabbinic idea. I suspect someone had to go that far only to counter the other view: that the human was the best of God's creations. The Bible is not particularly impressed with human goodness. It may not be possible, in biblical terms, to characterize human beings as "good" at all. A bit later in Genesis, in connection with the flood, we are told that God sees that "The inclination of the human's heart is only evil, from his youth." (Gen 8:21; cf. also 6:5). This is the source of the word *yetser*, "inclination" or "tendency." It is only the rabbis who much later soften this biblical judgment on humanity and add a *yetser tov*, a "good inclination" to balance off the will to evil. Both the biblical and rabbinic authors seem to be sufficiently familiar with the endless human capacity to do evil to avoid superficially rosy depictions of human nature.

Perhaps surprisingly, this tendency toward doing evil in no way lessens the Bible's insistence that the human being is created in God's very own image and likeness. I believe this to be the most important moral statement in the Jewish tradition, the basis of our concept of human decency and the single most clear guide to proper behavior that

---

[1] *Midrash Bereshit Rabbah* 9:5, 12. See further in that chapter for a series of "surprising" readings of *me'od*.

Judaism offers. We define human decency as treating the other, every other, as the image of God, and therefore as an embodiment of holiness. Our task, as the only ones of God's creatures who are reflections of the divine self in this way, is to increase the image of God in this world. We do so by propagating the species, fulfilling the first commandment, but also by living, acting, and treating one another as images of God's own self.

This belief that the human being is God's own and only image is also the reason for the most basic prohibition or taboo in the Jewish religious consciousness: the forbidding of idolatry. It is not because God has no image that we are not allowed to make depictions of God's likeness. Precisely the opposite! God has but one image and likeness in the world: that of every living human being. We are to fashion an image of God in this world; that is our task. But the medium in which we are to do it is the entirety of our lives. To take anything less than a living person—a canvas, stone sculpture, wooden statue—and to see in it God's image would be to demean our own Godlike humanity, and thus to lessen God.

The same connection to faith in the human as God's image is found also in the two other absolutes of the Jewish moral code. All commandments may be violated, indeed should be violated, for the saving of even a single human life. All except for these: idolatry, murder, and sexual degradation. Idolatry, because you are and therefore cannot "make," the image of God; murder, because the other is also the image of God; sexual degradation, because you are both the image of God, and you are enjoined not to degrade or diminish that image.

But what does the divine image have to do with *goodness*? The Bible can describe sun and moon, trees, plants, and animals as "good" in its account of Creation. Humans are in the image and likeness of their Creator, but they are not described as good. How can we be in God's image if we are not even good? Here we must recall some of the range of meanings attached to the divine likeness. We are creatures who bear moral choice, the only ones of God's creatures who were tempted (or some would say: destined) to eat of the Tree of Good and Evil. With moral choice goes responsibility, hence the possibility of being judged either good or evil, according to our deeds. The divine image also means that we are possessed of imagination and the spark of further creativity, the only creatures with the power to continue and participate

in God's own creative act. Here too the question of moral culpability
will loom large: we humans are responsible for that which we create.
We should also recall with some trembling that God's own goodness is
not beyond question in our tradition. Isaiah's God is the single source
of both good and evil, the One who "forms light and creates darkness,
makes peace and creates evil" (45:7). To be a monotheist is to believe
that there is a single source for all that comes to pass in this world. Of
course we may question the nature of evil, its relationship to God, how
the divine creation comes to be evil—and all the rest. But we may not
say that there is a second, independent source. The Kabbalists tell us
that God too is engaged in an ongoing struggle for self-purification, an
attempt to remove the dross that exists near to the very highest levels
of cosmic existence. *Our human struggle for goodness is thus not ours
alone, but our way of participating in God's owns search for a perfect
universe*, one in which *shalom*, peace and wholeness, will reign
throughout. We do this by following the way of Torah. That is the best
measure of goodness we have as we are to realize it in ordinary day-to-
day human life.

"And now, o Israel, what does the Lord your God demand of
you?" (Dt 10:12) is the root-question posed, and supposedly answered,
by religions of revelation. God has spoken. This is the key claim of
classical Judaism.[2] Contemporary theologians, among whom I count
myself, may offer elaborate theories of what those three words mean.
Leaning on the works of Jewish esoteric theologians over a thousand
years, we will try to tell you that the *event* of revelation, or revelation
as *process*, is what is central, and that the contents of revelation are
secondary, are unclear, or emerge from human interpretation of a
revelation that is in itself beyond content or beyond language. Such
notions have taken deep root in the intellectual life of thinking religious
Jews, and they are by no means exclusively modern. Both philosophical

---

[2] See Franz Rosenzweig's letter to Martin Buber, included in Rosenzweig's *On Jewish Learning*. On the Buber-Rosenzweig debate over
revelation and law, cf. Paul Mendes-Flohr, in *Jewish Spirituality*, II, ed. by
Arthur Green (New York, 1987), pp. 317 ff.

and mystical theologians, medieval as well as modern,[3] are interested in what they can learn and teach from revelation about the nature of the divine self, the relationship of that self to its creatures, and especially the ways in which divinity is manifest in the human soul, and particularly in the soul of the prophet

But this is not the dominant voice in the Jewish tradition. While philosophers, mystics, and their teachings have come and gone, the Jewish legal tradition, continuing to build and grow with each succeeding generation, has been interested precisely in the *content* of revelation, concerning itself little with exactly what we mean by the terms "reveal," "speak," "hear," or "will of God." It is this tradition, that of *halakhah*, the way or the path, that has shaped the contours of the classical Jewish community, including its ethics ("the commandments between person and person"), its devotional forms ("the commandments between person and God"), the delimiting of its borders, and its ability to confront an ongoing array of new circumstances in every phase of its existence. This has been the tradition of the rabbis and the people, both of whom often show distressingly little interest in the theological implications or deeper meanings of their own actions. They live out their spiritual life by great faithfulness and devotion—occasionally even to the point of martyrdom— to the *halakhah*, which to them is fully identified with faithfulness to Torah as divine word or to the will of God.

As is well known, Torah contains two bodies of teaching: the written law and the oral law. This formulation, probably originating in about the fourth century, embodies a reality that is still older. The written law, given to Moses either on Mount Sinai or over the course of his lifetime (there are differing views on this in the rabbinic sources, though the former view later comes to dominate[4]), consists of the first five books of the Hebrew Bible; the oral law is the interpretive and later codified tradition. The rest of Scripture occupies a somewhat intermediary position, but since it contains relatively little by way of specific

---

[3] On the role of mysticism in the revelation-theology of twentieth century Jews, cf. Rivka Horwitz in ibid., p. 346 ff.

[4] This debate is the central subject of Abraham J. Heschel's *Theology of Ancient Judaism*, vol. 2. This important book, currently available only in Hebrew, is now being translated into English.

legislation, determining its place in the system is not a crucial issue. It is quite clear that aspects of the oral tradition, that is, the interpretation of a written code within the community, go back to the biblical period itself, and this process in its early stages is sometimes witnessed in later biblical writings. The written Torah contains, according to a count first found in Talmudic sources,[5] six hundred and thirteen commandments, divided between two hundred forty-eight positive commands and three hundred and sixty-five prohibitions. Despite an explicitly stated stricture within the Torah (Dt 4:2) against adding anything on to the Torah God has given, the earliest rabbis were permitted under very restricted circumstances to add a few actual commandments. They also asserted the much broader authority to legislate as specific needs arose, occasionally even in contradiction to the agreed-upon meaning of a biblical injunction or prohibition. (Such legislation would be rabbinic dictum—termed *taqqanah, gezerah*, etc.—but not "command of God," except insofar as Torah enjoins one to listen to "the judge who will exist in those days" (Dt 17:9).) But by far the greatest portion of their work falls under the category of expansive interpretation, the reading first of sources in the written Torah, but later of authoritative and quasi-canonical rabbinic texts, and their deft manipulation to apply them to an ever-changing and expanding set of circumstances.

As I said above, this has been the Judaism of the people as well as the rabbis. For a very long time the Jews defined themselves as a community of praxis rather than one of particular faith or doctrine. Nowhere is this reality more dramatically indicated than in the Talmudic tale of Rabbi Meir, onetime disciple of Elisha ben Abuya.[6] The latter had become a "heretic" and had left the rabbinic community. The two of them were walking and talking one Sabbath day after Elisha had ceased living in accord with the ways of the rabbis. When they reached the Sabbath-border, that distance outside a town beyond which one is not permitted to walk on the Sabbath, Elisha warned his disciple to go

---

[5] b.(=Babylonian Talmud) Makkot 23b. The Talmudic sources do not list what the six hundred and thirteen actually are, but only fix the number. Listings of the specific commandments are disputed among the various medieval sages.

[6] b. Hagigah 15a.

back, lest he violate the prohibition. Taking the opportunity offered by his former teacher's still obvious awareness of the law, Meir responded: "You too, go back" meaning "recant your heresy." Elisha, however, would not do so, and the one walked on while the other returned, portraying in unusually graphic terms the "border" of life within the classical Jewish community.

The tradition that "membership in good standing" within the community of Israel is defined by religious practice (symbolized particularly by observance of the Sabbath) is still the case within today's observant community. Notice that I use the word "observant" here rather than "orthodox." As I have often explained to students in introductory courses on Judaism, there is no word for "orthodoxy" in pre-modern Hebrew or Yiddish. Jewish courts will accept the word of a witness who is known to be observant of the Sabbath; they will not ask him what he thinks is the nature of God or how he understands revelation. I remember my pious grandmother making discreet inquiries in the community about a certain butcher, trying to find out whether he was a Sabbath-observer before she would trust him to sell her properly prepared kosher meat. Again, the "orthodoxy" of his opinions was not a matter of public interest, but the strictness of his observance surely was. Here is where the line was drawn between a fellow-member of the House of Israel and one who had chosen to become an "outsider."

The careful reader of this paper may mote a certain wavering between the past and present tenses in my presentation of this situation. The reason for that is quite simple. The classical Jewish self-definition becomes deeply problematic in the modern world. Today some eighty-five percent of Jewry lives outside the authority of Jewish law, though a significantly higher proportion are selectively observant of certain traditions. This wholesale abandonment of legal boundaries has been the case increasingly since the beginning of the nineteenth century, with the faithful core shrinking at different times and to various degrees in each of the far-flung Jewish communities. The leadership of those remaining communities (now indeed often defined as "Orthodox") has been at great pains both to sharply denounce the unacceptable behavior of the majority and at the same time to find ways to keep them within the Jewish community. One strategy has been to distinguish between leaders and followers in viewing these "outsiders": it is the wicked "rabbis" and teachers of the non-Orthodox who have led the flock astray; the folk themselves are to be considered like "babes captive amid the heathen,"[7] who can hardly be held responsible for their own deeds. Another has been to refer to "the Jewish soul" which still exists among such people, leaders as well as followers, and to try by means of patience and kindness to develop that soul[8]—including elements of remaining religious conscience—in order to lead those Jews to penitence and return to "authentic" (meaning legally bounded) observance of the tradition.

Therefore we ask: "What does the Lord your God demand of you?" The Scripture here answers quite clearly: "Only this: to revere the Lord your God, to walk only in his paths, to love him, and to serve the Lord your God with all your heart and soul, keeping the commandments of the Lord which I command you this day, for your good." The "good" here is the reward Israel is to receive in return for living in accord with the divine commandments.[9]

It would appear, then, that classical Judaism's vision of the good life is at once very clear and almost infinitely complex. "To do good" is to live out all the commandments as the sages have interpreted them over the generations, combined with an attitude of piety and a loving acceptance of this rule of law. This is not an entirely inaccurate description, and it should not be dismissed. It is the most ancient and "native" response to this question implanted by the tradition in those who follow its ways, reflecting life as lived by those considered "religious" within the Jewish community. It especially accords with such a well-known dictum as "Be as careful with a minor commandment as a major one, for you do not know the true weight of the commandments"[10] and others in its spirit.

The problem with such a view is that is entirely dispiriting to discussions such as our own. All it would leave us to do is to wend our way through such a tome as Maimonides' *Book of the Commandments,*

---

[7] Based on b. Shabbat 68b.

[8] On the development of this strategy in later Hasidism, cf. M. Piekarz in *Studies in Jewish Mysticism...Presented to Isaiah Tishby* (in Hebrew) (Jerusalem, 1986), pp. 617 ff.

[9] RASHI, ad loc.

[10] m. (=Mishnah) Avot 2:1.

or perhaps Joseph Caro's *Set Table*, and only after mastering these (one a listing of the biblical commandments; the other the key code of religious law on a practical basis) would we be empowered to speak of Judaism's vision of the good. But much more seriously, of course, such a view also gives insufficient guidance to the religious Jew who has daily to make choices among the commandments, since no one can observe all the laws of God at the same time. What does God want of me?—to study Torah day and night or to work to support my family? What does God want of me when I see my people desecrating the name of God and Israel? Shall I fulfill "Openly reprove your neighbor" (Lev 19:17) or shall I say "all its path are peace" (Prov 3:17), and therefore opt for scholarly quiet and uninvolvement?

Fortunately our position is not quite so severe as that. *Halakhah* in Judaism always lives in tandem (and sometimes tension!) with *aggadah*, those narratives and teachings that constitute the non-legal portion of traditional wisdom. There we have many summary statements, re-formulated in almost every generation, of the "values of Judaism." There are numerous statements, and even compendia of statements, that allow one to go beyond the simple enumeration of commandments. One of the most famous of these from within the very Talmudic passage that first mentions the numbers of six hundred and thirteen commandments, should be quoted here:

> Rabbi Simlai expounded: Six hundred and thirteen commandments were spoken to Moses, three hundred and sixty-five prohibitions, corresponding to the days in the solar year, and two hundred and forty-eight positive precepts, corresponding to the limbs of man's body...
>
> David came and reduced them to eleven, as it is written: "A Psalm of David. Lord, who shall sojourn in Your tabernacle? Who shall dwell in Your holy mountain? (1) He who walks uprightly, (2) works righteousness, (3) speaks truth in his heart; (4) he who has no slander upon his tongue, (5) nor does evil to his fellow, (6) nor takes up reproach against his neighbor, (7) in whose eyes a vile person is despised. But (8) he honors those who fear the Lord, (9) he swears oaths at his own

expense and does not violate them; (10) he does not lend money at interest (11) or take bribes against the innocent. He that does these shall never be moved" (Ps. 15:1-4).

Isaiah came and reduced them to six, as it is written: "(1) He who walks righteously and (2) speaks uprightly, (3) who despises profiting from oppression (4) and shakes his hand loose from holding bribes, (5) who stops his ear from hearing of blood and (6) shuts his eyes from looking upon evil" (Is. 33:15-16).

Micah came and reduced them to three, as it is written: "It has been told to you, O man, what is good and what the Lord requires of you: only to do justice, to love mercy, and to walk humbly before your God" (Mic. 6:8).

Again came Isaiah and reduced them to two, as it is written: "Thus says the Lord: Keep justice and do righteousness" (Is. 56:1).

Amos came and reduced them to one: "For thus says the Lord to the house of Israel: Seek Me and live" (Am. 5:4). But to this Rabbi Nahman ben Isaac raised an objection: [Might this not be taken to mean] Seek me by observing the entire Torah and live? Rather it is Habakkuk who came and [properly] based them all on one, as it is written: "The righteous shall live by his faith" (Hab. 2:4).[11]

The biblical language here is quite lofty in tone, using prophetic phrasing to point to what seems to be the "real meaning" of the religious life. But we should not permit the use of biblical language to divert our attention from the rabbinic origins of this passage. The passage in the Talmud that first codifies the number of six hundred thirteen commandments is essential for the later development of *halakhah*. The medieval discussions of the list of commandments, hence, of which acts (or non-acts, such as faith in God!) are required by Torah, all depend upon this passage. Yet the Talmud itself responds to this numbering of the commandments by a series of attempts to get at the moral or religious

---

[11] b. Makkot 23b-24b.

127

essence of the *mitzvah* system. It is asking not "what are the things commanded?" but "what is the moral essence of the divine command?"

As lawyers, the rabbis were not generally fond of such broad and lofty statements. More typical of rabbinic language is the following formulation of "the highest Jewish values." I juxtapose it to the Makkot passage because it too seems to rise in protest against the quantification of divine command. Here the Mishnah lists those commandments that are without fixed measure ("the more the merrier," in other words). Joined to it is a list of observances so beloved by the human community as well as by God that they are claimed to be double in their form of reward. This passage is quoted in the daily prayer book and thus is familiar to any observant Jew:

> These are things which have no [prescribed] limit: the corner of the field [to be left for the poor], the first fruits [brought to the Temple], appearances [at the Temple on pilgrimage], bestowing kindness, and the study of Torah.
>
> These are things the fruits of which a person enjoys in this world while the principal remains for him in the world to come: honoring father and mother, bestowing kindness, coming early to the study-house morning and evening, hospitality to guest, visiting the sick, dowering [poor] brides, attending to the dead, devotion in prayer, and bringing peace between fellow-persons. But the study of Torah surpasses them all.[12]

The first of these two statements (the Makkot passage) clearly belongs to the realm of *aggadah*. While it refers to an ordering of commandments in various prophetic teachings, it does not seem to have any normative function. The second inhabits an intermediate status between *halakhah* and *aggadah*. While its Mishnaic language sounds like that of law, we would be hard pressed to claim it as a truly legal formulation of the highest values within the rabbinic tradition. But within *halakhah* proper there are also necessarily statements that prefer

---

[12] m. Peah 1:1.

one normative act over another. The well-known use of Lev 18:5 ("You shall live by them") to indicate that in most circumstances human life takes precedence over other commandments is perhaps the prime example. Halakhic authorities throughout the ages were also well aware that it is possible to be a "knave within the domain of Torah," that is, to technically fulfill all the demands of the law and still be a miserable human being, worthy of condemnation. As detailed as the law seemed to be, in itself it could not fully shape one into being a "good person." Thus the Torah contains certain passages that themselves demand that one go beyond the letter of the law. It is to two of these that I would like to turn our attention.

"Do what is right and good in the sight of the Lord (Dt 6:18) is taken as a catch-all to determine behavior that is not specified elsewhere in the law. Here is the comment of Nahmanides, the thirteenth-century Catalonian sage who was certainly one the most respected Jewish personages in his era and who remains a major figure in any discussion of *halakhah*. Nahmanides is expounding on an earlier rabbinic teaching:

> "What is right and good" refers to compromise and [willingness] to go beyond the letter of the law. The intent of this is as follows. First Moses stated that you are to keep God's statutes and testimonies as commanded you, give thought as well to doing what is right and goodly in God's eyes, for God loves the right and the good. This is a basic rule. It was impossible that the Torah specify all aspects of a person's conduct with neighbors and fellows, all of a person's interactions, and all the ordinances of various countries and societies. But since many of them were mentioned, such as, "You shall not going about telling tales" (Lev 19:16); "You shall not take vengeance or bear any grudge" (ibid.18); "You shall not stand idly by the blood of your neighbor" (ibid.16); "You shall not curse the deaf" (ibid.15); "You shall stand up in the presence of the white-haired" (ibid.32)—and so on, the Torah goes on in a general way to say that in all

> matters we should do what is right and good, including
> compromise and going beyond the letter of the law.[13]

Compromise in legal cases, especially within the civil code, is not enjoined by the law itself. If the judges find for me, after all, then the full sum is mine and I have a right to demand it. But the rabbis realized (in days long before insurance) that litigation could ruin individuals and families, and thus they urged compromise in such cases as constituting "the right and the good." The same was true with going beyond the letter or, more literally, staying "within the line" of the law. There are situations when the right thing is for one to do other than assert one's full legal rights, and the decent person is to know when those times are.

The *hasid* or lover of God is defined by the Talmud as one who lives well within that line, doing and giving more than the law demands, both to God and to one's fellow. It is the heart's sensibility, trained, to be sure, by a lifetime of living within the law, that tells such a *hasid* when to do more. Just as the doors of inner prayer come to be more readily opened by a life of regular fixed prayer, so do the inner instincts of caring and generosity of spirit come to be more highly attuned by a life of daily concern for demands of the moral law. The constant training of that moral sensitivity is central to what Judaism views as piety or *hasidut*.

The next passage to which we turn is found a bit farther on in Deuteronomy, amid the prohibitions of divination and augury. There (18:13) the text says "You must be *tamim* with your God. The term *tamim*, sometimes translated here as "wholehearted," is the same word translated as "unblemished" in references to both priests and the animal sacrifices they offered. The verse will offer to Samson Raphael Hirsch, the key figure in nineteenth-century German-Jewish Orthodoxy, a chance to say some important things about the Jewish religious "ethos." The call to be *tamim* is a

---

[13] Commentary on the Torah ad loc. Translation adapted from that of C. Chavel.

demand for the completeness of our devotion, the devoting of every phase, without exception, of our being to God. This is the most direct result of our consciousness of the "oneness" of God, the realization of the *'am segulah* mission, the mission of a nation belonging exclusively, in every phase, to God. We are not to cut the slightest particle of any phase of our life away from God; we are to be with God with our complete life, with every fibre of it. Thereby the whole of the heathen attitude toward life depicted in the preceding verses is banned from the Jewish sphere. God, the sole Director of our fate and Guide of our deeds, alone decides our future; His satisfaction is the sole criterion by which we are to decide what to do and what to refrain from doing. Not blind chance, the Moloch "luck," rules over our lives or the lives of our children...the *tamim* is so completely engrossed in God that he lives entirely in the thought of doing his duty all the time; he leaves the rest, including his own entire future, to God.[14]

While Hirsch does get a bit "preachy" (here as frequently), he shows us another occasion where a verse in the Torah carries us far beyond its seeming intent. *Tamim* here really means "whole" or "unblemished" in the life of faith, going far beyond the specific prohibitions of the immediate context. The knowing reader of Scripture in the Hebrew will immediately be carried back to the Bible's first use of *tamim*, that which God says to Abraham in Genesis 17:1" "Walk before me and be *tamim*." The contemporary translators'(JPS, RSV, Jerusalem Bible) "blameless" is inadequate in this case; there is nothing negative about *tamim*. I rather prefer the King James' "perfect." Of course this is the language introducing Abraham to the commandment of circumcision; it is the (paradoxical) perfection of his body that he is about to undertake, as an outward sign of the moral or religious being he is to become. *Tamim* as "perfect" would be rather close to *shalem-*

---

[14] The Hirsch Humash, vol. 5, ad loc. Minor changes in style are my own.

shalom as "whole" or complete." This is as close as we come to the possibility of a person's "being" as well as "doing" good in the Bible.[15]

But Abraham is very much to the point in this discussion. He lives before the commandments are given, and therefore would seemingly have to lead a religious life without them.[16] Might his example then be able to tell us what it means to be a good person without going through the entire list of the commandments? A great deal is made in Christian Scripture and tradition, ranging from Paul to Kierkegaard, of Abraham as the ideal figure of faith, living before the law was given. But the rabbis are aware of the Christian claim, and therefore the Talmud insists, based on Genesis 26:5 ("inasmuch as Abraham obeyed Me and kept My charge: My commandments, My laws, and My teachings") that "Abraham our Father observed the entire Torah"[17] even before it was given. They go so far as to say that he knew every detail of the law, even the clearly rabbinic device for preparing Sabbath-food on a festival, a matter that admittedly has not a shred of biblical basis. The point is that for the rabbis there is no piety outside the law, and they will not allow our own patriarch to be used to show otherwise.

Despite the rabbis' claim of our ancestor, however, he remains important as a model for the religious life, and not just as a faithful follower of the law. Throughout Jewish history Abraham is the ideal type of piety, much as Moses is of learning or Solomon is of wisdom. The less naive among later writers, while not openly challenging the rabbinic claim, set it aside to return to the pastoral image of the patriarch who lived as close to moral and devotional perfection as human life seems to permit. Here is Maimonides, in a famous passage from his *Guide for the Perplexed*:

---

[15] Cf. also Job 1:1, where the hero of that book is described as *tam we-yashar*, "perfect and upright". If we want a biblical description of a "good man," that verse and its parallels in the Psalter and Proverbs are key passages.

[16] Cf. my discussion in *Devotion and Commandment: the Faith of Abraham in the Hasidic Imagination* (Cincinnati, Hebrew Union College Press, 1989).

[17] b. Yoma 28b.

And there may be a human individual who, through his apprehension of the true realities and his joy in what he has apprehended, achieves a state in which he talks with people and is occupied with his bodily necessities while his intellect is wholly turned toward Him, may He be exalted, so that in his heart he is always in His presence, may He be exalted, while outwardly he is with people, in the sort of way described by the poetical parables that have been invented for these notions: "I sleep but my heart wakes; the voice of my beloved knocks" (Cant 5:2) and so on. I do not say that this is the rank of all the prophets; but I do say that this is the rank of Moses our Teacher...This was also the rank of the patriarchs, the result of whose nearness to Him, may He be exalted, was that His name became known to the world through them: "the God of Abraham, the God of Isaac, the God of Jacob...this is My name forever" (Ex 3:15). Because of the union of their intellects through apprehension of Him, it came about that He made a lasting covenant with each of them. Also the providence of God watching over them and over their posterity was great.

Withal they were occupied with governing people, increasing their fortune, and endeavoring to acquire property. Now this is to my mind a proof that they did these actions with their limbs only, while their intellects were constantly in His presence, may He be exalted. It also seems to me that the fact that these four were in a permanent state of extreme perfection in the eyes of God, and that His providence watched over them continually even while they were engaged in increasing their fortune—I mean while they tended their cattle, did agricultural work, and governed their household—was necessarily brought about by the circumstance that in all these actions their end was to come near to Him, may He be exalted, and how near! For the end of their efforts

during their life was to bring into being a religious
community that would know and worship God.[18]

This of course is the *vita contemplativa*, descriptions of which
are to be found in the devotional classics of all our traditions. What is
particularly interesting here is the combination of contemplative and
active life, or the way in which the patriarchs go on about their this-
worldly work while their minds are wholly with God.

The figure of Abraham and his religious life was especially
inspiring to the Hasidic masters, who saw in him a model for their own
"spiritual" fulfillment of the commandments. In addition to living in
accord with the ways of the law, they wanted to find the inner root of
each divine command, which they were quite sure also collectively
made up the inner root of the human soul. By devotion to the commandments in a spiritually aware way, they would come to do what they
saw Abraham as having done. The would discover the entire Torah as
it is inscribed within their own souls and would thus come to know the
commandments as a deep inner map of the spiritual journey that God
has given to those who truly seek. The word *mitzvah* ("commandment"),
they taught, is actually the name of God in half-hidden, half-revealed
form. It is by turning in to the *mitzvah* (which they sometimes derived
from the Aramaic *tsavta* or "togetherness") that one comes to meet God.
This emphasis on the "inner commandments," accompanying and
enriching their outward fulfillment, is a highly characteristic path within
the Jewish mystical tradition.

What kind of person is it the tradition is trying to create? What
is its vision of the good life as it is to be lived by Jews who follow it?
We have had a glimpse of Abraham, the ideal type of the *hasid*, loving
God and always ready to do even more than the law demands. We
should join to him the figure of Moses, teacher and prophet, for the
rabbis the idea of the original sage and master. If the Abraham-ideal is
one of pastoral simplicity, the image of Moses is one of student-scholar-
teacher, the *talmid hakham* or wise disciple as leader of the people. It
was such scholar-sages of the law whom traditional Jewish society most
came to venerate over the centuries, people about whom countless tales

---

[18] 3:54, Pines translation, pp. 623f.

were told to show that in every detail of their lives they embodied the way of Torah, especially in its ethical ramifications.[19]

The *hasid* and the sage stand in interesting tension with one another. One is a potentially extreme figure, jumping forward to do more than the law requires. The *hasid* loves God; that love is the single center of his religious life. For the sake of this love he is ever ready for martyrdom; sometimes one has the sense that he even seeks it out. Purity of devotion and boundless giving are his hallmarks. The sage is a figure of significantly greater sobriety. He will not act without consulting the sources, without seeking precedent in the generations that have come before. The sage imitates God in loving both the Torah and the people Israel, carefully balancing these two loves as he tries to show Israel how to live the life of Torah. His own love of God is quiet and understated, realized mostly in this life of *imitatio Dei*, "walking in His ways," as it is said in Hebrew. In a classic moment of confrontation between these two ideals, the Talmudic discussion of Sabbath-law notes that: "One who kills [life-threatening] snakes or scorpions on the Sabbath, the spirit of the *hasidim* is not pleased with him." The Talmud adds, thanks to an editor with just a bit of a sardonic touch: "The spirit of the sage is not pleased with such *hasidim*."[20]

With room for some notable exceptions, I think it fair to say that the spirit of the sages triumphed in Jewish history. Commitment to the rule of law became a chief virtue within this tradition, one strangely upheld by the large number of Jewish attorneys, legal scholars, and judges throughout the Western world who may not practice our own native legal traditions but nevertheless hold fast to the broader ideal. (In the modern world, of course, it was often the power of law that saved Jews from persecution and upheld the protection of minority rights that were so important to them.) Judiciousness and sobriety, the virtues of the judge, are very much those of the pious Jew. Spontaneity and self-expression are to be held in check until one sees whether the expression is appropriate to the dignity of one who proudly upholds an ancient law,

---

[19] Cf.E. Urbach, *The Sages: Their Concepts and Beliefs*, (Jerusalem, Magnes, 1975) and Gershom Scholem, "Three Types of Jewish Piety" in *Eranos Jahrbuch*, vol. 38 (1969).

[20] b.Shabbat 121b.

until one knows whether there is any danger of being misunderstood, until one sees whether the expression will help or harm the ever-endangered house of Israel.

There is a stoic influence to be noted in the mores of Judaism, one that comes to penetrate Jewish ethics through both of the two great contacts Judaism had with Greek civilization. In the first two centuries of the Common Era, when the Jewish-Christian sects eventually crystallized into a new religion that was deeply Hellenistic in both mythos and ethos, emerging rabbinic Judaism managed to maintain a relatively more purely Semitic mythic structure, but in ethos it too became a part of the broadly Hellenistic philosophic world. The very figure of the sage himself, and his way of knowing God through an understanding of ancient texts, has been seen as belonging, *mutatis mutandis*, to the intellectual world so extensively developed by Alexandria and all it represented. The moral teachings offered by these sages, recorded in the pages of Mishnah Avot and cognate sources, also reflect a good deal of Hellenistic school-wisdom only slightly dressed up in Jewish garb. The second contact of Judaism with the Greeks, mediated chiefly through the philosophy and ethics of Islam in the early Middle Ages, greatly reinforced an already somewhat developed stoic point of view. This will be clear if one opens almost any page of Bahya Ibn Paquda's *Duties of the Hearts*, perhaps the greatest moral treatise of medieval Jewry, written in Arabic in eleventh-century Spain. Patience, equanimity, and self-control are high on the list of virtues in this and the many works that followed it. There is a passion in the love of God (especially in the later and Kabbalah-inspired treatises), but this passion is to be given proper expression by the love of His creatures, by walking in His ways by following the counsel of the sages.

A part of this enshrining of sobriety as a virtue is a strong sense of the ongoing battle every person fights with *yetser ha-ra'*, the human inclination toward evil. Even for the rabbis, it appears that the two *yetsarim* (moral inclinations) are not quite balanced in the human being, the negative force naturally having something of the upper hand. The fact that human instincts and passions are both real and powerful is not something that Jewish moralists have sought to deny. But the reality of a drive does not make for its goodness or even its permissibility. *The law is there as God's gift to help one achieve the self-control needed in order to become a more perfect and whole vessel for the service of God.*

In this area, I might add, the traditional ethos of rabbinic and later Judaism is sharply at odds with the contemporary popular post-Freudian tendency (very much not that of Freud himself!) to accept and affirm every aspect of our inner selves. The clearest example that occurs to me is in the treatment of anger and aggression. Our aggressive drives, in the rabbinic view, are part of our *yetser ha-ra'*, that libidinal energy reserve which may be called the "evil" inclination, but which they also knew full well to be vital to our survival and to the propagation of the species. Aggression runs deep in all of human existence; the task with which we are faced is that of finding proper channels for expression of this aggressive drive. Anger, the most ordinary and readily available expression of aggression, is universally recognized by Jewish ethicists as a bad outlet. Anyone who "lets off steam" in an aggressive outburst against another human being is committing the ultimate double sin of "lessening the divine image" in both the receiver and the giver of that anger. Traditional moralists will urge us to convert the energy behind that anger into virtue, perhaps using it to defend the faith or to reprove the wicked. But such reproof, they hasten to add, cannot be offered in anger. There is no greater act of love than that of seeking to bring a fellow-human back into relationship with God. One cannot engage in such work until one has "uplifted" rage, or "sweetened it in its root," in the Kabbalistic formulation.

This work, and much of the religious living that goes with it, can only be achieved in humility, a virtue not much spoken of in our contemporary world. Ultimately I believe the prophet Micah was most right: He was the one who reduced the commandments to three: "Do justice, love mercy, and walk humbly before your God." This statement of virtue is one that preserves the best of the ancient Hebrew moralistic tradition. Its ancient roots in Judaism are widely seen in the Psalter, whence it also came to have a key role in the teachings of Jesus and the Sermon on the Mount. I would like to see it take the place it deserves in the encounter among our three sister-faiths and in the activities undertaken in the spirit of such encounter. I therefore close by quoting a few words from a lovely essay on humility by our teacher Martin Buber:

The humble man lives in each being and knows each being's manner and virtue. Since no one is to him "the other," he knows from

137

within that none lacks some hidden value; knows that "there is no man who does not have his hour."...

"God does not look on the evil side" said one zaddik. "How should I dare to do so?"

He who lives with others according to the mystery of humility can condemn no one. "He who passes sentence on a man passes it on himself."

He who separates himself from the sinner departs in guilt...Only living with the other is justice...

He who lives with others in this way realizes with his deed the truth that all souls are one; for each is a spark of the original soul, and the whole of the original soul is in each.

IX. NEW PHASE IN JEWISH SELF-UNDERSTANDING?

Nancy Fuchs-Kreimer

1. Personal and Social Ethics

In Paul Mojzes' self-critical reflections in this volume he spoke about the difficulty in balancing personal and social ethics in Christianity. He suggested that the Christian right has a tendency to emphasize the personal aspects and to deny social responsibility, while the left sometimes suggests that Christianity deal with social issues to the exclusion of personal values. I wonder if that dichotomy might be overdrawn. It is my sense that Christians on the right and left often see a connection between personal ethics and social ethics but what they advocate in the public forum differs because their agendas differ.

Be that as it may, in the Jewish world today both right and left agree that the political/social arena is a domain which must be addressed. Jewish law from its biblical origins always placed matters of ritual, personal morals, social ethics and political visions cheek by jowl (see, for example, the Holiness Code in Leviticus). Today, one can hear a rabbi give a sermon on a political issue in a left wing synagogue or in a right wing one. I don't believe there is serious division on the question of the religious responsibility of Jews to advocate for what they believe is good in society or in international relations. The division comes over the definitions of the good.

2. Universalism and Particularism

A fault line which divides Jews (and which runs across all the religious denominations as well as across secular Jewish movements like Zionism) is that which separates Jews who are primarily committed to a universal ethical vision (which they derive from Judaism) from Jews who are primarily committed to the Jewish people and its survival. There are Orthodox, Conservative, Reform, Reconstructionist and secular Zionist Jews of both stripes. While this dichotomy posits two stances which in their extreme versions are equally absurd (of what value is a Jewish vision if we do not preserve the body of the Jewish people? But what is the point of survival if there is no vision?), it serves to illuminate what I see as the source of much division among Jews as they struggle with the question of "the good," with matters of social ethics.

For example, in the fall of 1992 I heard arguments for and against the then recent Israeli deportations of over 400 Arabs in which issues of Jewish survival were played off against questions of values derived from Judaism. None of the participants in these discussions would have denied either the necessity of self protection or the relevance of values to the decisions of a Jewish state, but they disagreed in emphasis.

I would like to suggest that the question of "Judaism and the good" is about to break open in new and very exciting ways, that we are poised on the brink of a new era in our understanding. Let me backtrack. Prior to political emancipation in the eighteenth and nineteenth centuries, Jews were a corporate entity in Europe and the question of defining Judaism was not salient. It was only with the acceptance of Jews as individual citizens of modern nation states that the question was raised: What is Judaism? What is the reason for the ongoing existence of a Jewish community? Reform Judaism's response to this question was that Judaism's unique way of conceptualizing the good (ethical monotheism) was its *raison d'etre*. In a variety of ways, Jews developed understandings of Judaism which placed ethics at the center or the "essence" of Judaism.

3. Jewish Peoplehood Stressed

In contrast to that response was one that emphasized peoplehood, Jewish identity, and survival in the face of victimization. Let me be clear. I am not suggesting that believing that peoplehood is the core of Jewishness precludes a sense of ethics. Mordecai Kaplan, the founder of Reconstructionist Judaism, who championed the centrality of peoplehood thirty years before Hitler ("belonging comes before believing"), also wrote a great deal about what Judaism teaches about values and ethics. What I am suggesting is that many Jews, especially since the Nazi Holocaust, have answered the question "What is Judaism?" primarily through recourse to the notion of group identity and national survival.

In the last half century, many Jews abandoned efforts to define the "essence of Judaism." Jewish peoplehood, ethnicity, the struggle against victimization and for survival, group identity have become their own justification. Nahum Goldmann, the late president of the World

Zionist Organization, related that the Nazis stole his library and with it fourteen definitions of the essence of Judaism. He regretted the loss of the books, he said, but not the loss of the definitions, since he had since learned that the Jews are first and finally a unique people. Emil Fackenheim has written, "I used to criticize the idea of survival for its own sake. After confronting the holocaust, I have changed my mind."

4. Universalist Ethics Stressed

I believe that era is coming to a close. It seems possible to me that the new era we are entering will once again see an interest in defining Judaism in terms of its teachings concerning the good. It seems possible that universal ethical teachings derived from the traditions and experience of the Jewish people will again become central, while survival will become the handmaiden—the necessary tool to the larger end. It seems possible that the post-holocaust enthusiasm with ethnic Judaism may have begun to run its course.

a) A New Community Make-up
There are two reasons for this hypothesis. First, our community is becoming less and less ethnic. The combination of intermarriage (50% or higher in some communities), conversion into Judaism, adoption, new reproductive technologies, the entrance into synagogue life of gay and lesbian couples and their children is producing a Jewish community that looks less and less like an ethnic family. This change is profound. Ten years ago I sat in rabbinical school and listened to Kaplan's teaching that we are Jewish because...we are Jewish. Nobody demurred. Now, when I teach that, my students (one, a convert, another a woman who was adopted as an infant by Jews, another a woman who plans to adopt a third-world child) do not accept it. They want to know why they are Jews, why they should tell congregants to be or become Jews. Ethnicity is not enough. Also, keeping the Jewish people going is not sufficient for the community. We are gradually shifting from being a community of fate—this may lead us back to the earlier responses to modernity and emancipation: being a community of (ethical) faith.

b) The Influence of Feminism
The second influence, surprisingly not treated by Paul Mojzes

in his report on the Christian world, is the rise of feminism and the potential impact on Christian thought of significant numbers of female religious leaders and thinkers. A field of feminist religious social ethics is developing and I would be eager to hear more about how it is effecting the various issues Paul Mojzes' paper delineated for Christianity.

In the case of Judaism, it seems to me that many of the themes of feminist social thought are already part of the way Jews have thought about these issues. In particular, I would note the emphasis on specific relationships rather than abstract principles and the conceptualization of human beings as fundamentally connected with one another rather than separate. Indeed, I think one of the ways we will envision Judaism in the emerging era is as a special (not superior, but unique) way of approaching the pursuit of the good—one that is consonant with feminist approaches.[1]

The impact of feminism on the Jewish world may be profound. Women as leaders will bring to the issue of Jewish universalism-particularism a new perspective that may break open the entire discussion and take it in new directions. I speak hesitantly since I am only beginning to think through these ideas.

Almost all post-holocaust Jewish thinking has been infused with our sense of victimization, which has reinforced particularism. Women bring to this discussion their participation in a different community of victimization—their sense of sisterhood with women from all religious and national groups with whom they share a spiritual history not only of discrimination but also of rape, sexual abuse, domestic violence, sexual harassment, and the constriction of freedom created by the awareness of the possibility of these crimes. The Jewish community may be moving to a new stage in its appropriation of the holocaust, one in which it wrestles the blessing from the horror, the possibility that our pain can become a window into the pain of others. The empathy of a woman for another woman, her sense of connection with a sister whose son is deported or killed may bring a different perspective to the

---

[1] For a fuller statement of these cryptic assertions, see my article "Holiness, Justice and the Rabbinate," *Cross Currents*, 42, 2 (Summer 1992), pp. 212-227.

discussion. When women become major players in Jewish life, it may hasten the shift I am predicting toward a Judaism more focussed on universalism than we have seen in recent decades.

X. CHRISTIAN VIEWS ON HOW TO CONCEIVE AND IMPLEMENT THE GOOD A SELF-CRITICAL REFLECTION

Paul Mojzes

1. Statement of Purpose

The main purpose of this paper is to provide an overview of various Christian conceptions and implementation of the good. That description will be followed by a few critical remarks, primarily of the weaknesses or problems displayed in these Christian efforts. No attempt will be made to come up with novel approaches. Without claiming comprehensiveness, the attempt will be to suggest the scope of varieties of Christian ways to understand and put into practice the good. The author is also aware of the limitation of the bibliography; the essay is based almost entirely on sources published in America. Though the paper deals with ethical approaches, the author did not intend to survey Christian ethics *per se* but deal more with how some ethicists envision the good and how these insights were applied historically to shape practical life.

2. Introductory remarks

Christians are often entreated to do good and to be good. One of the common prayers before a meal in America is:

God is great. God is good.
Let us thank God for our food.

A common admonition at departure in the USA is "Be good!" though it seems to be rapidly displaced by "Have fun," which may well be a commentary of the changing times. The search for truth, beauty, and goodness is a motto of many Christian universities.

The creation story in Genesis 1 routinely ascribes to the various stages of God's creation a comment attributed to God, "And God saw that it was good." On the surface it would seem that religion in general and Christianity in particular have much to do with recognizing and promoting goodness.

Therefore, it comes as a surprise that a very large number of theological books consulted for this paper did not have in their table of contents anything about the good or goodness, though a larger number dealt with evil and sin—which may or may not be the antonyms for good. A few of the books had the word good in the index but provided very few page references. This is all the more astonishing since in the Bible, both the Hebrew Bible and the Christian Scriptures, previously referred to as the Old and New Testament, the word good was used frequently and with a variety of connotations (e.g., "we know that all things work together for the good" Rom. 8:28 or "none is good, save one, that is God" Lk 18:9). Perhaps the reason why the term appears seldom in many standard, general works of systematic theology is that it is seemingly so broad or self-evident that little direct attention is given to it. It is more likely, however, that the notion of love is regarded as so central in association with God in Christian writings as to replace the word good.

Others go even further by totally separating God and good. The play writer, Archibald MacLeish, wrote in his powerful drama *"J.B.,"* which is reminiscent of the biblical Job:

If God is God He is not good;
If God is good He is not God.[1]

Certainly for many, especially in times of great distress and agony, the relationship between God and goodness is unclear. Is everything that God does to be defined as good? Or must God do only that which is good? Or does God do both good and its opposite, evil? Is sin the opposite of good or the opposite of love?

3. Conceptions of the Good

There are three clear sources of the Christian understanding of reality. One is Judaism as it was formulated until the end of the first century C.E. The second is the person and teachings of Jesus Christ along with the witness of the apostolic or primitive Christian community. The third is the Hellenistic thought of the Greco-Roman world into

---

[1] As quoted in George A. Buttrick, *God, Pain, and Evil* (Nashville: Abingdon Press, 1966), p. 19.

which Christianity expanded. Christians have relied on all three of these sources but different Christian interpreters or communities tended to rely sometimes on one source more than others. That may well be one of the major reasons why Christians of the past and the present often expressed themselves in significantly different ways. The Judaic, primitive Christian, and Hellenistic traditions were sometimes contradictory. In addition, we recognize that each of these traditions were heteronomous, i.e., that a great variety of views, not all of them consistent, were espoused within each of these units.

Since Christians are rooted in all three of these modes of thought, it is clear that they would say that the good comes from God. Some might say that all goodness is rooted in God alone; others will claim that humans (and perhaps other cosmic creatures) also can be creators of good. Plato's words were easily appropriated by Christians:

> Let me tell then why the creator made this world of generation. He was good, and the good can never have any jealousy of anything. And being free of jealousy, he desired that all things should be as like himself as they could be. This is in the truest sense the origin of creation and of the world: God desired that all things should be good and nothing bad, so far as this was attainable.[2]

The words "good" and "value" are synonyms and it is clear that the Jewish, Christian, and Muslim religions associate values with divinity. However, some religious interpreters ascribed disvalues as well to divine origin. When it came to interpreting the ultimate origin of disvalues, some Christians tended to follow the pattern of the Hebrew scriptures and assert that God is the locus of all that is, including evil, while another Christian tradition denied the existence of intrinsic evil preferring to give evil the status of instrumental good—ultimately all evil yields some good and therefore all that is, is good. The vast majority of Christians were of this so-called absolutistic theistic orientation which denied ultimate reality to evil, rendering all evil into instrumental good. A much smaller group became "finitistic" theists who believed that

---

[2] *Timaeus*, 30-31.

while God's goodness is perfect, God's power is not unlimited; there was *surd* evil, namely, an uncreated reality or force (the Given) located in God's own being which obstructed the perfect expression of God's good will.[3]

At the Atlanta ISAT (International Scholars' Annual Trialogue) in January, 1992, we agreed, I believe, not to enumerate what is regarded as good in our tradition. We decided to focus primarily or solely on how we can know or conceive what is good and to focus on good as it applies to human behavior, namely, the area of ethics and morality. It should be noted at least in passing, without enumerating here all the concrete virtues which Christians hold in common with Jews and Muslims, that a tremendously large number of notions of the good, i.e., virtues, such as loyalty, justice, peace, thoughtfulness, honesty, and so forth, are, indeed, affirmed by all three religious communities. But *Christianity does make one virtue or approach entirely central to its understanding of the good, namely, self-giving and self-sacrificing love (agape)*.

Common to all Christians is to acknowledge that their understanding of what is good is based on the Holy Scriptures of the Hebrew Bible and New Testament, generally seen as a source of divine self-disclosure and unveiling of what is to be done by humans primarily by those who are in a covenantal relationship with God as well as, at least in some instances, also by those who are not Christians. From this common acknowledgement Christians diverge on how one can know what is good.

The Eastern Orthodox and Eastern Apostolic Churches did not restrict revelation to the Holy Scriptures or to the creeds of the councils but made it directly accessible to all humans who faced God's presence in the Church. While direct and immediate contact with God is possible, says John Meyendorff,

> The mainstream of Eastern Christian gnosiology, which indeed affirms the possibility of direct experience of God,

---

[3] L. Harold DeWolf, *A Theology of the Living Church*, (New York: Harper & Brothers, rev. ed, 1960), pp. 140-142. The latter view is promoted by Edgar S. Brightman, *A Philosophy of Religion*. (Englewood Cliffs, NJ: Prentice-Hall, 1958), pp. 240-341.

is precisely founded upon a sacramental, and therefore hierarchically structured, ecclesiology, which gives a Christological and pneumatological basis to personal experience and presupposes that Christian theology must always be consistent with the apostolic and patristic witness.[4]

In Eastern Orthodox understanding nothing new conceptually or in content could be added to that which was received by the apostles from Christ once and for all; only identical confirmations of revelation is possible. In that sense there can be no development of new information though there can be growth in our understanding of that which is revealed.

As to interpreting the meaning of the Scripture (exegesis) the Orthodox have agreed that,

> It is necessary for those who preside over the churches [bishops]...to teach all the clergy and people... collecting out of the divine Scripture the thoughts and judgments of truth, but not exceeding the limits now fixed, nor varying from the tradition of the God-fearing Fathers. But if any issue arises concerning Scripture, it should not be interpreted other than as the luminaries and teachers of the Church have expounded it in their writings; let them [bishops] become distinguished for their knowledge of patristic writings than for composing treatises out of their own heads.[5]

On those issues where there is no firm apostolic teaching the Eastern Orthodox have tended to avoid making definite dogmatic decisions and allow for a significant diversity of opinion not only on issues such as whether there is a purgatory but also whether artificial birth control is permitted. There are, indeed, many Greek Orthodox

---

[4] John Meyendorff, *Byzantine Theology: Historical Trends and Doctrinal Themes*, (New York: Fordham University Press, 1974), p. 9.

[5] Canon 19 of the Council in Trullo (692) quoted in ibid., p. 20.

theologians, as Demetrios Constantelos pointed out, who do not view the Orthodox tradition as legalistic or restrictive but tend to give to its believers a wide range of discretion as part of the concept that God and human beings cooperatively work in the creation of the good.

The *Roman Catholic* position is in fundamental agreement with the Eastern Orthodox approach in that it also relies on Scripture and Tradition, but it deals with Tradition in a more assertive way. Roman Catholic theologians have contended that God does not reveal God's self only in the special revelation of the Holy Scriptures, but that there is also the general revelation of God in nature from which it is possible by reason to extrapolate God's will. This is usually called natural theology. The eternal law of God is perceived to be behind the law of nature, and therefore it is possible to deduce the will of God from observing these laws. This enlarged the scope of biblical ethics because,

> If everything to which human nature tends derives from God, then God's goodness is implicit in every good.... And if the seeking of God's gifts leads to awareness of human nature's tending towards their giver, then the reasonable seeking of any good must be consistent with the seeking of God.[6]

The primary precept of natural law is that we ought to do what is good and avoid what is evil. Behind this precept is the conviction "that basic human awareness of good and evil...underlies all ethical thinking"[7] and is expressed at least rudimentarily in conscience.

Roman Catholicism has sometimes placed a greater stress on Tradition than on Scripture and emphasized the *Magisterium*, i.e., the teaching office of the church residing primarily in the episcopal office, and in an even more pronounced way in the papal office, culminating in the teaching of papal infallibility in certain *ex cathedra* matters of faith and morals. This has, at times, led to either a neglect in the use of Scripture or a use of Scripture simply as a proof-texting for views

---

[6] James Gaffney, *Newness of Life: A Modern Introduction to Catholic Ethics* (New York: Paulist Press, 1979), p. 170.

[7] Ibid., p. 159.

149

Scripture or a use of Scripture simply as a proof-texting for views derived from natural theology. Thus some Roman Catholic theologians found it necessary to defend recourse to Scripture—something Protestant theologians find strange. Edouard Hamel writes, for instance, the following:

> Scripture poses a series of problems for moral theology which are not so readily solved. To begin with, why go back to the Bible in moral theology?...Is the Gospel of salvation not written by the Spirit in the hearts of Christians (Jer 31:33)? Have not moral standards been impressed by the creator on the conscience of human beings (Rom 2:15)? Would recourse to the Bible to find moral standards not constitute pointless redundancy?...And what value will the concrete moral standard contained in the New Testament actually have? A permanent value, or just a historical value? Are they binding norms or just an ideal to which one should strive?[8]

While Hamel himself makes a case for Catholic moral theology to go back to Scriptures, it is primarily because it confirms the natural law in a way that is unspoiled by sin and rationalization to which a concrete conscience or reason may be subject.

Charles Curran points out that in Catholic teachings there are those who suggest that Christian ethics adds nothing to the material content of human ethics and those who do.

> Most of Catholic ethics in the past has been based on natural law. Contemporary official church documents speak of Christian morality as being the truly, or fully, or perfectly human, so that even what is different from the human must not be opposed to the human but rather be in

---

[8] Edouard Hamel, "Scripture, the Soul of Moral Theology?" in *Readings in Moral Theology No. 4: The Use of Scripture in Moral Theology*, ed, by Charles E. Curran and Richard A. McCormick, (New York: Paulist Press, 1984), pp. 105-106.

continuity with it and ultimately the fulfillment of the human.[9]

What is curious is that often what the Roman Catholic *Magisterium* had proposed as universal ethical norms based on the reasonable interpretation of natural law is often contradicted or denied by many others who do not come to the same conclusion from the same data.[10]

Protestants, as one may expect, do not agree among themselves on how to derive their conceptions of the good. Originally the Lutheran and Reformed traditions denigrated both Tradition and reliance on reason and based their views on Scripture alone. Human reason as the result of the Fall was so thoroughly corrupted and sinful that it was not regarded as a reliable source of what is good; only God can disclose such insights.

Anglicans and theological traditions arising out of Anglicanism tended to retain a greater reliance on traces of human goodness and rationality in their gnosiology. George Fox, the founder of the Quakers, relied on the "inner light" or "that which is of God" in every human for guidance on matters of right and wrong. John Wesley, the founder of Methodism, spelled out the quadrilateral, namely reliance on Holy Scriptures, Church tradition, reason, and experience in figuring out what is good. Some other, more recent religious movements even added the writings of their founders (e.g., Mary Eddy Baker's writings for Christian Science, Ellen White's for Seventh-Day Adventists, or the Book of Mormon for the Church of the Latter-Day Saints, or the Divine Principle in the Unification Church) as keys to interpret Scripture and God's will for humans.

Christian perfectionist and holiness movements (expressed in various charismatic churches and movements) tend to look at the example of Jesus and the early Christian communities and to imitate

---

[9] Charles E. Curran, *Ongoing Revision: Studies in Moral Theology* (Notre Dame, IN: Fides, 1975), p. 21.

[10] See for instance "The Vatican Declaration on Sexual Ethics" issued by the Sacred Congregation for the Doctrine of the Faith in 1975 which has elicited disagreement not only by non-Catholic ethicists but even by many Catholic ethicists and faithful.

their example in their personal and communal lives, distinguishing themselves from the general population in rigorous ethical behavior that is unwilling to make many if any allowances to current mores. For instance, they become dedicated pacifists and will literally rather be killed than carry weapons. Moral example of the minority is their approach, hoping to lure others by the purity of their lives into the ranks of believers.

Currently, Protestants seem to be divided no longer by denominational adherence as by theological orientations. Conservatives or evangelicals (and fundamentalists) tend to give great priority to the Holy Scriptures and use reason only deductively to apply biblical insights to the contemporary situation. The liberals give high regard to reason, particularly critical thinking and methodological tools developed since the Enlightenment to apply to insights gained from Holy Scripture and nature as well as contemporary human experience and tend to seek to apply and adapt Christian insights to the contemporary situation. In a rebellion against what were seen as too many concessions of liberal theologians to contemporary intellectual currents, the Neo-reformation or Neo-conservatism (under great influence from Karl Barth) sought to restore biblical primacy, suggesting that only the revelation of God through Jesus Christ is determinative for the Christian faith.

Most recent currents, such as liberation theology, black theology, and feminist theology, contributed the insights that many conceptions of the good were actually culturally derived and failed to take into consideration the interests of the oppressed, the people of color, and women and that theology done based on the experience of the oppressed tends to be more universally human than the theology of privileged white male clerics.

There is still another way by which one can categorize Christian ethical approaches to how to do good. It is the division of ethics into normative, antinomian, and situational ethics. Normative or rule ethics (some call it "old morality") contends that eternal norms have been revealed or discovered to which all people everywhere ought to conform. An example par excellence of these might be the Ten Commandments. Violations of such norms is always wrong—unless there are conflicts of norms in which a lesser norm must give way to a greater norm.

The Roman Catholic ethical tradition holds that in the application of universal rules one must employ four distinguishable ethical factors:

(1) the motive of the agent; (2) the intrinsic nature of the act; (3) its foreseen effects; (4) the modifying circumstances. For an action to be morally good, all four factors must be good; for it to be evil, it suffices that a single factor be evil.... Determine that an action is good, and you say only that it *may* be done; numerous other good options are available. Establish that it is evil, and you say that it *must not* be done.[11]

Protestant normative ethics is generally based on biblical rules, but a relatively recent powerful application of normative ethics is Martin Luther King, Jr.'s "Letter from the Birmingham Jail" in which he distinguishes various levels of law, the highest of which is God's universal law and that lesser laws are subject to correction or abolishment by higher laws if they are bad laws, i.e., they apply only to a segment of the community rather than to all people. Martin Luther King, Jr. operated in the liberal Protestant tradition which shares the Roman Catholic belief that human reason can discover eternal verities as to what is good and what is not from nature as well as from the Bible.

A fairly elaborate system of rewards and punishments (more of the latter than the former) were instituted to make sure that the rules were obeyed. Some of these were afterlife rewards or punishments, heaven for the obedient or hell for the disobedient. Roman Catholic theology provided an in-between stage as an opportunity for purification called purgatory. In this life the rewards were fewer, mostly the opportunity to be considered saintly, while the punishments were many, specified in canon law or church discipline , consisting of warnings, temporary suspensions, various forms of penance, withholding the sacraments, silencing, defrocking of clergy, and the most serious, excommunicating, though in the past the imprisonment, torture and even

---

[11] James Tunstead Burtchaell, *Philemon's Problem: The Daily Dilemma of the Christian*, (Chicago: Life in Christ, 1973), p. 77.

killing of the alleged culprit occasionally took place. Such punishments are less fashionable in the twentieth century, though in some instances some of these punishments are applied today.

The second approach is antinomian, i.e., moral decision-making is without any principles or maxims but by some intuitive knowledge of what is right (or what God wills) at this particular moment: "their moral decisions are random, unpredictable, erratic, quite anomalous."[12]

Situation or contextual ethics uses with respect the ethical principles of the Christian and wider human community as a guide, yet is willing "in any situation to compromise them or set them aside *in the situation* if love seems better served by doing so."[13] Thus, situation ethics uses ethical norms and rules as guidelines for usual behavior but judges as good that behavior which is the most loving (agapeic) option toward others in a given circumstance. Love here is defined as goodwill coupled with reason, and the emphasis is on decision-making under various circumstances, suggesting that a Christian moral choice, and a good one at that, is available whenever any decisions are to be made.

The appearance of "situation ethics" infused considerable liveliness in Christian ethical discussions. Some criticized it sharply; some embraced it enthusiastically; and some rejected it while accepting certain of the notions of situation ethics.

Some Christian thinkers want to avoid being clearly placed into one of these three ethical approaches and make a case for a different way of discovering and implementing the good. James T. Burtchaell, a Roman Catholic, for instance, criticized situation ethics in being a "praise-and-blame ethics" which

> ignores the dialectic between singular acts and overall orientation, deed and intention. A morality that is con-
> cerned with guilt or innocence thinks of acts only as

---

[12] Joseph Fletcher, *Situation Ethics: The New Morality* (Philadelphia: Westminster Press, 1966), p. 23.

[13] Ibid., p. 26.

responsible expressions of the self, and neglects that they
are also shapers of the self.[14]

Morally, according to Burtchaell, one may be destroyed by actions into
which one enters without an evil intention. Stanley Hauerwas, a
Protestant ethicist, faults situation ethics for contending that decision is
the central act rather than our moral notions, which include "the nature
of the moral self, the conception of Christian existence, and the nature
of moral authority."[15]

Hans Küng suggests that Jesus was a critic of legalism and
specified that the "the supreme norm *is the will of God*."[16] As per the
Lord's Prayer, it is "Thy will be done on earth as it is in heaven." The
law may declare God's will, but often people hide from God's will
behind the law, i.e., people often prefer to keep an item of the law
rather than make personal decisions which take God's will seriously.
Küng concludes

> The Sermon on the Mount of course by no means aims at
> a superficial situation ethics, as if only the law of the
> actual situation could be the dominating factor. The
> situation cannot decide everything. What is decisive in the
> particular situation is the absolute demand of God him-
> self, claiming total possession of man. In view of the
> ultimate and definitive reality, the kingdom of God, a
> fundamental transformation is expected of man.[17]

It is self-evident that Christian thinkers would not assert that
people should do anything but the will of God. The problem is not
whether to do God's will but *how* to know what the will of God is.

---

[14] Burtchaell, *op. cit.*, p. 81.

[15] Stanley Hauerwas, *Vision & Virtue: Essays in Christian Ethical
Reflection* (Notre Dame: Fides, 1974), p. 12.

[16] Hans Küng, *The Christian Challenge*, transl. by Edward Quinn
(Garden City, NY: Doubleday, 1979), p. 137.

[17] Ibid., p. 142. Küng does not clarify how this transformed person
would make concrete decisions, unless it be in an antinomian manner.

Paul Mojzes

to say there are vigorous, if not vicious conflicts in the Christian community about the appropriateness of using this or that ethical approach in figuring out God's will. It is not unusual for someone to pronounce that if people follow this or that ethical approach they simply cannot be real Christians. And if they have difficulty accepting the conception and implementation of the good by other Christians, it follows that they have at least as great difficulty with the conceptions and implementation of the good by other persons from other religions.

There is another division observable in Christian ethics and that is between personal ethics and social ethics. Personal ethics deals with the behavior of individuals. Historically Christianity paid much attention to this aspect of ethics, especially to sexual ethics, with which Christianity seems to have had a morbid preoccupation. Social ethics deals with what the Christian response ought to be to social crises and problems created by the various social systems. Some Christians contend that the churches as corporate bodies have no business in addressing themselves to social problems and issues, such as war and peace, poverty, social justice, racism, sexism, and so forth, while others contend that this is even more important an area than the issue of personal behavior, which does not affect as many people as do social policies. These two concerns, however, should not be separated but need to be coupled.

> Those who concentrate on the church's role in promoting social change may miss the aspects of faith that provide personal comfort and support—grace in times of brokenness, healing in times of suffering, meaning in times of anxiety. Those who see only an individual gospel or a church whose only task is spiritual miss the element of God's judgment and the Gospel imperatives to minister to the oppressed and the powerless. These two dimensions of the church's message are necessary to each other.[18]

4. Implementation of the Good

Over the centuries, Christianity used and changed a number of

---

[18] Paul T. Jersild and Dale A Johnson, eds., *Moral Issues and Christian Response* (New York: Holt, Rinehart & Winston, 3rd ed., 1983), pp. 32-33.

156

strategies in implementing the good. A convenient, though somewhat oversimplified, division of the twenty centuries of Christian history discerns three models of implementing the good, namely, the 1) Primitive Christian, 2) Constantinian, and 3) Post-Constantinian or pluralistic.

1) By the Primitive Christian model is meant the early Christian period from the inception of Christianity until the formal legalization of Christianity under the Roman emperor, Constantine the Great in early fourth century C.E. There was a great variety of Christian ways of implementation of the good, but most of it centered upon following the example of Jesus Christ. The Jewish Christians continued for a time to implement the good in the manner of their Jewish heritage, often not departing either in their conception or implementation from Judaism but simply tacking on to it a messianic, eschatological interpretation. Many Christians of the period had very strong apocalyptic expectations, and they sought no long-term implementation of the good. With a sense of urgency they tried to convince through evangelization and personal witness those who did not share their conviction that they needed to mend their ways, to turn away from self-centeredness and turn to the new law of Christ, turn to God and to fellow human beings. A slow process began of Christianizing Hellenism (and also Hellenizing Christianity, though the former was the more profound of the two processes). For them, Pauline theology seemed to have been more, though not exclusively, formative. Often conflicts would arise due to the different conceptions of what is good between the Jewish Christians and the various groups of Hellenists, which frequently gave rise to certain New Testament judgements on what is good and what is not. Apparently, they were meant by the biblical author as specific counsels for particular situations rather than a sweeping generalization valid for all times. In any case, the ethos and ethics were changing from a rural ethos of the Galilean Jesus to the urban ethos of Paul of Tarsus.[19] In Hellenistic Christianity, the methods of implementing were the same as

---

[19] Leander E. Keck, "Ethos and Ethics in the New Testament," in *Essays in Morality and Ethics*, ed. by James Gaffney (New York: Paulist Press, 1980), pp. 29-49.

in Jewish Christianity, a response to Jesus Christ in faith spread by means of preaching, witnessing, and modelling personal behavior by those members of the community who led particularly saintly lives. We have no evidence of Christian communities attempting to implement their idea of good upon the rest of society by law, though at times they anathematized their rivals and suggested that the rest of the world will eternally perish unless it follows God as interpreted by Christ. By the second century a group of educated Christian apologists emerged who attempted to demonstrate the superior way of Christianity.

2) What is now called the Constantinian model was in truth not formed completely under Emperor Constantine, but it evolved gradually over the centuries until codified by emperor Justinian in the sixth century C.E. Nevertheless, a pattern emerged under Constantine the Great whereby Christianity became first the legal, then the privileged, and later almost the only legal religion of the Roman Empire.[20] Constantinianism was practiced, and in some countries continues to be practiced even today, in a number of specific forms, but it is generally characterized by a close cooperation of church and state with a certain division of responsibilities between the spiritual and secular realms in which the church would generally teach what is good, and the state would legally implement it throughout the empire, by force if necessary. Christian values were codified and enforced not only under canon law but by the law of the state as well. To violate Christian virtue was punishable by law.

In the East there were several caesaro-papist patterns of the model but the prevalent model was that the secular Christian kingdom is sacred as it is a reflection of the heavenly kingdom.

> One monarch on earth was the reflection of the one God's sovereignty in heaven. The church was incorporated into the imperial structure, and this incorporation assumed institutionalised forms. The Synod of Bishops comple-

---

[20] In fact the so-called Constantinian pattern is actually pre-Constantinian, starting with the formal acceptance of Christianity by the King of Armenia for his entire people in the third century C.E. This did not, however, leave as lasting an imprint on world Christianity as did the Constantinian process.

mented the Senate, thus providing Byzantium, and later on the Russian empire, with the symbolism of the double-headed eagle. The Senate codified the political decrees of the emperor and was responsible for their orderly applications, while the Synod of Bishops legislated theologically for both the church and the Empire—for, if approved by the emperor, its degrees were recognised as laws.[21]

The emperor was frequently actively interested in theological issues and sometimes even initiated the formulation of Christian conceptions of the good and certainly enforced their implementation, although churchly patriarchal and episcopal power to balance the particularly unsaintly emperors were not altogether wanting.

However, when Christian churches of the East fell under Muslim rulers, especially the Ottoman Turkish Empire, this pattern was broken and the Turkish *villayet* system replaced it. In that system the patriarch of Constantinople became responsible for the implementation of the Christian legal system among the Christian populace who lived under the sultan.

In the West papal authority over the secular realm developed until it culminated in claims to papal absolutism under Innocent III and Boniface VIII in the thirteenth century. Later this was reversed as the papacy was brought under royal control in the period of absolutist monarchy and the papal captivity in Avignon. The sixteenth-century Catholic Reformation initiated the slow change to a modern relationship between papal and state power that nevertheless found different expressions, for instance, eighteenth-century Gallicanism, Febronianism and Josephinism and nineteenth-century Aufklärung Catholicism and Liberal Catholicism on the one hand and the absolutism of the First Vatican Council (1870). But for all of them, until recent times (particularly with Vatican Council II—1962-65) it was a characteristic common conviction that church and state must cooperate in implementing the good.

---

[21] Michael A. Meerson, "The Political Philosophy of the Russian Orthodox Episcopate in the Soviet Period," in *Church, Nation and State in Russia and Ukraine*, ed. by Geoffrey A. Hosking (New York: St. Martin's Press, 1991), p. 210.

There were some non-state forms of implementing the good. People were taught in the churches by means of liturgy, the sacraments, particularly the confession, homilies, and artistic "audio-visuals" (painted church walls, stained glass windows, sacred music, church architecture). They also witnessed the life of the clergy, particularly the monastic communities, male and female, who became the reservoirs of saints and the teachers in how to live a good life. The life of lay people was sometimes in contrast distressingly difficult but certainly not devoid of examples of courageous goodness.

The Protestant Reformation, especially its Magisterial branch, did not bring a change in the Constantinian model. Luther's two-kingdom theology brought the German princes deeply into the working of their *Landeskirchen*. Calvin's bourgeois theocracy in Geneva expressed the belief that the state and the church share responsibility for the implementation of the good.

Only the radical reformers (Anabaptists, Mennonites, etc.) begged to differ and sought to deliver believers out of the clutches of the state, suggesting that Christians must implement their conceptions of good without recourse to state coercion. Rather, they believed in the power of conviction and the power of example leading to a conversion experience on part of sinners. Neither the Catholics nor the Magisterial Reformers would accept this radical design and vigorously persecuted the "sectarians" just as they persecuted each other.

The Constantinian model knows of no or little toleration. If forced to grant some toleration through a stalemate in battle, it certainly does not show appreciation for pluralism. Under the Constantinian model, which even today is manifested in a number of European and Latin American societies, certain religious groups or churches receive a privileged and protected status, including financial and educational benefits.

3) The Post-Constantinian (or the emerging pluralistic) pattern is characterized by the separation of church and state and by religious liberty for all (at least on paper). It was initiated by the American experience but has found adherents in many places, and many think that it is a desirable system for all. The church loses its privilege and institutionally defined secular power, but is no longer under the dictates of the secular power and, thus freed, can sometimes amass a great deal of power in society. The church then not only can embody the epitome

of a certain concept of good, but also has the possibility freely, and if necessary vigorously, to enter the political process and fight for its conceptions and urge the implementation of the good.

In a society where a fairly large number of different concepts of what is good exists (e.g, how and when to celebrate the sabbath), it becomes a blessing to minority churches and religions that the major ones cannot legislate and impose their specific conceptions. Some have described this process as the feminization of religion[22] and point to the loss of influence of religion over the moral tenor of the nation. Others see it as a victory of freedom and the free expression of various notions of good seeking through democratic processes to arrive at some consensus on how to preserve and protect the good as variously conceived.

Under this last system the task of each religious group is to teach its adherents the good by means of the church-related educational system, the Protestant Sunday Schools (or Catholic CCD or Jewish Sabbath School or other religious instruction),[23] by means of literature, speeches, and media communications, as well as through political processes (not as uniquely privileged but as one of the players among many) and thereby advocate the acceptance and implementation of their ideas.

5. Self-critical reflections

Part of a critical response is to point out the good as well as the bad features of a phenomenon or process. I start with the assumption that we Christians have sufficiently disseminated or advertized our positive accomplishments so that it is not appropriate to advertize ourselves any more. In addition, our partners here in the Trialogue have

---

[22] A term used by Rabbi Dr. Rebecca Alpert of Temple University, Philadelphia, at a lecture at Rosemont College in the Spring semester 1992 to describe what she envisioned as the loss of power and prestige to religion with the separation of church and state and the marginalization of religion. I do not agree with her assessment of the position of religious institutions in the USA.

[23] The Sunday Schools, which include adult education, have been a particularly effective way of promoting a church's vision in a society dominated by public education which divorced itself from "sectarian" views.

had a chance to observe the strengths of the Christian conception and implementation of good, and I leave it to their discretion to discern and express what to them seem the strong points. Therefore, in this self-critical segment of the paper it seems more helpful to point out areas of weakness or trouble in the Christian approach.

1) One of our foremost problems has been an arrogant assertion that our conceptions and implementations of good are the best—certainly superior to others. This has been maintained not only vis-a-vis non-Christians, particularly our closest rivals, the Jews and Muslims, but also one denomination over against the others.

2) Love is the central good from the Christian perspective, and we have often acted as if we have a monopoly on self-giving love. The average Christians habitually uses the term "Christian love" for *agape*. Part of the reason for the adjective "Christian" is perhaps to distinguish this kind of love from filial or erotic love, but part of it also stems from the subliminal conviction that the Christian notion of love is superior to other people's notion and practice of love. Getting to know Jews and Muslims from closer range would demonstrate to many Christians that, indeed, they have no monopoly on such love but can learn from examples of self-sacrificial and self-giving love of other religious and even non-religious people.

3) In the past, and occasionally still even today, Christians have tried to implement their notion of the good by force, used either by ecclesiastical or secular authority. This was particularly true in the Constantinian model. While there were some benefits in the state providing support for the implementation of the good, those who did not have the same conception of the good were often repressed and even persecuted. Here we need only to recall the massacres and pogroms of Jews, the Crusades against Islam, the Inquisition against just about everybody who did not agree with the inquisitors, the exile and the burning at the stake of heretics, and the religious wars, particularly between Catholics and Protestants. One might say with Paul Tillich that a demonization of the Christian religion took place when the ultimate concern shifted from God to the conformist implementation of the perceived truth about God. There was far too much certainty that our conception is true and right and far too little humility in the face of the awesome mystery that is God and God's truth.

4) The experience of repression under the Constantinian model brought about the current post-Constantinian pluralistic society in which all religions can express and promote their view of the good, but none is given the sole authority to implement and impose it. That is good. But a corresponding malaise crept in which might be called relativism and passivity. Having given up the notion that we are the sole conceivers and implementers meant that many of us have given up altogether on being conceivers and implementers. We often experience frustration and impotence for not having it completely our own way, and then we stop trying, thereby giving the arena of public decision to those groups that tend to be more assertive and more dogmatic. It is not unusual in countries in which Christians make up a significant number of the populace that only the more extreme[24] voices are heard while the greater number of moderates are by-passed in the decision-making. Since ethical decision-making was always difficult, particularly when one does not have the support of prevalent social mores and social pressure, many Christians have abdicated altogether the need to implement their vision of the good.

5) Christians have had a difficulty in balancing personal and social ethics. At times the social aspects of Christian life prevailed, but mostly it was presumed that the Christian life consisted mostly of the personal affirmation of the good and the individual application of it as an example unto others. Indeed, Christianity did raise many good people—some of them authentic saints. But the general tendency has been to emphasize the personal aspects and deny the validity of any social responsibility (in the American spectrum this tended to be characteristic of the Christian right wing, the fundamentalists, the evangelicals, the "silent majority," and many other pious people, although less so at the present time). On the other hand, there are some on the Christian left who sometimes suggest that Christianity ought to address only the great social issues of the day and see salvation in only corporate (or revolutionary) action. Great utopian dreams have been born of this approach, and interestingly, despite the severe blow to the

---

[24] I am using the word here in a descriptive rather than judgmental sense, though often the extreme positions can be extremist. But I am operating here with the conviction that an "extreme" point could be true.

Marxist vision by the collapse of etatist socialism in the Soviet Union and Eastern Europe, there are still some who dream of the fusion of the Marxist and Christian utopias, i.e., visions of the good, ideal society.[25]

6) In the contemporary world Christians have not found a way to appeal effectively to others, both among their own members and to others for a common social ethos and ethics.[26] Christians are often quite concerned about the direction in which a modern secular society develops but have found it difficult to address the issues in a convincing manner. Some Christians issue shrill warnings and threats that society will self-destruct if it does not return to the "good old days." Others criticize any attempt to make a social witness to address grave problems, though privately they may complain about the development of social ills such as crime, graft, greed. So far the best we have done is to write about it. The writing is in the form of books and articles by individual authors as well as ecclesial letters and addresses (e.g., bishops of various churches have addressed the issue of nuclear war) and it has had some impact. On some issues, such as abortion, their interventions tended to shed more heat than light on the issue.

7) Another problem too long associated with Christians of all variations was that we believed we knew *the* will of God on what is good and how to put it to effect rather than realize that we possess only human conceptions of what the will of God may be in regard to the good, and that some notions may be better than others. In other words, infallibility was not only a notion applied to the papacy but somehow the entire Christian tradition was infected at least implicitly by various sorts of infallibility claims. In so far as such claims reflect the desire for assurance that what we do know of God and the good is not misleading,

---

[25] E.g., John Marsden, *Marxian and Christian Utopianism: Toward a Socialist Political Theology* (New York: Monthly Review Press, 1991), and Bas Wielenga "Letter to the Editor" *Occasional Papers on Religion in Eastern Europe*, vol. XI, no. 1 (1991), pp.48-49.

[26] Attempts have been made recently by Hans Küng and Leonard Swidler. See in this volume Leonard Swidler, "Toward a Universal Declaration of Global Ethos," and the responses to it; and in more detail by Hans Küng *Projekt Weltethos* (Munich: Piper Verlag, 1990); English translation, *Global Responsibility. In Search for a New World Ethos* (New York: Crossroad, 1991).

these sentiments are understandable. But regretfully too often they turned into arrogant claims of absolute certainty. The language of religion, which is more like the language of poetry and the language of love, came to be treated as the language of prosaic certitude about definitive observations.

8) Many Church authorities and theologians have frequently treated the laywomen and laymen as children who must be told what is good and right and how they must practice it. There is a real reluctance to treat church members as mature adults (for fear of loss of power to the clergy?), and many church members are extremely frustrated and are leaving the churches because they think that the good as advocated by the churches is out of tune with their needs, and they simply refuse to implement it consistently in their lives, though they often suffer guilt and condemnation. It is high time that church members, who are increasing better educated—not infrequently better educated than their clergy—assert their will to search for the good and implement it the best they can.

9) Many Christians operate on the system of reward for the good and punishment for bad behavior rather than regarding the search for and doing the good for its own sake a sufficient reward unto itself. Too frequently, Christians feel threatened into being good out of fear of eternal punishment or are enticed into doing good because of the hope of eternal life in heaven, many of whom envision these two states of being vividly as places of burning fire or golden mansions in the sky. While the well trained theologians do not see it this way, it is easy to encounter relatively well educated and sophisticated people unable to tear themselves free from such crude imagery, which they envision literally. The churches are doing too little to alter these images.

6. Conclusion

On the whole the Christian record on the topic is rather mixed. Yet despite the weaknesses and failures, it seems to me that perhaps on the whole there were more pluses (upon which I did not dwell) than minuses. The great proliferation of conceptions and the variety of attempted methods of implementation of the good practically guaranteed that out of the tensions of the contest maturation would take place and more evident errors would be either critiqued or abandoned.

Paul Mojzes

In this dialogical age, we Christians need to address these issues jointly with other faith communities such as Judaism and Islam rather than against them, although from time to time we shall probably select different approaches, hopefully without becoming antagonists. Jointly, we may see the good more fully and implement it more effectively, rejecting, however, coercion both of the ecclesiastical and secular sort (except in dealing with crime, terrorism, and war). Not merely for our own benefit but for the sake of the world, we need to find better ways to cooperate in order to create and preserve greater values and diminish disvalues.

XI. THE "GOOD" IN THE SOURCES OF ISLAM ITS CONCEPTION AND IMPLEMENTATION BY MUSLIMS

Fathi Osman

1. The "Good" in the Qur'an

A significant name given to the "good" in the Qur'an is "the known" (by the human nature), *al-ma'ruf*, while the "evil" is called "the rejected" (by human nature), *al-munkar* [e.g., 3:104, 110, 114; 7:157; 9:71; 22:41; 31:17]. This underlines the common grounds of moral conception and commitment among human beings. All the followers of God's guidance have been bound with this common morality, including the "People of the Book"—the Jews and Christians [3:114], and the Muslims [3: 104; 110; 9:71].[1] According to a *sura* (a "chapter") of the Qur'an revealed in the middle of the Meccan period, an ancient wise man known as *Luqman* advised his son a long time before Islam, to enjoin the doing of *ma'ruf* and forbid the doing of *munkar* [31:17]. Judaism underlined seven commandments that are considered obligatory for all people regardless of belief, known as the "Noachide Laws" in which Talmudic scholars have seen a road to a wider religious perspective and tolerance. They are: prohibition of eating the flesh of a living creature, blasphemy, robbery, murder, paganism, perversion, and the precept to do justice.[2]

The Qur'an repeatedly teaches that it is not only the individual's observance of the good and avoidance of the evil which is required, but also the spreading of this in the society through words and deeds. The prominent commentator on the Qur'an, Al-Qurtubi (d. 1272), stated that the enjoining of doing good and the forbidding of doing evil had been taught in previous messages of God, and is the main benefit of these messages for humanity as well as for those who carry out this duty to follow the conveyors of the divine guidance in widening and

---

[1] For a brief survey of the parallel texts about the basic moral values in the Torah (especially the Ten Commandments), the Gospels, and the Qur'an see: Deraz, Mohamed Abdullah, *Initiation au Koran*, a dissertation submitted to La Sorbonne in December 1947, Arabic translation: *al-Madkhal 'ila al-Qur'an al-Karim* (Kuwait, 1971), pp. 91-105.

[2] Dagobert D. Runes, *Concise Dictionary of Judaism* (New York: Philosophical Library, 1959).

Fathi Osman

deepening it.³ Relating the "good" and the "evil" to a common consciousness of humanity is emphasized in this Qur'anic verse: "And
consider the human self, and how it is formed properly, as it is inspired
to distinguish between the moral failure and the righteousness" [91:8].

In other verses, the Qur'an gives the "good" another name:
"righteousness," *al-birr*. It is comprehensive, not restricted to the
superficial observance of certain practices of worship, but in its true
sense means a genuine faith in God which has its practical implications
in human relations such as: helping the poor and needy and freeing
those in bondage, keeping one's promises, being patient and steadfast
in times of hardship and peril—"It is they that have proved themselves
true, and it is they who are really conscious of God" [2:177]. Al-
Qurtubi—the prominent commentator on the Qur'an (d. 1272)—mentioned that "righteousness" encompasses all the good, and the verse was
revealed in Medina to teach the Muslims, after being well settled and
established, that morality is the essence of religion and that such
morality cannot mean a mechanical observance of certain rituals or
formalities⁴ (e.g., material requirements about cleanliness, food, drink,
dress, etc.) In cases of confusion about what is moral and righteous the
Prophet Muhammad directed women and men to look to their own heart
and conscience, "even if others, and others may, advise you differently."⁵ Moreover, the Prophet underlined the fact that morality is an
outcome of an individual and social accumulation of concepts and
practices; thus who were morally among the best before Islam would be
among the best of Muslims when they embraced Islam.⁶ He once
praised an Arab who had been widely known for his generosity and
hospitality before Islam. Muhammad's message was summed up by him
merely as a "complement to moral values."⁷

---

³ Muhammad ibn 'Ahmad al-Ansari al-Qurtubi, *al-Jami 'li-Ahkam al-
Qur'an* (Cairo), comment on the verse 3:22, vol. IV, p. 47.

⁴ Ibid, vol.II, comment on verse 2:177, esp. p.239.

⁵ A Prophet's tradition reported by al-Bukhari, Muslim, Ibn Hanbal and
al-Tirmidhi.

⁶ Reported by al-Bukhari, Muslim and Ibn Hanbal.

⁷ Reported by al-Bukhari, al-Hakim and, al-Bayhaqi

As it is repeatedly stressed in the Qur'an, genuine faith is connected and always interacts with doing the good.[8] It happened later that Muslim theologians argued about one who has faith but no good deeds, whether s/he may be considered a believer or not. The faith ought to inspire various good deeds that benefit others; even to remove an object which may obstruct the way and hurt someone proves a true faith.[9] All acts of worship aim merely to nurture morality through God-consciousness: "prayer restrains [a person] from loathsome deeds and from all that is rejected by human nature and common sense *(munkar)*" [29:45].[10] A Prophet's tradition states that the really bankrupt person is the one who comes on the Day of Judgement with many practices of worship such as prayers and fasting while his/her account also records slanders and frauds and assaults against others which would be subtracted from her/his assets until nothing remains.[11]

Moral responsibility is *individual* [The Qur'an 6:154; 17:15; 19:80, 95, 35:18; 39:7; 53:36-38], and it is based on *one's intention*,[12] not on what appears to others' senses on the surface. That is why the true judgement about one's morality *rests only with God* on the Day of Judgement [e.g., The Qur'an 2:77, 235; 3:29; 9:78; 11:5; 20:7; 21:110; 27:74; 33:51; 40:19; 47:26; 87:7]. Personal judgments, of course, will have to be made, as is necessary for the individual, the society and the state; however, this should never be considered an absolute or final

---

[8] Faith, *iman*, was connected with doing the good, *amal alsalihat*, in about eight Qur'anic verses.

[9] A Prophet's tradition reported by Muslim, 'Abu Dawud, a-al-al-al-Nisa'i and Ibn Majah.

[10] All practices of worship are meant to develop moral values, e.g., 2:183, 197; 9:103; 22:37. A Prophet's tradition reads: "Fasting is a protection; whenever one is fasting s/he should not lose his/her temper, and when s/he faces those who may their lose temper s/he should practice self-restraint and say, 'I am fasting'"; reported by Ibn Hanbal, al-Nisa'i, ibn Majah and al-Bayhaqi.

[11] Reported by Muslim and Ibn Hanbal.

[12] A Prophet's tradition states, "Deeds are judged only according to one's intentions"; reported by al-Bukhari, 'Abu-Dawud, al-Tirmidhi and al-Nisa'i.

169

judgement, but only a relative one according to the best knowledge of a certain individual in given circumstances. Such a judgement naturally has to rely on what is concrete and can be surely discerned by human faculties.[13] One has to be fair and should resist all bias in favor or against [The Qur'an 4:135; 5:8]. Realizing that the absolute and final judgement rests only with God develops a climate of common tolerance and stands against human arrogance and claims of moral superiority.

Although a state has to guard the common interests of the people and forbid by law certain immoral deeds which are harmful to others, such as assault, slander and fraud, the effects of morality that go to the depth of human intention are far beyond legal procedures. Jurists made a distinction between what the judge has to rule in court and what true religiosity should guide the concerned parties themselves to. The Qur'an stresses that *the moral change of the individual is the goal*, not just the enforcement of a law, and if such an internal reform can be proved before a defendant is reached by the authorities, the illegal deed, and even the legal procedure, should be disregarded.[14] Believers are urged to go beyond their legal rights to forgiveness, forgoing and altruism [e.g., 2:109, 178, 237; 3:109, 114; 4:86; 5:13; 16:90; 23:96; 24:22; 41:33; 42:40; 60:8; 64:14]. Even in case of avoiding a repulsive person, one is urged to make one's avoidance decent and discreet [Qur'an 73:10], and one is urged to practice "goodly patience" [70:5], and "goodly forgiveness" [15:85]. *Human magnanimity goes beyond any legality* and knows no limits [35:32], and people are urged to compete with one another in such virtues [3:133; 57:21; 83:26].

---

[13] A Prophet's tradition states that he is merely a human being and rules according to what is apparent to him in a case from the submitted evidence, but what counts for God's judgement may not be obvious to him and is known only by the concerned parties in the case, who have to settle their dispute morally, and not be content with what the legal judgment may bring out; reported by Malik, al-Bukhari, Muslim, Ibn Hanbal, 'Abu Dawud, al-irmidhi, al-Nisa'i and Ibn Majah.

[14] The Qur'an exempts from punishment for a specific crime "those who repent before you can have power over them" [5:34]. The prominent jurist Ibn al-Qayyim generalized the rule to include any defendant who may be accused of any offence and is proved to have repented genuinely before being seized by the authorities; see *'I'lam al-Muwaqi'in* (Cairo), vol.II, pp. 48-49.

Diversity is characteristic of human nature, and the followers of different faiths can compete only in doing the good regardless of their different ways of life. "And if God had so willed, He could surely have made you all one single community, but [He willed it otherwise] in order to test you through what God has given you in this life. Vie, then, with one another in doing good deeds. Unto God you all must return; and then He will make you understand all what you differed on" [5:48]. Competition should not negate cooperation for implementing the good and furthering it [5:2]. Unless there are common human means for different individuals or groups to know the good, regardless of their religious differences, how would they co-operate or compete in doing it, as the Qur'an guides?

A social change cannot be achieved from above through the state authority and its legal measures and compulsive powers, but from the depths of the human hearts and minds, as "God does not change a people's condition unless they change their inner selves" [13:11], and there can be "no compulsion in matters of faith" [2:256]. Rights of privacy cannot be violated for any moral claim [2:189; 17:36; 24:27-29; 49:12] and human dignity, integrity and reputation are protected morally and legally [22:30; 24:15-19; 25:72; 49:6].

2. Muslim Intellectual Approaches to "Universal Morality"

Being inspired by the Qur'anic presentation of the "good" as *what is known by human nature and common sense to be so*, that is, *ma'ruf*, Muslim thinkers tried to articulate such a concept of universal morality and make it obvious and understandable. While Muslim theologians and philosophers found in the human *mind* the common vehicle for such a universal morality, the Muslim mysticism-oriented "Sufis" believed that the only common ground for all humanity is the *heart*, or the *spirit* which has been breathed by God into the material components of the human being in order to create this species [Qur'an 15:29; 38:72].

a) In Theology
Supported by Greek philosophy, especially logic, Islamic theology was developed initially to defend the faith *'ilm al-kalam*; while

171

discussing the faith independently from emerging arguments, "science of monotheism," *'ilm al-tawhid* developed gradually afterwards.

This argumentative approach was represented clearly by the *Mu'tazila*, a word with several explanations for its origin, but they all indicate a "split,"[15] whether from the main doctrinal stream or from a certain circle of doctrinal studies. They emerged already in the second century of Islam and survived for several centuries, but flourished especially under the Abbasid Caliph al-Ma'mun (d. 833) and his successors al-Mu'tasim (d. 842) and al-Wathiq (d. 847). Their schools in Basra and Baghdad had their differences, as did their prominent leaders, but they all had a common ground in their efforts to provide a rational presentation of the Islamic faith. They so vigorously defended the oneness of God that they rejected the eternity of many of God's attributes, because He in His own self is the only eternal reality, and many of His attributes such as "speech" occur merely incidentally on certain occasions when He wants to speak to someone. This view resulted in denying the eternity of the Qur'an, although they never denied that it is the word of God. Besides, they stressed the human free will in what one chooses or does, and this is essential in their view for the human accountability and the divine justice. For the same reason, in the view of the *Mu'tazila*, good and evil can be known according to their own merits by the human being independently, as judged by the *human mind*. While divine messages and laws would help or support the human knowledge in this respect, they did not initiate it. God has always to choose the good, does not desire evil, and never ordains it; rather, it is the human being who creates evil.[16] It is a pity that the *Mu'tazila*, in spite of such pioneering liberal thinking, used their influence and power in horrible ways to oppress those who differed with them on the grounds that they were defending the true faith against heresy.

---

[15] See the different explanations for the origins of the name *Mu'tazila* in 'Ahmad 'Amin, *Fajr ul-'Islam* (Beirut, 1969), pp. 288-296.

[16] Al-Shihristani, Al-Milal wa-l-Nihal (Beirut, 1975), pp. 45-85, esp. pp. 45, 52, 58, 70, 72; Muhammad Miqdad Yalgen, al-Ittijah al-Akhlaqi fi al-'Islam (Cairo, 1973), p.198; Georges C. Anawati, "Philosophy, Theology and Mysticism," in: The Legacy of Islam, ed. by Joseph Schacht and C.E. Bosworth (Oxford, 1979), pp. 354-55; 'Ahmad 'Amin, ibid, p. 298.

The *Mu'tazila* also stated that the believer in God who commits evil and does not repent is in a state between the true believer and the denier of God, and thus they stood between two previously held views: the one by *Murji'a*, who considered such a person a believer in this life according to his/her words, leaving the final judgement to God in the life to come, and the second by the *Kharijis*, who emerged as rebels against the fourth Caliph Ali and continued to fight against successive Umayyad and Abbasid Caliphs, and considered such a person a rejector of the faith. This issue was an enormously heated issue with regard to the political differences and civil wars, one that resulted in the bloodshed of Muslims from the time of the third Caliph Uthman (d. 644). The *Mu'tazila*'s middle position may explain why they were not considered irritating by the later Umayyads or early Abbasids—indeed, were even supported by some of them.[17]

Al-Zamakhsari, the prominent linguist and commentator on the Qur'an (d. 1143), whose *Mu'tazili* attitude was known, stated in his commentary on the verse 3:104 about enjoining doing good and forbidding doing evil: "All evil is bad and should be forbidden, *and the obligation of forbidding it is determined by the human mind and the divine message as well,* according to 'Abi 'Ali (Muhammad ibn "Abdel-Wahhib al-Jubba'i, d.907)."[18] He reflected in his commentary on verses 91:7-10, "And consider the human self, and how it is formed properly, and how it is inspired to know moral failure as well as righteousness" as follows: "*The meaning of inspiring moral failure and righteousness is making both understandable and reasonable* [for the human mind], so they are recognized as good and bad, *and thus the human self is enabled to choose what one wishes [freely]. And so the human being is put in the next verses as the agent of purification or profanation.*"[19]

---

[17] 'Ahmad 'Amin, ibid, pp. 291-5.

[18] Mahmud ibn 'Umar al-Zamakhshari, al-kashshaf (Cairo), vol. I, p. 452; see also: al-Jubba'i, quoted by Muhammad 'Abu Zahra, Tarikh al-madhahib al-'Islamiyya (Cairo, 1976), vol. I, pp. 144-145.

[19] al-Zamakhshari, ibid, vol.IV, pp. 258-259.

Fathi Osman

This fits with the general trend of many ethical philosophers that the human moral conscience exists in every human being by nature,[20] rather than with those who believe that it is a result of education or society. However, even most Muslim theologians who believed that good and evil can be essentially known by God's guidance, did not deny that the human being can understand the divine wisdom subsequently.[21]

b) In Philosophy

Besides by the Qur'an and the Prophet's traditions, *Hadith* and *Sunna*, the Muslim thought was greatly influenced by its encounter with Christian theological thinking and Greek philosophy in the Fertile Crescent. The Christians, especially perhaps the Syrians of Antioch, had already "Christianized" certain passages from the ancient writers, or made them seem more religious.[22] Muslim philosophy benefitted from the Aristotelian philosophy and neo-Platonism, but it could not live long as it began and ended in the twelfth century; yet it produced among Muslims three outstanding philosophers and had an immense influence on the history of thought in Christendom and Judaism, as it is under-lined by S. Pines from the Hebrew University of Jerusalem.[23] These three philosophers were Ibn Bajjah (d. 1138), Ibn Tufayl (d. 1185) and Ibn Rushd (d. 1198). Muslim philosophy contained religious elements

---

[20] Oswald Kulpe, *Introduction to Philosophy*, Arabic translation by 'Abu-l-'Ila 'Afifi (Cairo), pp. 311-312.

[21] The *Mu'tazili* views were opposed severely by many theologians, traditionists [*Muhaddithin*] and jurists, especially by Abi al-Hasan al-Ash'ari (d. 936), al-Matridi (d. 945); and by the *Hanbalis*, especially Ibn Taymiyya (d. 1327) and his disciple Ibn al-Qayyim (d. 1350) who represented the *Salafi* trend. See: al-Shihristani, ibid, I: pp. 92-103; Ibn Khaldun, *al-Muqaddima* (Beirut, 1978), pp. 463-6, Yalgen, ibid, pp.315-320. For a lengthy argument that the human mind by nature knows the good and evil see: Salih ibn al-Mahdi al-Muqbili (d. 1696), *al-'Alam al-Shamikh* and its supplement: *al-Arwah al-Nawafikh* (Damascus, 1981), pp. 31, 216-263 and continued to 373.

[22] Anawati, op. cit., pp. 352-3.

[23] S. Pines, "Philosophy", in the *Cambridge History of Islam* (Cambridge, 1970), vol. II, pp. 814-815.

from the Qur'an, and sought sincerely to reconcile religion and reason, although it aroused the suspicion of traditional believers and 'ulama.[24]

Ibn Tufayl considered that *morality is related to the area of nature, not the area of religion*, and the good in his view is merely that the human being should not obstruct nature in its process.[25]

Ibn Rushd's view was that *the faculty of the human intellect called the hylic or material intellect, is one and the same in the whole of humanity, participated in by each individual human being*, and it is permanently actualized. Thus, the existence of philosophers in every generation is part of the nature of things. Beside the common folk who enjoy their beliefs presented in a simple way, the philosophers are capable of grasping the truth. However, the argumentative defenders of the faith, the *almutakallimun*, do not grasp the truth correctly through philosophy and, with dangerous results, propagate false interpretations of the Qur'an among the ignorant masses.[26] One of Ibn Rushd's works had a significant title: "A Decisive Approach to the Relation Between Wisdom (Philosophy) and *Shari'a* (Islamic Law): (*Fasl ul-Maqal fi-ma bayna al-Hikma wa-l-Shari'a mina-l-Itisal*). He stated that wisdom is the sister of Shari'a, and those who are related to each are companions by essence and nature, in spite of all hostility and fighting. Shari'a was hurt most by those ignorant friends who are related to it."[27]

Ibn Maskawih (d. 1030), a Muslim philosopher of ethics, stated that "the human essence is related to a creative power (God), while improving this essence is assigned to the human being and related to his/her will."[28]

Ibn Rushd and other Muslim philosophers presented the "human mind" as common ground for knowledge and morality but meanwhile limited those who can use the human intellect to philosophers. It is

---

[24] Anawati, op. cit., pp. 358-359.

[25] Farrukh, *'Umar, Tarikh al-Fikr al-'Arabi* (Beirut, 1981), pp. 642-3.

[26] Pines, op. cit., pp. 817-819.

[27] Quoted by Farrukh, op. cit., p. 678.

[28] 'Abu 'Ali 'Ahmad ibn Muhammad ibn Ya'qub Ibn maskawih, *Tahdhib al-Akhlaq* (Cairo, 1959), p. 39.

natural that such an elitist attitude could not gain popularity among the masses, and it raised the doubts of traditionists (*Muhaddithin*), theologians and jurists. It had less influence among the Muslims than in Europe. On the contrary, Christian theologians such as Thomas Aquinas (d. 1274) felt more comfortable in dealing with Greek philosophy than with the Christian masses.

Ibn Khaldun (d. 1406) strongly attacked philosophy and considered its approach and principles false and useless, as philosophers restricted true knowledge to the human mind and ignored the possibility that what exists may be beyond the human mind and senses, although he admitted one benefit of philosophy, that is, intellectual training.[29]

Shaykh Muhammad Abduh, the prominent Egyptian Islamic reformer (d. 1905), believed that theologians were harsh in criticizing the philosophers when they knew about their concepts related to theology, such as the eternal nature of matter and what is essential and accidental, and the late theologians went beyond all moderation in this respect.[30]

c) In Mysticism (Sufism)

The *"Spirit"* which God has breathed in the clay that He shaped to form the human being [15:29; 38:72], is able then—according to the Qur'an—to know good and evil initially and instinctively, and is able even to know God Himself prior to any of His messages [7:172-3]. Therefore, this "Spirit" has been the Sufis' means to universal morality. Muhyi al-Din ibn 'Arabi (d. 1240), who represented intellectual Sufism, stated that "the 'perfect man' is a miniature of reality; he is the macrocosm, in whom are reflected all the perfect attributes of the microcosm... The 'perfect man' was the cause of the universe, being the epiphany of God's desire to be known; for only the 'perfect man' knows God, loves God and is loved by God."[31]

---

[29] Ibn Khaldun, in ibid, pp. 514-519.

[30] Quoted by Mustafa 'Abd-ul-Raziq, *Tamhid li-Tarikh al-Falsafa al-'Islamiyya* (Cairo, 1966), p. 84.

[31] A.J. Arberry, "Mysticism," in: *The Cambridge History of Islam* (Cambridge, 1970), vol. II, p. 623.

Whatever the sources from which Sufism originated might be, it is obvious that Ibn 'Arabi mixed Aristotelian and neo-Platonic and other philosophical sources with Islamic beliefs derived from the Qur'an and the Sunna. The human, and especially the human heart, represent the best temples in which to worship God; they are far better than temples built of stone. The different faiths are but different sides and angles of one faith in the One God. A Sufi tries hard to make ethics close to God's attributes or merits. The human being is naturally universal and has the ability to encompass the truth, and in this respect s/he is like the eye's pupil (which is called in Arabic *'insan*, the same word for a human being).[32] Some Sufis said that there are as many ways to God as the number of human beings on earth.[33] However, implementing the good interacts with the faith, and immoral and unethical deeds produce pressures and obstacles for the faith.[34] Ibn Taymiyya (d.1328) and his disciple Ibn al-Qayyim (d. 1350) believed in a Sufism that is directed and controlled by the Qur'an and Sunna. Sufis considered ethics an essential goal in their approach to God.[35]

As Georges Anawati has put it, "the man who was to contribute most to get mysticism accepted by 'official' Islam and to break down the prejudices of an Islam too exclusively juridical was al-Ghazali" (d. 1111).[36] He was not an absolute enemy of the human intellect, as he devoted a full chapter in his great work *'Ihya' 'Ulum al-Din* to the high value of the human mind and its nature and functions. The human mind is what distinguishes between human beings and animals. However, he devoted a considerable part of his work to the *heart* and/or the *spirit*, which represents the real value of the human being as the center of knowledge and that part of the human being which is addressed by God and is accountable before Him. They represent a universal power in all

---

[32] Farrukh, op. cit., pp. 528-535.

[33] Reported and opposed by Ibn Taymiyya, *Majmu'at al-Fatawa* (Riyad), vol. X, p.454.

[34] Ibn Taymiyyah, op. cit., pp. 628-629.

[35] Yalgen, op. cit., p. 44.

[36] Anawati, op. cit., p. 372.

Fathi Osman

humanity, and can be trained and developed morally and spiritually to
know the truth through another way rather than formal education. The
basic moral values are wisdom, courage, and chastity, in addition to
fairness in using these three. However, the Sufi master with a group of
followers had to make differentiations in guiding his followers through
their spiritual development, as there is no one pattern for developing the
human self—although its nature and general functions are the same.[37]

Al-Ghazali's works proved that he mastered theology, jurisprudence and Sufism, as well as being familiar with the main philosophical
issues. He analyzed and categorized what the philosophers' views which
were different from the Sunni mainstream into seventeen illegitimate
innovations (*bida'*) which could not be considered to be in contradiction
to the main faith, while most other differences were merely semantic.
But the three points which the philosophers held and contradicted the
Islamic faith, in al-Ghazali's view, were: the eternity of the universe,
restriction of God's knowledge to general principles excluding the
emerging particulars, and spiritual resurrection which means that the
body will vanish for ever and is not resurrectible.[38] Ibn Khaldun
supported al-Gazali in his strong attack against philosophy as expressed
in his two well-known works, "The Purposes of the Philosophers"
(*Maqasid al-Falasifa*) and "The Incoherence of the Philosophers"
(*Tahafut al-Falasifa*).[39]

d) The Present Situation

What has happened to this universal attitude of relating good
and evil *al-ma'ruf, al-munkar* to the human "mind" or the human
"spirit"?

The elitist intellectual approaches could not deepen their roots
in the mainstream, among the masses or the *'ulama*. The *Mu'tazila* and
their belief about the natural merits of the good that can be conceived
by the human mind were not able to survive for a long time among

---

[37] 'Abu Hamid Muhammad ibn Muhammad ibu Muhammad al-Ghazali,
'Ihya' 'Ulum al-Din (Cairo, 1957), vol. I, pp. 82-89, vol. III, pp. 2-77.

[38] 'Abdul-Raziq, op. cit., pp. 83-84; Farrukh, op. cit., pp. 503-508.

[39] Ibn Khaldun, op. cit., pp. 514-519.

178

Sunnis, after they lost the Abbasid support when al-Mutawakkil became Caliph [847-861]. Although their main concepts continued to exist among the *Shi'is*, these became a part of the *Shi'i* doctrine and the *Mu'tazila* could not be identified as a living independent school of theology any more.

Those who could win the Sunni mainstream were the *Ash'aris*, whose leader 'Abu-l-Hasan al-'Ash'ari (d. 935) split from the *Mu'tazila*, and tried to gain the support of the masses and the *'ulama*, benefitting from his earlier argumentative training among the *Mu'tazila*. In his view, God produces the human actions, and what is good or evil is determined by God. While the human being does not perform his own actions, he/she can *acquire* them (*kasb*), and such "acquisition" of an act can occur in every particular case through a power of "acquisition" especially created by God in this human being.

Al-Ash'ari's doctrine dominated, and was elaborated on by prominent theologians such as al-Baqillani (d. 1013) and al-Juwayni (d. 1085).[40] However, later works in this field, went far in mixing philosophy with their theological approaches—as ibn Khaldun noticed—and thus became so alienated from the public religious culture, that a prominent scholar like ibn Khaldun stated that such approaches had become in his time neither necessary for the students nor for the faith.[41]

Ibn Taymiyyah judged that the *Ash'ari* approach deviated from that of the Qur'an and Sunna, and stressed that the faith should only follow the revelation in all its details, but he did not think that this would contradict the human reason.[42] His approach represented what became known as the *Salafi trend*, which is noticeable not only in the field of faith but also in the field of law, Shari'a, and thus he did not adhere to one particular juristic school, not even the *Hanbali* school in which he was educated. Salafism was strengthened later by the movement of Muhammad ibn "Abd-el-Wahhab (d. 1792) in the Arabian

---

[40] Pines, op. cit., pp. 812-813.

[41] Ibn Khaldun, op. cit., pp. 465-467.

[42] Ibn Taymiyya had a voluminous work with a significant title: "The Accordance of True Rationality with the Authentic Tradition" (*Muwafaqat Sarih al-Ma'qul li-Sahih al-Manqul*).

peninsula, which influenced in different ways and degrees modern Islamic thinking and movements.[43]

The philosophers could not gain a foothold in the first place, especially after the strong attack of al-Ghazali against them. Although al-Ghazali pointed out that only three philosophical theses contradict the Islamic faith, and the philosopher Ibn Rushd was also a recognized jurist, the influence of Muslim philosophers could not be felt among the Muslim masses or the *'ulama*. The modern Egyptian reformer Muhammad 'Abduh— as previously mentioned—considered that the late attacks on philosophy had exceeded all limits of moderation. A more recent Azharite scholar has considered theology (*'ilm al-kalam*) and the fundamentals of jurisprudence (*'usul al-fiqh*) the true representatives of the Muslim philosophical mind.[44] The rationalist attitude of Muhammad 'Abduh was able to influence some intellectuals in Egypt, but it could not reach the masses and most of the *'ulama* in al-Azhar. Its influence could also be followed in some other Muslim countries from North Africa to South East Asia. Recent rationalist attempts may be traced among some Muslim intellectuals here and there, but they cannot—in my view—represent a consolidated wave.

Intellectual Sufism could not also be more successful in propagating a universal morality, as it aroused the juristic opposition, while the "non-esoteric sufism, which held to the essential parts of Muslim dogma could spread among the people, appealing to their religious feeling and their devotional impulses. What it sought was to touch men's hearts, to draw near to God in a heartfelt manner.... It was thus that the 'confraternities', which had originally been groups made up of a master and his disciples, spread among the masses."[45] However, such a popular Sufism had a local flavor wherever it could develop,

---

[43] 'Abu Zahra, op. cit., pp.180-220. About the *Salafi* trend in contemporary Islam see: Fathi Osman, *'al-Salafiyya fi al-Mujtama'at el-Islamiyya al-Mu'asira'* ("The Salafi Trend in Contemporary Islam") (Cairo, 1980), and M. Sa'id Ramadan al-Buti, *'al-Salafiyya Marhala mina al-Tarikh la Madhab 'Islami'* ("Salafism: A Period of History not a Muslim doctrine") (Damascus, 1988).

[44] 'Abdu-l-Raziq, op. cit., pp. 26-27.

[45] Anawati, op. cit., p. 376.

although it might nurture a limited feeling of universality within Muslims. The Prophet Muhammad was identified by Sufis as "the Perfect Man," which encouraged a cult of the Prophet,[46] which in turn nurtured Muslim self-centeredness. Salafism—which has stressed adhering to the teachings of the Qur'an and Sunna as understood and practiced by the Prophet and the "good preceding generations"—has strongly attacked Sufi innovations and deviations from the early Islamic model, and contributed to the decline of Sufism in modern times. However, some scattered signs of Sufi intellectual and behavioral activities can be traced recently.

3. Some Contemporary Reflections

The following are some observations about the understanding and implementation of the "good" among contemporary Muslims. Of course such generalizations are enormously broad and are naturally subject to my limited knowledge:

1. *The "good" may be restricted in many contemporary Muslim minds and practices* to observing the daily prayers, yearly fasting, and certain dietary rules and women's dress code. In addition, there are some segregative and restrictive rules in sex relations—which may be related to social traditions rather than Shari'a—giving the man a privileged place in his family and social position and with regard to what may be considered a sexual offense.

The "good" in its original comprehensive, rich and inspiring sense of *ma'ruf* and *birr*, or virtue and righteousness, is not widely conceived or implemented. The narrow vision of morality has its effects in making judgements about or dealing with non-Muslims or Muslims who may not observe the above mentioned "formalities" of behavior. Many emerging ills, such as those of corruption, drugs, sexual offenses, family conflicts and generation gaps, are not put in their full social perspective, but are considered mere consequences of ignoring Islam and following other patterns of behavior.

---

[46] Arberry, op. cit., p. 628.

181

2. Following contemporary Muslim thinking and movements, one notices more concentration on *a moral reform that comes from above*, through the state and the law, rather than a moral reform that develops from below, through the individual, the family, and society. Consequences of colonization, internal and external exploitation, secularization and Westernization on one side, and industrialization, urbanization, modernization and democracy on the other, have become mixed together and confusing to the contemporary Muslim mind. Therefore, it has been pushed by frustration to a simplification which crystallizes all vices in the authorities, and sees the way to change in the removal of those who are in power, while doing nothing about what is below the top, even in one's own family. Many of those who condemn dictatorship or autocracy may be dangerous dictators and autocrats in their own families over their wives and children. Liberation must be deeply rooted and morally directed, so that it may mean simultaneously: liberation from one's own self and its whims, as well as from pressures from the outside.

Inconsistently, although many Islamists believe in the excessive role of the government in moral and social reform, they are reluctant to secure by law the equality between men and women in the family and society, or the equality between Muslims and non-Muslims in political and civil rights. They argue that Muslim moral traditions and their justice and magnanimity have always achieved—and will continue to achieve—in such fields more than legal obligations.

As public schools, universities and mosques are mostly run by the government in many Muslim countries, this may add more justification to the idea that reform should come from above. Enjoining doing the good and forbidding doing evil by the authorities [Qur'an 22:41] was understood out of context, however, by ignoring that the fact that the concepts of *ma'ruf* and *munkar* have to be developed initially through the society itself [3:110] and by certain specialized institutions [3:104], if any support of a government may have any effect.

Besides, any governmental support for moral values should be practiced itself in a moral way when such measures become necessary, as Islamic morality should never mean a totalitarian or police state. Governmental measures have to be restricted to what is seen to be harmful by the people and their legislative representatives, without violating any human rights. Lying is a central evil which may cover or lead to more evils, and it is considered in the Qur'an as contradictory to the faith [16:105], but it is not considered legally felonious by Shari'a except in certain forms which bring out in a direct way a concrete harm to individuals or society, such as in the cases of slander, false testimony and fraud.

The general principles of Shari'a and its goals ought to prevail over any particular rule in case of any legal contradiction, and on the top of these principles are what the Qur'an states: "There is no coercion in matters of faith" [2:256], and what the Prophet's tradition states: "No harm can be allowed from one to another, whether it may be intentional or through negligence, initial or reciprocal."[47] The goals of Shari'a have to secure and develop: Human life, the family and the offspring (continuity of human life), the human mind, the freedom of belief, and the rights of private and public ownership.[48]

Morality should go beyond legality and ought to prevail over it as it has been indicated before [e.g., 2:279-280]. Jurists have pointed out in several cases that something can work in court for a certain party, but such a party is urged religiously to drop his/her case. Many Muslim minds are overwhelmed by a legalistic simplicity that can magically cure the social ills, ignoring the reality that the fundamentals of social reform and moral education provide the base for a genuine justice and morality, otherwise mere legalistic and suppressive measures would develop hypocrisy and evasion of the law.

3. The bitter memory of the colonial period revived the previous one of the Crusades, and both had their impact on the Muslims' moral view of the "others," especially Christian Europe, which has been extended afterwards to the Christian West. In addition, while the concept of morality among Muslims has become more rigid and narrow, the Christian West has begun to experience an attitude of permissiveness, and thus a sharp contrast between the two concepts of morality has come out and has damaged the confidence of both parties in finding common moral grounds.

---

[47] Reported by Ibn Hanbal and Ibn Majah.

[48] al-shatibi; 'Abu Ishaq Ibrahim ibn Musa, *al-Muwafaqat* (Cairo), vol. II, pp. 8-12.

Fathi Osman

As a result of the technological revolution in mass production, marketing, transportation and communication, humanity is living in an era of pluralism and globalism. Pluralism is now national and universal, as human movement from land to land for different reasons has become more possible and easier, and thus various ethnicities and faiths are being brought close to one another. The Muslims may still be living in the psychology of a "closed shop" entity that may allow some openness to others on its own terms, protected by certain political power, however, heavy handed or symbolic it may be.

In the contemporary world with its global pluralism, Muslims have to adhere to and develop the universal, rational and spiritual attitude of the Islamic morality. They have to realize that while their grievances from the past and the present and their aspirations for change are very legitimate, an essential requirement for a long, successful struggle for this great and noble cause is moral responsibility in its depth and width, without which no rights can be maintained, and no change or reform can be achieved. "Verily, God does not change people's condition unless they change their inner selves." [Qur'an 13:11].

XII. SYNTHESIS OF THE CONCEPTION
AND IMPLEMENTATION OF THE GOOD
IN THE THREE ABRAHAMIC TRADITIONS

Denise Lardner Carmody and John Tully Carmody

Let us develop this topic under five headings: 1) overlap among
the three Abrahamic traditions; 2) what remains distinctive in each
tradition; 3) present lacunae on the way to political cooperation; 4)
present lacunae on the way to sharing worship; and 5) how best to
orient future intellectual exchanges. Throughout our development, we
shall assume that all parties to the discussion value both one another's
traditional views of the good and the high points of one another's
traditional achievements of the good. If here we stress future prospects
more than past accomplishments, it is not to disparage what our
predecessors have accomplished but rather to remind ourselves of what
God asks now, in this our hour.

1. Overlap Among the Three Abrahamic Traditions

The papers by Arthur Green, Paul Mojzes, and Fathi Osman
deal fairly fully with, respectively, the traditional Jewish, Christian, and
Muslim conceptions of the good. In the process, they make it clear that
none of the Abrahamic religious families has neglected either study of
what constitutes the good life or serious effort to produce that life.
Perhaps this clarity about the imperative character of the good life is
itself the most striking and hopeful overlap among the three sister faiths.
From the One God whom they associate with the figure of Abraham,
Jews, Christians, and Muslims all believe that they have suffered strong
claims on their conscience. None has felt that how they behaved was a
matter of indifference. All have rather judged that God expected them
to act in some ways and avoid acting in other ways. Thus, to live under
the One God, by faith, traditionally has been to feel called upon to do
good and avoid evil—immediately, without any intervening two-step or
shuffle. Pursuing justice and extending mercy have been requisite, not
optional.

Arthur Green's several citations of biblical epitomes of the
moral life offer good examples of the constant concern down the
Abrahamic centuries to lay out a practicable ideal. Isaiah 33, for

example, sketches indelibly the ways of the pious, good person: "...walks righteously, speaks uprightly, despises profiting from oppression, shakes his [or her] hand loose from holding bribes, stops his ear from hearing of blood, and shuts her eyes from looking upon evil." To follow the God of Abraham, Isaac, and Jacob, one has had to imitate this sort of behavior. Not to imitate this sort of behavior, on the contrary, has been to mock the God of the patriarchs, to bring into contempt the covenant struck with the ancestors.

Paul Mojzes has gathered some of the Christian equivalents to the rabbinic views of the good life. Despite the self-criticism that deficiencies in the Christian ethical tradition ought to provoke, one can observe down the Christian ages considerable effort to develop principles for social justice, concern for the poor, and, above all, love of neighbor as oneself. The model that traditional Christians have found in the life of Jesus, as reported in the New Testament, has beckoned them to such virtues as healing the sick, teaching the ignorant, uplifting the downtrodden, and bearing themselves meekly, kindly, without arrogance.

Moreover, the beatitudes have placed at the center of the Christian sense of the good life a strongly eschatological reminder. Those who live on the margins of society may well be the apple of God's eye. In the reign of God, the realm of the One whom Jesus called "Father," people poor in spirit and concerned with making peace may well rank higher than the wealthy, the powerful, those who tend to feather their own nests. For Christian biblical ethics, only God's favor has made something good. To be prosperous in worldly terms but lack God's favor has left a person stranded morally.

As Fathi Osman's thorough study of the ethical terminology favored by the Qur'an makes plain, at the foundations of Islam lies a similarly great, Abrahamic concern for the good life, the life pleasing to Allah. Human beings ought to know what is good and what is bad. God expects us to live by such knowledge. Just as in Judaism both the learned and the pious concerned themselves with doing good and avoiding evil, so in Islam both those who gained a legal expertise in the Qur'an and those who sought a Sufi warming of the heart sought to help Muslims live well and please God. Nothing merely extrinsic or forensic could please either the scholars or the Sufis who looked into the burning holiness of God. Only a genuine purity of heart, an

186

authentic goodness of soul, could make the believer into what she or he ought to be. One could no more speak of shortcuts in Islam than in Judaism or in Christianity. The venture associated with Abraham entailed a faith, a trust, a submission that was wholehearted.

Last, it bears noting that all three traditions think that human beings are intrinsically moral. In virtue of having reason, and so being able to scan a range of options, and thus not being determined by their animal instincts, human beings ought to know what is right and do it. Similarly, they ought to know what is wrong and avoid it. Certainly, the rabbis, fathers, and sufis have not downplayed the importance of tradition and education. They have not said that people do not have to develop their moral capacities, just as they develop their abilities to think mathematically or weave with skill. But the Abrahamic masters have said that at the heart of being human lies a connatural feel for what is fitting and what is not, what squares with the way that God has made the world and what does not. It demeans the human being to lie, steal, or do bodily harm to others. It is shameful not to control one's tongue or one's sexual appetite. Equally, it tears social groups apart, brings woe to both family and town, when either individuals or cohorts live without control, go on rampages like wild animals. All this Jews, Christians, and Muslims accept, assume, with little fuss.

The final overlap among the three Abrahamic traditions is their common failure to achieve their ideals, to live up to their high standards. Prescinding from legitimate differences of opinion about what these failures have been historically, in either kind or scope, we find regret central enough in the Judaisms, Christianities, and Islams of all historical eras to be certain that trying to live by faith has never been easy. In addition to the obscurity that faith forces upon the human spirit, the necessity of our learning again and again that God is no thing, never comes under our control, it confronts us with a dauntingly high moral ideal. In terms passed down by the Bible, we human beings are images of God, and we are supposed at all times to remember our high status. What would reflect badly on God, whose image we are, we ought not to do.

Yet frequently, in ways either small or great, we do act to the shame of our Maker. We do do what is selfish, or destructive, or irrational. We injure people we profess to love. We ride roughshod over the poor and the vulnerable. And in the process we hurt ourselves, making it unclear whether God was wise to have created our kind. Jews, Christians, and Muslims have all beaten their breasts and raised laments of this sort. Women and children, men in their prime and men gone to seed—all have wept, cursed, asked the hills to bury them. Far beyond the evils that nature has visited upon us have been the enormities of our own human wars, rapes, unconcern for the starving, abuse of children, and casual contempt for the less fortunate.

The more keenly the spiritual leaders of the Abrahamic traditions have sensed the wonder that God should have made a world or called human beings into covenants, the more sharply they have regretted the failures of their kind to perform well morally. In all three traditions a prophetic religious sensibility has kept burning a flame of indignation that so much which might have been healthy and right has been allowed to sicken and lead to wrong. The biblical Abraham is a wily figure, but at his best, when he is fleeing idolatry and defending Sodom, he proves a worthy prophetic forebear. The Jews, Christians, and Muslims who look back to this figure are at one in thinking that living by faith is suspect unless it leads to social justice.

2. What Remains Distinctive

Jews remain distinctive for the Torah that they derive from Abraham and, even more, from Moses. Christians remain distinctive for the confession they make that Jesus was fully divine as well as fully human. Muslims remain distinctive for the prophecy that they associate with Muhammad and the Qur'an. Each of these distinctions colors the given tradition's sense of the good life. In no case does an adherent of a particular tradition have to feel that adherents of other traditions, either Abrahamic or non-Abrahamic, have nothing in common with them, no portion in their inheritance and God. But in all three cases the good life, the ethical venture, so takes its shape from what is distinctive (Torah, Jesus, or the Qur'an) that the tradition's morality emerges as characteristic as its doctrine or worship.

The Torah comes from God. To be a Jew is to live from, in, by a cultural heritage going back to Abraham and the Bible. This heritage opposes other gods and supreme treasures, calling them idols. They are not real as the God of Abraham, Isaac, and Jacob has been real. They are not similarly valuable. The 613 commands of Torah constitute a distinctive program for both honoring God and affirming, exercising, and maintaining Jewish peoplehood. Torah-talmud has been the hallmark, the characteristic architecture, of Jewish history and culture. To live as God's people, Jews have striven to sanctify their entire lives: space, time, diet, and more. This has not meant that Jewish conceptions of good and evil have borne no relation to Christian, Muslim, or other conceptions. It has meant a different construal of ethics, a different style, method, and traditional education. The great cultural treasure of Jewish history has been the Torah, an intellectual heritage intimately bearing on how to comport oneself in a community referred centrally to the Lord associated with Abraham, Moses, and the rabbis.

Christian ethics has been distinctive because of the distinctive Christian belief that Jesus of Nazareth was, indeed continues to be, fully human and fully divine. Moreover, the fate of Jesus, his death and resurrection, has stamped Christian doctrine, piety, and ethics indelibly, setting them apart from the equivalents of Jews, Muslims, and the adherents of other religious traditions. For example, historically the ordinary Christian faithful have taken the moral teachings attributed to Jesus as the words of one who is the living confluence of the human and divine. Hence, they have not been on a par with any other words or teachings. They could not be, if Jesus were "the Word made human—*et Verbum caro factum est*," as John's Gospel put it. In modern times, when historical and literary studies revealed the complexity of all the biblical sources, including those of the New Testament, educated Christians began to place more nuance on how they interpreted the sayings of and about Jesus, but that was a fairly recent phenomenon, coming long after Christian moral sensibilities had developed a deep and vigorous life. For most of Christian history Jesus was thought to possess unique words of everlasting life.

The Christian conception of the good can no more wander far from the life, teaching, death, and resurrection of Jesus than the Jewish conception of the good can wander far from the traditions of Torah or the Muslim conception of the good can wander far from the Qur'an. To be true to itself, each of the three Abrahamic traditions has to honor the history and conviction that have shaped its identity to this point. In the Christian case, the unique status accorded Jesus remains of paramount importance. Naturally, how this status ought to be understood in the future is a further question, and one that interreligious dialogue ought

189

to influence considerably. But a Christian whose worship is not oriented by Jesus is as anomalous as a Jew whose worship is not shaped by Torah, or a Muslim whose worship is not focused by the Qur'an.

There is no Islam without the Qur'an. That is where Allah makes fullest provision for the instruction of human beings, shaping the submission that God wants from all. It is only right and proper, therefore, for Muslim ethicists to take their stand primarily on the teachings of the Qur'an. Those teachings are bound to be canonical in Islam. If they did not make Muslims distinctive, Muslims would have lost their savor and efficacy. The Qur'an, along with the legal and ethical traditions which have arisen for studying it, the practice of the Prophet, and the other traditional sources of Muslim faith and life, is what people interested in genuine dialogue with Muslims expect to deal with. Not to deal with the good as the Qur'an understands it, or with the evils that the Qur'an most hates, would be to deal with something not Muslim, just as to deal with a Jewish understanding of the good not shaped by Torah would be to deal with something hard to recognize as Jewish, or to deal with a Christian understanding of good not centered in and directed by the teachings and life of Jesus would be to deal with something hard to recognize as Christian.

It is obvious, of course, that each of these distinctions has a history, rich and complicated and often painful. It is also obvious that how each Abrahamic faith has thought about its distinctiveness has varied over time and offers us numerous options today. For present purposes, though, there seems no reason to think that either Jews, Christians, or Muslims are forced to make their distinctiveness a great impediment to either dialogue or cooperation. Each tradition can point to several powerful justifications for speaking with members of the other two traditions respectfully and collaboratively. In each tradition the others can have considerable standing before the One God. None of the three faiths is unique in harboring reasons for respecting the others. Neither dialogue nor collaboration is one of the singularities that a comparativist has to attach only to Judaism, or to Christianity, or to Islam.

Moreover, each tradition can point to things of which it may rightly be proud, but also to things of which it does well to be ashamed. No tradition is uniquely holy, free of ethical wrongdoing or underdevelopment, and so no tradition finds itself without peer or partner. Neither the Torah, nor the traditional Christology, nor the Qur'an has solved all the moral problems that the Abrahamic faith with which it has been associated has had to face. None of the sources of distinctiveness has fashioned a people fully holy, containing no sinners or criminals. Thus nothing distinctive in any of the three traditions need abort the fruitful dialogical future for which many Jews, Christians, and Muslims now find themselves longing. If that future miscarries it will be less because past history determined it would do so than because our own generation proved unequal to the moment that God offered us.

3. Political Cooperation

The three major papers presented in this volume offer many hints of the richness of their traditions' understandings of how human beings ought to live together. With more than a nod to the stance in the world that we now associate with the name Abraham and the word "faith," Jews developing Torah, Christians reflecting on how best to imitate Christ, and Muslims listening for the Word of Allah in the Qur'an can offer all people of good will, all men and women with eyes to see and ears to hear, rich instruction in the things necessary for human prosperity and peace.

Nonetheless, as these three papers also suggest, to this historical point the Abrahamic faiths have done less to encourage trans-traditional cooperation than what the future would seem to require of them. World history has now evolved to the point where international cooperation is not a luxury but rather the bare requisite for survival. As different peoples strive to uncover or develop bases for understanding one another and collaborating, it becomes clear that they are foolish not to take advantage of whatever similarities or sympathies the past centuries have created.

So, for example, Jews, Christians, and Muslims can judge that they have ready to hand many religious likenesses. Whether or not they stress their common indebtedness to Abraham and faith, they can underscore the singleness of the God whom they worship, the call for justice at the center of their ethical codes, their common conviction that all human beings are made in the image and likeness of God, and their common conviction that God will judge the world at its consummation, rewarding the good and punishing the wicked.

191

In the past, the relatively narrow horizon in which they tended to regard their interactions, especially their conflicts, often inclined Jews, Christians, and Muslims to stress their differences and neglect their likenesses. The attitude that Christians had superseded Jews, and that Muslims had superseded both Jews and Christians, put a competitive edge on all cultural, economic, and military interactions. Great amounts of suffering resulted from this state of affairs. The question most pressing today is whether the lessons of history, combined with the new international situation, will make us wiser than our predecessors. Will we choose to stress what we hold in common, as bases for political cooperation, and to downplay frictions from either the past or the present that tempt us toward conflict? Without denying that we continue to believe significantly different things, and that we ought never to try to escape our past histories, will we choose to focus on what we can say and do together, cooperatively, to improve political and other conditions around the world, especially in the places (such as the Middle East) where our three different Abrahamic traditions remain powerful moral influences?

In this context, a minimal contribution might be reflection by scholars from each of the three traditions on the legitimate grounds for cooperation with outsiders, especially adherents of another Abrahamic faith. Whatever study would make it clear that confessing the primacy of the one God and working for civil, religious, and other political rights flow together fittingly and naturally could be a significant contribution to improving relations in many geographical situations. To be sure, political cooperation has to be fully concrete, proceeding case by case as local conditions require. But a pluralism of a different sort already obtains in various situations, and we may hope that more pluralistic situations will arise in the near future. "Pluralism" need not imply that a given cultural and religious heritage loses its dominance. It need only imply that all citizens or residents in a particular locale ought to enjoy basic civil, legal, political, religious, economic, and other freedoms—that these come with human nature, ought to be in force, in play, wherever men, women, or children live, move, and have their being.

Now, clearly there is considerable experience relevant to this question available in all three of the Abrahamic traditions. All three have wrestled with the question of the relations that ought to obtain among them—the political, religious, economic, and other rights that any human being ought to enjoy. It does not minimize the achievements of the past to suggest that such experience has yet to produce the complete clarity of either conception or execution that idealists tend to desire. Similarly, it does not detract from the achievements of our major papers to suggest that their equivalents in the future might profitably devote more concern to reasons for cooperating with outsiders.

For example, the contributions of Jews will only be richer if they reflect on the implications of the covenants with Adam and Noah for future political cooperation. Relatedly, Jewish moral thinkers ought to receive a warm invitation from Christians and Muslims of good will to develop the rabbinic teachings about political rights, economic freedoms and responsibilities, the respect for the image of God in every human being's heart, and the like so that they started to color a pluralistic political praxis—a pluralistic ethics that was fully dialogical and cooperative. Such an ethics would not be minimal, prescinding from everything particularly Jewish. Rather it would thrive from an invitation to develop precisely the genius of Jewish, rabbinic moral reflection in the lineaments of Torah. Christians and Muslims would make it plain that they wanted to know what the leading rabbinic voices suggest about their own citizenship, even their own religious practice, because they greatly respected the wisdom of high Jewish tradition, finding it a voice of their own God—of the one God they have inherited from Abraham.

The parallels for the other two traditions are obvious. Jews and Muslims would encourage Christians to develop the riches of the moral life, both reflection and practice, that Christians have found revealed, laid bare, set forth aglimmering in the example of Jesus, Francis of Assisi, and the other stunning Christian paradigms. Jews and Christians would encourage Muslims to suggest what the Qur'an implies for their own political and religious practice—what is common, for all human beings, in qur'anic moral revelation, and what is distinctively Muslim but in such wise that it ought to provoke well-disposed Christians and Jews to a proper, analogous emulation.

The point should be clear. If we are in fact at a pregnant dialogical moment, then the wisdom of each tradition becomes part of the treasury of all traditions. Then the rabbis and the fathers and the mullahs do not speak only to their own people. They speak as well to all other people, because they are relevant to, potential benefactors of, any people who cherish learning, wisdom, and holiness. Beneath this practical orientation lies a theological commitment of considerable moment: God appears wherever we find wisdom and goodness. We cannot cordon off the Word of God to suit our historical prejudices. We have to break our stiff-necked pride, humble our spirits to meet our great, manifest need. Otherwise, we neglect the gifts of God, run the risk of abusing the providential moment in which God has placed us.

It makes sense, of course, that religious teachers should stick to their own traditions, preach to their own sisters and brothers. It could seem presumptuous to do otherwise—unless one received an invitation to address, teach, enrich outsiders. If Jews and Christians want to know what Muslims think Jews and Christians ought to do, how Muslims regard what Islamic morality might mean for the lives of Christians and Jews, then Jews and Christians ought to ask Muslims about these things—ought to request, humbly yet urgently, that Muslims give them the benefit of qur'anic counsel. The same, *mutatis mutandis*, with how Christians and Muslims ought to deal with Jewish ethical teachers, Jews and Muslims ought to deal with Christian ethical teachers.

In a round-robin situation such as this, each person or group asked could know that the request was both sincere and limited. If the three-way instruction began with political matters, steps toward closer political cooperation rooted in religious and ethical ideals, it might eventually advance toward further sharing in worship and theological reflection. The goal would never be to remove historical, cultural, or religious differences, except inasmuch as such differences stemmed from misinformation or underappreciation. But the realistic goal could be to mount more programs for practical action on behalf of richer human rights. And the realistic effects could include both a fuller appreciation of the wisdom that the God of Abraham has inspired and a fuller enjoyment of that God's peace.

4. Toward Sharing Worship More Fully

Each of the three Abrahamic traditions recognizes the prayer of the others. Looking out with some self-knowledge, each realizes that the same urge to worship the divine Creator and Lord, to let the soul break forth in pure praise, that has driven its own great saints has driven the best and the brightest in the other two traditions. For, in the beginning of the life of the spirit, and at its end, the faithful child of Abraham

194

turns out to be a psalmist. Before asking God for anything, he or she proposes a bare, beatific acknowledgement. God is, and is beautifully, splendidly, magnificently. There is no worthy prosperity for the human being without basking in the glow of God's splendor. Indeed, the delight of the angels is to praise the splendor of God. The holier the child of Abraham, the hungrier the desire for worship.

Two lacunae in the present dialogue stand out, when one reflects on these propositions. First, the good life, the way to live that beckons most imperatively, is a life of worship and praise. Whether five times a day, or ideally continually, the devout person of faith meditates on the law of God, communes in spirit with God, asks God primarily that God's own will be done. Thus we offer only a truncated version of the good, in any of the Abrahamic traditions, as long as we do not situate what people of faith do, how they act, in the context of their lives of worship, of the deepest passions of their soul, which are to proclaim the divine glory.

Second, we miss a great opportunity as long as we do not mine from our own traditions, and extend for this our day, encouragement to outsiders, stimuli for the worship of others. If we all honor and worship one God, we must all desire with might and main the praise of God by all God's people. There is only one Lord of creation. There is only one Father in heaven, one Mother of us all. Whatever in our own traditions encourages us to think of outsiders as people bent on the worship of God, and encourages them to fulfill this vocation, has to benefit us all.

In this context, the further obvious consideration is common worship. What have Jews, Christians, and Muslims done in the past to facilitate praying together? What ought we to do in the future? Have we been hampered by pseudo-barriers, customs that could easily cede to an imaginative, creative will to proceed otherwise? If we take seriously the oneness or soleness of God, and let others define for themselves what common prayer they find compatible with Jewish, Christian, or Muslim traditions of monotheistic worship, we should not find it difficult to create either patterns of speech or patterns of silence through which to offer praise to God, to ask God's blessings, and to beg of God forgiveness for the wrongs we have done in the past.

In fact, it is strange that common worship should ever have posed serious problems. Inasmuch as all developed theologies acknowledge the mysteriousness of God, none tends to seek a monopoly on worship. The more religious a given tradition tends to be (the more concerned to praise God from the heart), the happier it is to see any people expressing their love of the divine beauty, their gratitude for the divine largess. Certainly, the part of prudence in planning ecumenical services for worship may be to begin sparely. But it would not take huge amounts of imagination to encourage each Abrahamic group to think through what traditional forms of prayer it could open to outsiders without feeling compromised. Jews could think about both what new words they would feel comfortable saying, or hearing, in worship with non-Jews, and what from their standard traditions they could offer outsiders for their free use. The same for Christians and Muslims.

The most obvious initial problem—Christian traditions about the worship and Jesus—is neither small nor simple. If Jews and Muslims want to deal with orthodox Christians, followers of Jesus whose faith hands on what their ancestors have held for centuries, then Jews and Muslims must want to deal with people who confess Jesus to be the divine incarnate, even as they confess him also to be fully human, like them in all things save sin.

To negotiate this problem, however, one need not detour into heavy analysis of the Trinitarian patterns of traditional Christian worship. In our opinion, one need only take orthodox Christians at their word when they claim to bow before the God of Abraham, Isaac, and Jacob, and to love the holiness of the God revealed through Muhammad and the Qur'an. The Christian conviction that God is One, as well as Three, can cover what common monotheistic worship requires. Christians need require no trinitarian formulas, nor any formulas that solicit common prayer to Jesus the Christ. Jews and Muslims need require, we suspect, no thought-policing of their Christian fellow worshipers, whom the one God clearly has admitted to his or her sanctuaries for numerous generations.

Though worship is good in its own right, for its own sake, and ought never to be approached pragmatically, as a means to some other end, it is a simple fact that common worship can strengthen bonds among people in ways that seem later to pay political dividends and make them warmer intellectual friends. If we take "dialogue" in a broad sense, then, worship can be an important component part. Just as a dialogue that never gets down to political cases is suspect, so is one that never stops the participants' babble by turning all their souls toward silent praise.

God is always more, *semper major*. Not to confess this, love this, is to trivialize one's theology. Worship is a major way in which human beings honor the majority of God. Common praise and petition of God can be a direct path toward the realization that Jews, Muslims, and Christians are indeed at least as alike as we are different, have in fact grounds for mutual love much deeper than either political need or intellectual interest. The papers on the good that we have been served in this volume do less with the call to worship that our dialogue might sponsor than what the future will require of us. We shall not be the full children of Abraham that we might be, the kith and kin close and warm, unless we start to encourage one another's worship, now and then by bowing and singing together.

5. Future Intellectual Exchanges

Just as there are achievements to celebrate, when one considers where Jewish-Christian-Muslim intellectual exchange now stands, so there are advances for which to hope. The advances may well come in the measure that the trialogue expands into common worship and joint political action, but however they come, such intellectual advances will be welcome. Perhaps the most profitable exercise for this occasion would be to imagine the style and mood in which they might come most handsomely.

Parallel to the invitation that Jews and Christians will have to extend to Muslims, if they want to learn what Muslims think Islamic wisdom has to offer Christians and Jews toward a richer moral practice, we see an invitation, repeated around the Abrahamic trialogue, from each tradition to the other two to share its sense of where our traditions' intellectual exchanges now stand—where the obstacles to fuller mutual understanding now lie. For example: What in the Christian and Jewish doctrinal complexes now causes Muslims the greatest difficulty? Where do Christians now find the sorest problems, when they consider Torah and Shar'ia? What in Muslim and Christian teaching is still most painful for Jews?

Each group has to answer for itself, and of course no group is likely to answer univocally. But if all three groups can create sincere invitations to the others to speak their minds, bare their hearts, our future intellectual exchanges could be both exciting and consoling.

Framing such invitations could be the sense we all share, from our symbolic parents Abraham and Sarah/Hagar, that it is always imperative to live by faith. The sole living God never comes into our hands, never becomes the possession of our minds. Even if our traditions have fashioned truths for which, in certain circumstances, we may feel we ought to be willing to die, we know, in the measure that we are religious, that our formulations of such truths are imperfect.

Thus, what we find contradictory, incompatible, may not be that for God. The more we have entered into the experience of faith, entered upon the living presence of the real God who never surrenders the divine name, the less the discussion of our traditional doctrines will frighten us, the freer we shall feel to say, "I don't think so, but perhaps at the end of the day you will be proved right."

Naturally, no individual or group entering upon interreligious discussion is immune to political pressures, sometimes including threats to life itself. There is no need to be foolhardy, especially concerning what we give out for public consumption. In itself, however, interreligious dialogue can occasion a fuller appreciation of the riches of the divine mystery, the unfathomable character of the divine nature. In itself, interreligious discussion that reaches the point of a frank exchange of difficulties can become a fuller appreciation of how much less than God all our doctrines always remain.

Having invited representatives of the other Abrahamic traditions to express their puzzles, difficulties, problems with one's own Jewish, Christian, or Muslim doctrines, a given group could move on to still a further invitation. What have these difficulties prompted internally? What second or further thoughts have they sponsored about Torah, or Christology, or the theology of the Qur'an? Naturally, the particular group in question has to shape a given matter as it finds best. The point is simply that, when dialogue has become the cast of mind that, in maturity, it has the potential to become, there will be a steady rebound from the questions which one asks of others, and which others ask of oneself, upon the elaboration of one's own faith. In other words, one's own religious reflection, theological construction, will tend to change, under the pressure of new questions that interreligious dialogue has stimulated.

Christian theologians who discuss religious matters regularly with Muslims and Jews will tend to think thoughts that do not occur to their Christian colleagues who do not engage in interreligious dialogue. The same for Muslim and Jewish theologians who do and do not interact with outsiders regularly.

The validity of this phenomenon, its justification, stems from the rights that Abrahamic faith bestows on outsiders. If all three traditions deal with the same, single God, then the reflections of the other two are germane to the reflections of one's own. Muslims and Christians do not become Jews, but their reflections become relevant to those of Jews who value their contributions to the Abrahamic dialogue. The same in the other two directions. The differences between "us" and "them" lessen, while the appropriateness of "their" making suggestions for "our" work increases.

Naturally, all this demands large amounts of tact and good manners. The greater the fund of experience and trust that given inter-religious groups have built up, the more likely their chances for success. When they have prayed together, and worked together politically, they shall find themselves in still better shape. But as soon as they take one another's offerings seriously, so that their dialogue is more than just an ecumenical gesture, more than something to which they are obliged by good form, their own internal theological work will have changed.

With such a change, dialogue will have become a new venture. It will no longer be possible for a given theologian, or group of theologians, to work as had been the case previously, before the views of his, her, or their partners had become important—an interior moment in the constructive process of their Jewish, or Christian, or Muslim religious reflection.

One cannot program this experience ahead of time. It only happens when and if and as it actually does. Until a given theologian truly finds what "outsiders" say relevant, so that he or she cannot ignore their voice any more than the voice of a fellow Jew, Christian, or Muslim who has come to require a full hearing, such outsiders exert no decisive influence and dialogue has yet to make a crucial impact. Until then, one's Jewish, Christian, or Muslim theology (or religious reflection, or whatever one wants to call it) remains indebted only to internal sources, criteria, authorities. One has yet to open it to external, outside authorities. One's partners in dialogue have yet to earn an effective hearing, make a real difference, actually function as sisters and brothers in Abrahamic faith.

XIII. TOWARD A UNIVERSAL DECLARATION OF A GLOBAL ETHIC

Leonard Swidler

Humans tend to group themselves in communities with similar understandings of the meaning of life and how to act accordingly. For the most part, in past history such large communities, called cultures or civilizations, have tended on the one hand to live unto themselves, and on the other to dominate and, if possible, absorb the other cultures they encountered. For example, Christendom, Islam, China.

1. The Meaning of Religion (Ideology)

At the heart of each culture is what is traditionally called a Religion, that is: "An explanation of the ultimate meaning of life, and how to live accordingly." Normally all religions contain the four "C's": Creed, Code, Cult, Community-structure, and are based on the notion of the Transcendent.

> *Creed* refers to the cognitive aspect of a religion; it is everything that goes into the "explanation" of the ultimate meaning of life.
> *Code* of behavior or ethics includes all the rules and customs of action that somehow follow from one aspect or another of the *Creed*.
> *Cult* means all the ritual activities that relate the follower to one aspect or other of the Transcendent, either directly or indirectly, prayer being an example of the former and certain formal behavior toward representatives of the Transcendent, like priests, of the latter.
> *Community-structure* refers to the relationships among the followers; this can vary widely, from a very egalitarian relationship, as among Quakers, through a "republican" structure like Presbyterians have, to a monarchical one, as with some Hasidic Jews vis-a-vis their "Rebbe."
> The *Transcendent*, as the roots of the word indicate, means "that which goes beyond" the everyday, the ordinary, the surface experience of reality. It

can refer to spirits, gods, a Personal God, an Impersonal God, Emptiness, etc.

Especially in modern times there have developed "explanations" of the ultimate meaning of life, and how to live accordingly" which are not based on a notion of the Transcendent, e.g., secular humanism, Marxism. Although in every respect these "explanations" function as religions traditionally have in human life, because the idea of the Transcendent, however it is understood, plays such a central role in religion, but not in these "explanations," for the sake of accuracy it is best to give these "explanations" not based on notion of the Transcendent a separate name; the name often used is: *Ideology*. Much, though not all, of the following will, *mutatis mutandis*, also apply to Ideology even when the term is not used.

2. From the Age of Monologue to the Age of Dialogue

Since the 16th-century "Age of Discovery" the earth has tended more and more to become, as Wendell Wilkie put it in 1940, "One World." This increasingly happened in the form of "Christendom" dominating and colonizing the rest of the world. In the 19th century, however, "Christendom" became less and less "Christian" and more and more the "secular West" shaped by a secular ideologies, alternative to Christianity. Still, the religious and ideological cultures of the West, even as they struggled with each other, dealt with other cultures and their religions in the customary manner of ignoring them or attempting to dominate, and even absorb them—though it became increasingly obvious that the latter was not likely to happen.

As the 20th century drew to a close, however, all of those ways of relating become increasingly impossible to sustain. For example: What happened in other cultures quickly led young men and women of the West to die on the volcanic ash of Iwo Jima or the desert sands of Kuwait. But more than that, the "West" could no longer escape what was done in the "First World," such as the production of acid rain, in the "Second World," such as the Chernobyl nuclear accident, or in the "Third World," such as the mass destruction of the Amazon rain forest, "the world's lungs."

At the same time the world has been slowly, painfully emerging from the millennia-long Age of Monologue into the Age of Dialogue. Until beginning a century or so ago, each religion, and then ideology—each culture—tended to be very certain that it alone had the complete "explanation of the ultimate meaning of life, and how to live according-ly." Then through a series of revolutions in understanding, starting in the West, but ultimately spreading more and more throughout the whole world, the limitedness of all statements about the meaning of things began to dawn on isolated thinkers, and then increasingly on the middle and even grass-roots levels of humankind: The epistemological revolutions of historicism, pragmatism, sociology of knowledge, language analysis, hermeneutics.

Now that it is more and more understood that the Muslim, Christian, secularist, Buddhist, etc. perception of the meaning of things is necessarily limited, the Muslim, Christian, secularist, etc. increasingly feel not only no longer driven to replace, or at least dominate, all other religions, ideologies, cultures, but even drawn to enter into dialogue with them, so as to expand, deepen, enrich each of their necessarily limited perceptions of the meaning of things. Thus, often with squinting, blurry eyes, humankind is emerging from the relative darkness of the Age of Monologue into the dawning Age of Dialogue—dialogue now understood as a conversation with someone who differs from us *primarily* so *we* can learn, because of course since we now growingly realize that our understanding of the meaning of reality is necessarily limited, we might learn more about reality's meaning through someone else's perception of it.

3. Need for a Global Ethic

When the fact of these epistemological revolutions leading to the growing necessity of interreligious, interideological, intercultural dialogue is coupled with the fact of all humankind's interdependency—such that any significant part of humanity could precipitate the whole of the globe into a social, economic, nuclear, environmental or other catastrophe—there arises the pressing need to focus the energy of these dialogues on not only how humans perceive and understand the world and its meaning, but also on how they should act in relationship to themselves, to other persons, and to nature within the context of

203

reality's undergirding, pervasive, overarching source, energy and goal, however understood. In brief, humankind increasingly desperately needs to engage in a dialogue on the development of, not a Buddhist ethic, a Christian ethic, a Marxist ethic, etc., but of a global ethic—and I believe a key instrument in that direction will be the shaping of a *Universal Declaration of a Global Ethic.*

I say ethic in the singular rather than ethics in the plural, because what is needed is not a full-blown global ethics in great detail—indeed, such would not even be possible—but a global consensus on the fundamental attitude toward good and evil and the basic and middle principles to put it into action. Clearly also, this ethic must be global. It will not be sufficient to have a common ethic for Westerners or Africans or Asians, etc. The destruction, for example, of the ozone layer or the loosing of a destructive gene mutation by any one group will be disastrous for all.

I say also that this *Universal Declaration of a Global Ethic* must be arrived at by consensus through dialogue. Attempts at the imposition of a unitary ethics by various kinds of force have been had aplenty, and they have inevitably fallen miserably short of globality. The most recent failures can be seen in the widespread collapse of communism, and in an inverse way in the resounding rejection of secularism by resurgent Islamism.

That the need for a global ethic is most urgent is becoming increasingly apparent to all; humankind no longer has the luxury of letting such an ethic slowly and haphazardly grow by itself, as it willy nilly will gradually happen. It is vital that there be a conscious focusing of energy on such a development. Immediate action is necessary:

1) Every scholarly institution, whether related to a religion or ideology or not, needs to press its experts of the widest variety of disciplines to use their creativity among themselves and in conjunction with scholars from other institutions, both religiously related and not, in formulating a Global Ethic.

2) Every major religion and ethical group needs to commission its expert scholars to focus their research and reflection on articulating a Global Ethic from the perspective of their religion or ethical group—in dialogue with all other religions and ethical groups.

3) Collaborative "Working Groups," of scholars in the field of ethics which are very deliberately interreligious, interideological need

to be formed specifically to tackle this momentous task, and those which already exist need to focus their energies on it.

4) Beyond that there needs to be a major permanent Global Ethic Research Center, which will have some of the best experts from the world's major religions and ethical groups in residence, perhaps for years at a stretch, pursuing precisely this topic in its multiple ramifications.

When the *Universal Declaration of a Global Ethic* is finally drafted—after multiple consultation, revision and eventual acceptance by the full range of religious and ethical institutions—it *will then serve as a minimal ethical standard for humankind, religious and non-religious, to be held to*, much as the United Nation's 1948 Universal Declaration of Human Rights. Through the former, the moral force of the world's religious and ethical institutions can be brought to bear especially on those issues which are not very susceptible to the legal and political force of the latter. Such an undertaking by the Religions and Ideologies of the world would be different from, but complementary to, the work of the United Nations.

After the initial period, which doubtless would last several years, the "Global Ethic Research Center" could serve as an authoritative religious and ideological scholarly locus to which always-new specific problems of a global ethic could be submitted for evaluation, analysis and response. The weightiness of the responses would be "substantive," not "formal." That is, its solutions would carry weight because of their inherent persuasiveness coming from their intellectual and spiritual insight and wisdom.

4. Principles of a Universal Declaration of a Global Ethic

Let me first offer some suggestions of the general notions that I believe ought to shape a *Universal Declaration of a Global Ethic*, and then offer a tentative draft constructed in their light:

1. The Declaration should use language and images that are acceptable to all major religions and ethical groups; hence, its language ought to be "humanity-based," rather than from

authoritative religious books; it should be from "below," not from "above."

2. Therefore, it should be anthropo-centric, indeed more, it must be anthropo-cosmo-centric, for we can not be fully human except within the context of the whole of reality.

3. The affirmations should be dynamic in form in the sense that they will be susceptible to being sublated (*aufgehoben*), that is, they might properly be reinterpreted by being taken up into a larger framework.

4. The Declaration needs to set inviolable minimums, but also open-ended maximums to be striven for; but maximums may not be required, for it might violate the freedom-minimums of some persons.

5. It could well start with—though not limit itself to—elements of the so-called "Golden Rule": Treat others as we would be treated.

Excursus: the "Golden Rule"

A glimpse of just how pervasive the "Golden Rule" is, albeit in various forms and expressions, in the world's religions and ideologies, great and small, can be garnered from this partial listing:

a) Perhaps the oldest recorded version—which is cast in a positive form—stems from Zoroaster (628-551 B.C.E.): "That which is good for all and any one, for whomsoever—that is good for me...what I hold good for self, I should for all. Only Law Universal is true Law" (*Gathas*, 43.1).

b) Confucius (551-479 B.C.E.), when asked "Is there one word which may serve as a rule of practice for all one's life?" said: "Do not to others what you do not want done to yourself" (*Analects*, 12.2 & 15.23). Confucius also stated in a variant version: "What I do not wish others to do to me, that also I wish not to do to them" (*Analects*, 5.11).

c) The founder of Jainism was Vardhamana, known as Mahavira ("Great Hero—540-468 B.C.E.); the various scriptures of Jainism, however, derived from a later period: "A man should wander about treating all creatures as he himself would be treated" (*Sutrakri-tanga* 1.11.33). "One who you think should be hit is none else but you.... Therefore, neither does he cause violence to others nor does he make others do so" (*Acarangasutra* 5.101-2).

d) The founder of Buddhism was Siddhartha Gautama, known as the Buddha ("Enlightened One"—563-483 B.C.E.); the various scriptures of Buddhism also derived from a later period: "Comparing oneself to others in such terms as 'Just as I am so are they, just as they are so am I,' he should neither kill nor cause others to kill" Sutta Nipata 705). "Here am I fond of my life, not wanting to die, fond of pleasure and averse from pain. Suppose someone should rob me of my life.... If I in turn should rob of his life one fond of his life.... How could I inflict that upon another?" (*Samyutta Nikaya* v.353).

e) The Hindu epic poem, the 3rd-century B.C.E. Mahabharata, states that its "Golden Rule," which is expressed in both positive and negative form, is the summary of all Hindu teaching, "the whole Dharma": "Vyasa says: Do not to others what you do not wish done to yourself; and wish for others too what you desire and long for for yourself—this is the whole of Dharma; heed it well" (*Mahabharata*, Anusasana Parva 113.8).

f) In the biblical book of Leviticus (composed in the fifth century B.C.E., though some of its material may be more ancient) the Hebrew version of the "Golden Rule" is stated positively: "You shall love your neighbor as yourself" (Lev. 19: 18).

207

g) The deuterocanonical biblical Tobit was written around the year 200 B.C.E. and contains a negative version—as most are—of the "Golden Rule": "Never do to anyone else anything that you would not want someone to do to you" (Tobit 4:15).

h) The major founder of Rabbinic Judaism, Hillel, who lived about a generation before Jesus, though he may also have been his teacher, taught that the "Golden Rule"—his version being both positive and negative— was the heart of the Torah; "all the rest was commentary": "Do not do to others what you would not have done to yourself" (*Btalmud*, Shabbath 31a).

i) Following in this Jewish tradition, Jesus stated the "Golden Rule" in a positive form, saying that it summed up the whole Torah and prophets: "Do for others just what you want them to do for you" (Luke 6:31); "Do for others what you want them to do for you: this is the meaning of the Law of Moses [*Torah*] and of the teachings of the prophets" (Matthew 7:12).

j) In the seventh century of the Common Era Mohammed is said to have claimed that the "Golden Rule" is the "noblest Religion": "Noblest Religion is this—that you should like for others what you like for yourself; and what you feel painful for yourself, hold that as painful for all others too." Again: "No man is a true believer unless he desires for his brother that which he desires for himself."[1]

k) The "Golden Rule" is likewise found in some non-literate religions: "One going to take a pointed stick

---

[1] Hadith: Muslim, chapter on iman, 71-2; Ibn Madja, Introduction, 9; Al-Darimi, chapter on riqaq; Hambal 3, 1976. The first quotation is cited in Bhagavan Das, *The Essential Unity of All Religions* (1934), p. 298.

to pinch a baby bird should first try it on himself to feel how it hurts"[2]

l) The eighteenth-century Western philosopher Immanuel Kant provided a "rational" version of the "Golden Rule" in his famous "Categorical Imperative," or "Law of Universal Fairness": "Act on maxims which can at the same time have for their object themselves as universal laws of nature.... Treat humanity in every case as an end, never as a means only."[3]

m) The late nineteenth-century founder of Baha'ism, Baha'ullah, wrote: "He should not wish for others that which he doth not wish for himself, nor promise that which he doth not fulfill."[4]

n) In 1915 a new version of Buddhism, Won Buddhism, was founded in Korea by the Great Master Sotaesan. In the teachings he left behind are found variants of the "Golden Rule": "Be right yourself before you correct others. Instruct yourself first before you teach others. Do favors for others before you seek favors from them." "Ordinary people may appear smart in doing things only for themselves, but they are really suffering a loss. Buddhas and *Bodhisattvas* may appear to be stupid in doing things only for others, but eventually they benefit themselves."[5]

---

[2] A Yoruba Proverb (Nigeria), cited in Andrew Wilson, ed., *World Scripture* (New York: Paragon House, 1991), p. 114.

[3] Immanuel Kant, *Critique of Practical Reason*, A 54; and *Groundwork of the Metaphysics of Ethics*, BA 66f.

[4] *Gleanings from the Writings of Baha'u'llah*, trans. by Shoghi Effendi (Wilmette, IL: Baha'i Publishing Trust, 2d ed., 1976).

[5] *The Scripture of Won Buddhism* (Iri, Korea: Won Kwang Publishing Co., rev. ed. 1988), pp. 309f.

It is clear that the core of the world's major Religions, the "Golden Rule," "does not attempt the futile and impossible task of abolishing and annihilating the authentic ego. On the contrary, it tends to make concern for the authentic ego the *measure* of altruism. 'Do not foster the *ego* more than the *alter;* care for the *alter* as much as for the *ego*.' To abolish egoism is to abolish altruism also; and *vice versa*."[6]

Authentic egoism and authentic altruism then are not in conflict with each other; the former necessarily moves to the latter, even possibly "giving one's life for one's friend." This, however, is the last and highest stage of human development. It is the stage of the (w)holy person, the saint, the arahat, the bodhisattva, the sage. Such a stage cannot be the *foundation* of human society; it must be the *goal* of it. The foundation of human society must be first authentic self-love, which includes moving outward to loving others.

Not recognizing this foundation of authentic self-love is the fundamental flaw of those idealistic systems, such as communism, that try to build a society on the *foundation* of altruism. A human and humanizing society should *lead* toward (w)holiness, toward altruism, but it cannot be built on the assumption that its citizens are (w)holy and altruistic to start with. Such an altruism must grow out of an ever developing authentic self-love; it cannot be assumed, and surely it cannot be forced (as has been tried for decades—with disastrous dehumanizing results).

6. As humans ineluctably seek ever more knowledge, truth, so too they seek to draw what they perceive as the good to themselves (that is, they love). Usually this self is expanded to include the family, and then friends. It needs to continue its natural expansion to the community, nation, world and cosmos, and the source and goal of all reality.

7. But this human love necessarily must start with self-love, for one can love one's "neighbor" only AS one loves oneself; but since one becomes human only by inter-human mutuality, loving others fulfills one's own humanity, and hence is also the greatest act of authentic self-love.

---

[6] Bhagavan Das, *The Essential Unity of All Religions* (1934), p. 303.

8. Another aspect of the "Golden Rule" is that humans are always to be treated as ends, never as mere means, i.e., as subjects, never as mere objects.

9. Yet another implication of the "Golden Rule" is that those who cannot protect themselves ought to be protected by those who can.

10. A further ring of the expanding circles of the "Golden Rule" is that non-human beings are also to be reverenced and treated with respect because of their being.

11. It is important that not only basic but also middle ethical principles be spelled out in this Declaration. Although most of the middle ethical principles that need to be articulated in this Declaration are already embedded in juridical form in the United Nations' 1948 Universal Declaration of Human Rights, it is vital that the religions and ethical traditions expressly state and approve them. Then the world, including both adherents and outsiders of the various religions and ethical traditions, will know what ethical standards all are committing themselves to.

12. If a Universal Declaration of a Global Ethic is to be meaningful and effective, however, its framers must resist the temptation to pack too many details and special interests into it. It can function best as a kind of "constitutional" set of basic and middle ethical principles from which more detailed applications can be constantly be drawn.

5. A Plan of Action

Such general suggestions need to be discussed, confirmed, rejected, modified, supplemented. Beyond that, it is vital that all the disciplines contribute what from their perspectives ought to be included in the Declaration, how that should be formulated, what is to be avoided —and this is beginning to happen. The year 1993 was the 100th anniversary of the 1893 World Parliament of Religions which took place in Chicago and marked the beginning of what became world-wide interreli-

211

gious dialogue. As a consequence, a number of international conferences have been taking place and in the center of them has been the launching and developing of a *Universal Declaration of a Global Ethic*.

The first was held in New Delhi, India in February, 1993; the second in August of the same year in Bangalore, India and the third that year in September in Chicago. For that huge (over 6,000 participants) September 1993 Chicago "Parliament of the World's Religions" Professor Hans Küng drafted a document entitled "Declaration Toward a Global Ethic," which the Parliament adopted.[7]

Beyond that, the text given below, after having been commissioned by the January 1992 meeting in Atlanta, Georgia of the "International Scholars' Annual Trialogue-ISAT" (Jewish-Christian-Muslim) was drafted by Professor Leonard Swidler and submitted to and analyzed at the January, 1993 meeting of ISAT in Graz, Austria; it was focused on during the spring 1993 semester graduate seminar Leonard Swidler held at Temple University entitled: "Global Ethics-Human Rights-World Religions"; it was also a major focus of the "First International Conference on Universalism" in August, 1993, in Warsaw; a Consultation of the American Academy of Religion in November, 1993, in Washington D.C. was devoted to the topic; the sixth "International Scholars' Annual Trialogue" in January, 1994, concentrated for a second year on the Universal Declaration; in May, 1994, it was the subject of a conference sponsored by the "International Association of Asian Philosophy and Religion—IAAPR" in Seoul, Korea; the "World Conference on Religion and Peace—WCRP" in part focused on it in its fall, 1994 World Assembly in Rome/Riva del Garda, Italy; and on June 20-21, 1995, it was the subject of a conference in San Francisco in honor of the "Fiftieth Anniversary of the Founding of the United Nations," entitled: "Celebrating the Spirit: Towards a Global Ethic."

At the same time it is imperative that various religious and ethical communities and geographical regions work on discussing and drafting their own versions of a possible text for a *Universal Declaration of a Global Ethic*. The draft given below and the one drawn up by Hans Küng should certainly be made use of in this process. But all

---

[7] Hans Küng and Karl-Josef Kuschel, eds., *A Global Ethic* (New York: Continuum, 1993).

communities and regions need to make their own contributions to the final Declaration, and in the process of wrestling with the issue and forging the wording they will make the concern for a global ethic their own, and will thus better be able to mediate it to their "constituents" and enhance the likelihood of the Declaration in fact being adhered to in practice.

What needs to be stressed as well, however, is that such a project cannot be carried out only by the scholars and leaders of the world's religious and ethical communities, though obviously the vigorous participation of these elements is vital. The ideas and sensitivities must also come from the grassroots.

Moreover, it is also at the grassroots, as well at the levels of scholars and leaders, that, first, consciousnesses must be raised on the desperate need for the conscious development of a Global Ethic, and then conviction of its validity must be gained. The most carefully thought out and sensitively crafted Declaration will be of no use if those who are to adhere to it do not believe in it. A Global Ethic must work on all three levels: scholars, leaders, grassroots. Otherwise it will not work at all!

As a stimulus to this discussion, I offer the following tentative draft of a *Universal Declaration of a Global Ethic*, already revised many times after consultation with scholars and grass-roots from many religious traditions, including Catholic, Protestant and Orthodox Christians, Jews, Hindus, Buddhists, Muslims and Sikhs and Bahais.

XIV. UNIVERSAL DECLARATION
OF A GLOBAL ETHIC

1. Rationale

We women and men from various ethical and religious traditions commit ourselves to the following Universal Declaration of a Global Ethic. We speak here not of *ethics* in the plural, which implies rather great detail, but of *ethic* in the singular, i.e., the fundamental attitude toward good and evil, and the basic and middle principles needed to put it into action.

We make this commitment not despite our differences but arising out of our distinct perspectives, recognizing nevertheless in our diverse ethical and religious traditions common convictions that lead us to speak out *against* all forms of inhumanity and *for* humaneness in our treatment of ourselves, one another and the world around us. We find in each of our traditions: a) grounds in support of universal human rights, b) a call to work for justice and peace, and c) concern for conservation of the earth.

We confirm and applaud the positive human values that are, at times painfully slowly, but nevertheless increasingly, being accepted and advocated in our world: freedom, equality, democracy, recognition of interdependence, commitment to justice and human rights. We also believe that conditions in our world encourage, indeed require, us to look beyond what divides us and to speak as one on matters that are crucial for the survival of and respect for the earth. Therefore we advocate movement toward a global order that reflects the best values found in our myriad traditions.

We are convinced that a just global order can be built only on a global ethic which clearly states universally-recognized norms and, that such an ethic presumes a readiness and intention on the part of people to act justly—that is, a movement of the heart. Secondly, a global ethic requires a thoughtful presentation of principles that are held up to open investigation and critique—a movement of the head.

Each of our traditions holds commitments beyond what is expressed here, but we find that within our ethical and religious traditions the world community is discovering elements of a fundamental minimal consensus on ethics which is convincing to all women and men of good will, religious and nonreligious alike, and which will provide us with a moral framework within which we can relate to ourselves, each other and the world in a just and respectful manner.

In order to build a humanity-wide consensus we find it is essential to develop and use a language that is humanity-based, though each religious and ethical tradition also has its own language for what is expressed in this Declaration.

Furthermore, none of our traditions, ethical or religious, is satisfied with minimums, vital as they are; rather, because humans are endlessly self-transcending, our traditions also provide maximums to be striven for. Consequently, this Declaration does the same. Maximums, however, are ideals to be striven for, and hence cannot be required, lest the essential freedoms and rights of some thereby be violated.

2. Presuppositions

As a Universal Declaration of a Global Ethic, which we believe must undergird any affirmation of human rights and respect for the earth, this document affirms and supports the rights and corresponding responsibilities enumerated in the 1948 Universal Declaration of Human Rights of the United Nations. In conjunction with that first United Nations Declaration we believe there are five general presuppositions which are indispensable for a global ethic:

a) Every human possesses inalienable and inviolable dignity; individuals, states, and other social entities are obliged to respect and protect the dignity of each person.

b) No person or social entity exists beyond the scope of morality; everyone—individuals and social organizations—is obliged to do good and avoid evil.

c) Humans are endowed with reason and conscience—the great challenge of being human is to act conscientiously; communities, states and other social units are obliged to protect and foster these capabilities.

d) Communities, states and other social organizations which contribute to the good of humans and the world have a right to exist and flourish; this right should be respected by all.

Leonard Swidler

e) Humans are a part of nature, not apart from nature; ethical concerns extend beyond humanity to the rest of the earth, and indeed the cosmos. In brief: this Declaration, in reflection of reality, is not just anthropo-centric, but cosmo-anthropo-centric.

3. A Fundamental Rule

We propose the Golden Rule, which for millennia has been affirmed in many religious and ethical traditions, as a fundamental principle on which to base a global ethic: "What you do not wish done to yourself, do not do to others," or in positive terms, "What you wish done to yourself, do to others." This rule should be valid not only for one's own family, friends, community and nation, but also for all other individuals, families, communities, nations, the entire world, the cosmos.

4. Basic Principles

1. Because freedom is of the essence of being human, every person is free to exercise and develop every capacity, so long as it does not infringe on the rights of other persons or express a lack of due respect for things living or non-living. In addition, human freedom should be exercised in such a way as to enhance both the freedom of all humans and due respect for all things, living and non-living.

2. Because of their inherent equal dignity, all humans should always be treated as ends, never as mere means. In addition, all humans in every encounter with others should strive to enhance to the fullest the intrinsic dignity of all involved.

3. Although humans have greater intrinsic value than non-humans, all such things, living and non-living, do possess intrinsic value simply because of their existence and, as such, are to be treated with due respect. In addition, all humans in every encounter with non-humans, living and non-living, should strive to respect them to the fullest of their intrinsic value.

4. As humans necessarily seek ever more knowledge and truth, so too they seek to unite their selves with what they perceive as the good, i.e., they love; usually their self is expanded/transcended to include their own family and friends, seeking the good for them. In addition, as with the Golden Rule, this loving/loved "self" needs to continue its natural expansion/transcendence to embrace the community, nation, world, and cosmos.

5. Thus true human love is authentic self-love and other-love co-relatively linked in such a way that ultimately it is drawn to become all-inclusive. This expansive and inclusive nature of love should be recognized as an active principle in personal and global interaction.

6. Those who hold responsibility for others are obliged to help those for whom they hold responsibility. In addition, the Golden Rule implies: If we were in serious difficulty wherein we could not help ourselves, we would want those who could help us to do so, even if they held no responsibility for us; therefore we should help others in serious difficulty who cannot help themselves, even though we hold no responsibility for them.

7. Because all humans are equally entitled to hold their religion or belief—i.e., their explanation of the ultimate meaning of life and how to live accordingly—as true, every human's religion or belief should be granted its due freedom and respect.

8. In addition, dialogue—i.e., conversation whose *primary* aim is to learn from the other—is a necessary means whereby women and men ceaselessly expand and deepen their explanation of the meaning of life and develop an ever broadening consensus whereby they can live together on this globe in an authentically human manner.

5. Middle Principles

a) Legal Responsibilities

Because all humans have an inherent equal dignity, all individuals and communities should treat everyone equally before the law, providing all with equal protection.

At the same time, all individuals and communities should follow all just laws, obeying not only the letter but especially the spirit.

b) Responsibilities Concerning Conscience and Religion or Belief
Because humans are thinking, and therefore essentially free-deciding beings, all individuals and communities should respect this aspect of human nature, granting that all humans have the right to freedom of thought, speech, conscience and religion or belief.

At the same time, all humans should exercise their rights of freedom of thought, speech, conscience, religion or belief in ways that will respect themselves and all others and strive to produce maximum benefit for both themselves and their fellow humans.

c) Responsibilities Concerning Speech and Information
Because humans are thinking beings with the capacity to perceive reality and express their perceptions of it, all individuals and communities should respect this aspect of human nature, granting that all individuals and communities have both the right and the responsibility, as far as possible, to learn the truth and express it honestly.

At the same time everyone should avoid cover-ups, distortions, manipulations of others and inappropriate intrusions into personal privacy; this freedom and responsibility is especially true of the mass media, artists, scientists, politicians and religious leaders.

d) Responsibilities Concerning Participation in All Decision-making Affecting Oneself or Those for Whom One is Responsible
Because humans are free-deciding beings, all individuals and communities should respect this aspect of human nature, granting that all humans have the right to a voice, direct or indirect, in all decisions that affect them, including a meaningful participation in the choosing of their leaders and holding them accountable, as well as the right of equal access to all leadership positions for which their talents qualify them.

At the same time, all humans should strive to exercise their right, and obligation, to participate in self-governance so as to produce maximum benefit for both themselves and their fellow humans.

e) Responsibilities Concerning the Relationship of Women and Men
Because women and men are inherently equal and because they

are frequently attracted to one another, all individuals and communities should respect these aspects of human nature, granting that all humans, women and men, have an equal right to the full development of all their talents as well as the freedom to marry, with equal rights for all women and men in living out or dissolving marriage.

At the same time, all men and women should act toward each other outside and within marriage in ways that will respect the intrinsic dignity, equality, freedom and responsibilities of themselves and others.

f) Responsibilities Concerning Property

Because humans are free, bodily and social in nature, all individuals and communities should respect these dimensions of human nature, granting that all individual humans and communities have the right to own property of various sorts.

At the same time, society should be so organized that property will be dealt with respectfully, striving to produce maximum benefit not only for the owners but also for their fellow humans and the world.

g) Responsibilities Concerning Work and Leisure

Because to lead an authentic human life all humans should normally have both meaningful work and recreative leisure, all individuals and communities should respect these dimensions of human nature and strive to organize society so as to provide these two dimensions of an authentic human life both for themselves and all the members of their communities.

At the same time, all individuals have an obligation to work appropriately for their recompense, and, with all communities, to strive for ever more creative work and re-creative leisure for themselves, their communities, and other individuals and communities.

h) Responsibilities Concerning Children and Education

Children are first of all not responsible for their coming into existence or for their socialization and education; their parents are. Where for whatever reason they fail, the wider community, relatives and civil community, have an obligation to provide the most humane care possible, physical, mental, moral/spiritual, social, for children.

219

Leonard Swidler

Because humans can become authentically human only through education in the broad sense, and today also increasingly in the formal sense, all individuals and communities should respect this dimension of human development and strive to provide an education for all children and adult women and men which is directed to the full development of the human person, respect for human rights and fundamental freedoms, the promotion of understanding, dialogue and friendship among all humans, regardless of racial, ethnic, religious, belief, sexual or other differences, and respect for the earth.

At the same time, all individuals and communities have the obligation to contribute appropriately to providing the means necessary for this education for themselves and their communities, and beyond that to strive to provide the same for all humans.

i) Responsibilities Concerning Peace

Because peace as both the absence of violence and the presence of justice for all humans is the necessary condition for the complete development of the full humanity of all humans, individually and communally, all individuals and communities should respect this human need and strive to further the growth of peace on all levels, personal, interpersonal, local, regional, national, international, granting that

i. the necessary basis of peace is justice for all concerned;

ii. violence is to be avoided, being resorted to only when its absence would cause greater evil;

iii. when peace is ruptured, all efforts should be bent to its rapid restoration—on the necessary basis of justice for all.

At the same time, it should be recognized that peace, like liberty, is a positive value which should be constantly cultivated, and therefore all individuals and communities should make the necessary prior efforts not only to avoid its break-down but also to strengthen its steady development and growth.

j) Responsibilities Concerning the Preservation of the Environment

Because things, living and non-living, have an intrinsic value simply because of their existence, and also because humans cannot develop fully as humans, or even survive, if the environment is severely damaged, all individuals and communities should respect the ecosphere within which "we all live, move and have our being," and act so that

i) nothing, living or non-living, will be destroyed in its natural form except when used for some greater good, as, for example, the use of plants/animals for food;

ii) if at all possible, only replaceable material will be destroyed in its natural form.

At the same time, all individuals and communities should constantly be vigilant to protect our fragile universe, particularly from the exploding human population and increasing technological possibilities which threaten it in an ever expanding fashion.

December 3, 1993 Revision
Send approval, disapproval, revisions to: Professor Leonard Swidler, Religion Department, Temple University, Philadelphia, PA 19122, USA; FAX: 215-477-5928; E-mail: DIALOGUE@VM.TEMPLE.EDU

XV. PEACE! PEACE! BUT THERE IS NO PEACE!
(Jeremiah 6:14)

Pinchas Lapide

The endless confusion of war, tumult of battles and mass murders, a brutal siege of the capitol, and constant aggressions by hostile Great Powers—that was the historical background of the proclamation of Isaiah as he exercised the calling of his office under four kings of Juda twenty-seven hundred years ago. Under circumstances, which vividly remind us of the pressing issues of our own time, he succeeded by threats and reprimands, but above all with energizing promises of salvation, to coax courage back into those who were abandoned in the land so that they could hold out and act justly according to the will of God in their political and social actions.

His messianic prophecies of future world peace, which are among the noblest visions of the Bible, stood in the sharpest contrast with the desperate situation of his people. Here, of course, the "messianic" future—a Hebraic notion to be understood as this-worldly in its effect—was expected as a human sprout springing up from the House of David. What did Isaiah prophesy? "In those days it will come to pass that all nations will hammer their swords into plowshares, their spears into sickles. Nation will not lift sword against nation, there will be no more training for war." (Isaiah 2: 2-4)

Indeed, the same thing befell Isaiah as our friend Swidler: Both promise fascinating visions of peace, which however appear too high and steep for the actual realities of world politics. However, this seemingly too great of a challenge must not discourage us.

We should not preach a shallow optimism, for "optimum" means the "very best"—which no one on earth can bring about. *Meliorism* should be our more modest goal: Faith in a slow but steady improvement which moves forward step by step to reach for the sought after ideal in a deliberate manner, matching our human abilities. Just as water in a constant flow is able to hollow out even great rocks, so also consciously focused small efforts can master the greatest tasks we set for ourselves. In the Talmud it says: There are indeed many tasks; you will never be done with them all. Knowing that, however, does not free you from giving your all at every moment.

The draft of the "Universal Declaration" by Swidler is fundamentally made up of a synthesis of the basic principles of the Ten

Commandments, the Jewish confession *Sh'ma Israel* (Dt. 6: 4ff.), the Our Father, and the Sermon on the Mount—foundation pillars of the biblical ethic, which he with discretion and skill adapted to the demands of today and correspondingly articulated.

Will, however, our world be made more ready for peace by statements, treaties or declarations? There is no question but that *doing* is by far the most prominent leitmotif in all of the preaching of the Rabbi from Nazareth: "Not whoever calls Lord, Lord, will enter into the Reign of Heaven, but whoever does the will of our Father in heaven," we read literally (Mt. 7: 21). Why, then, for example, should not all theologians, without distinction of confession, *hic et nunc* [here and now], with or without candles, but without any syncretism, come out of their ivory towers and march shoulder to shoulder to the people? Why should they not form a long chain of theologians, a chain which through its power of action would have a more infectious effect than all their "book larnin"?

This would really address the need of today! It would also be a blow for the liberation of a frustrated public which long has been tired and disgusted, too often been given empty prayer-wheels, cliche-shells of the day-before-yesterday's solutions for today's problems.

While all of us Jews and Christians face a grim present, the grim present of all believers, certain specialists entertain themselves by inventing new difficulties for already solved problems. A classic example of this came from leading professors of Protestant theology at the University of Göttingen who recently apparently were unable to find any more pressing problem in the community of faith to focus on than the need for a more intense Mission to the Jews—and that in Germany fifty years after Auschwitz!

The thirst for the Word of God in broad stretches of the grass-roots is as burning today as it was in Isaiah's day. For the human being is and remains a *homo religiosus*—who, however, if s/he does not encounter a credible faith, falls victim to an *ersatz* ideology, sectarian faith or crass materialism. Unfortunately the biblical message is often proclaimed in a repetitive, stilted, apodictic packaging which awakens frustration and disgust. Powerful and gripping is what the peace message of the Scriptures always is, but hair-splitting inevitably robs it of its original force. The evil lies not only in the alleged resistance to believe by the people, but also in the theological arteriosclerosis that so many preachers suffer from.

In the search for creative examples and attempts to make peace-making tangible I recommend the Rabbinic parable of the cooking pot as a model for all peacemakers. For the lowly cooking pot embodies, without the need for a lot of fancy rhetoric, a daily miracle which should stimulate even politicians and church leaders. Although its thin bottom separates two hostile elements, namely, fire and water, from each other, it in no way reconciles the two. Nevertheless, it brings it about that the two come together in peaceful and constructive coopera-tion, a culinary cooperation in which the good is turned out in the form of a tasty kitchen delight, a lip-smacking pleasure which sizzlingly gratifies all the conflicting parties—without demanding from them an unacceptable relinquishment or resignation. No small accomplishment in all the epochs of our splintered human history.

It is in this sense that the Rabbis responded already in Jesus' time to the ancient question of whether peace on earth is at all possible with a "*Theopolitik* of small steps," which even today loses nothing in validity. It consists of a balanced shrinking of conflicts, of a stepwise moderating of confrontations, of a challenge to forego some rights, of more than fulfilling the love commandment, of a graceful giving way—of all the 1001 ways of patient ant-like work *lemaan Shalom* (for the sake of peace), as one reads numberless times in the Rabbinic writings.

The promotion of peace is so highly regarded in the Bible that even an angelic message was altered for its sake: As the angel an-nounced the birth of her son to Sarah, Sarah snippily responded with incredulity: I am to bare a child by my grey-bearded *husband*?" For the sake of peace, however, the angel later reported to Abraham that Sarah said: "In *my* old age I should conceive children?" At all costs the angel wanted to retain and foster peace in the home. (Genesis 18:1-13)

Our cooperation in God's plan of salvation, however, is indispensable if the world is to attain peace. "All the commandments are to be fulfilled," it states in the Rabbinic writings. However, concerning peace the talk is more of necessity: "For you shall seek it [peace] and pursue it." This pursuing peace, as the psalmist as well stresses (Psalms 34: 14), is also called "peace making" (Isaiah 27: 5), as likewise in the words of Jesus in the Sermon on the Mount (Matthew 5: 9).

But what is the essence of this so highly prized peace that Moses, Isaiah and Rabbi Jesus do not tire of teaching and preaching? Both the Greek and Latin translation of the Gospels mislead us here into a narrowing of the meaning. For *Shalom* corresponds neither to the Greek *Eirene*, as a lack of war or an armistice, nor to the *Pax Romana* of the Latins, with its original forced-peace meaning. *Shalom* etymologically stems from *Shalem*, which means "complete," or "intact." Thus *Shalom* is first of all an integrated wholeness, the antithesis to all division and dualism. The three-dimensional wholeness of the *Pax Hebraica* sets forth an all embracing harmony: With ourselves, with God, and also with our environment, of which we are also a part (Psalm 85: 10).

Following biblical wholeness thinking here, the political, social and religious are as little separable from one another as for example body from soul or nature from culture. Thus, wellness and goodness, peace among nations and welfare, happiness and social harmony are complementary elements of the one *Shalom*, which is as indivisible as the areas of politics, society and faith are from one another.

Every peace prophecy also includes non-human creation. Indeed, it embraces a worldwide *Biophilia*, the protection of the flora and fauna, our fellow creatures under God. Biblically that is the kingdom of heaven on earth—whereby neither heaven nor kingdom are meant literally, but God's Rule over God's creation. For us monotheists Zachariah proclaimed it already: "On that day God will be one and his will be the only name" (Zachariah 14: 9)—which is echoed in Paul: On that day the Son will place himself under God; and thus God will be all in all." (1 Corinthians 15: 28)

All humans are called upon at all times to intensify the love of neighbor (Leviticus 19: 18) in order to cement it as a foundation stone of a lived Ecumene, which Swidler rightly likewise lifts up in his draft. This thematic thought of all human coexistence, which Jesus also designated as the greatest of all the commandments, echoes in almost all religions. "Love your neighbor as your self!" (Leviticus 19: 18) Thus it is stated in most European translations. Despite its universal currency, this key phrase suffers from three faulty translations from the Hebrew which distorts it greatly from its original sense.

1. *Rea*, which is the term used here, need not in the least be limited to "the neighbor" in the ethnic or religious sense.

225

Rather, it much more implies everyone who encounters me now. Correctly translated according to its content, "the neighbor" should be "the human being."

2. Connected to this narrowing of meaning in the translation is a faulty interpretation of the phrase "as yourself." The question arises whether a person who is not at one with her/himself is thereby dispensed from the command to love one's neighbor. By no means! For the Hebrew here says *Kamocha*, that is, "for s/he is as you yourself." Hence, the commandment is valid for those as well who are not in harmony with themselves.

3. The third translation error concerns the words "Love your neighbor." It was common among both the Rabbis and Jesus that the feelings of love could not be commanded. But the acts of neighborliness could. Ergo, the Hebrew has here a *Dativus Ethicus* whereby loving deeds are intended, which hopefully will then call forth the feelings of affection.

The so-called love of one's enemies of the Sermon on the Mount is likewise to be understood in parallel fashion. No abrupt excessive demand is intended here, but a powerful in action hostility-eliminating love (*Entfeindungsliebe* which through reconciling deeds and not through feelings—which, again, cannot be forced—may be able to reach out and persuade the opponent. In our unfortunately so hostile world, therefore, the rightly understood commandment of love can be a rational contribution to overcoming hostility. With all the particularism of the Hebrew Bible we should not overlook its likewise fundamental universalism. Like a red thread there runs throughout all the books of Scripture the command to care for the stranger, the refugee, the guest—for "I am your [plural] God" (Leviticus 19: 54) means: The Lord is God of the native born—but also of the foreigner.

The reaching out to the pagan cities of Niniveh, Sodom and Gomorrah and others evidences the equality in value of all human beings under God. Thus some leading figures of the Bible are pagans or foreigners and are set forth as models, as for example Jethro, Ruth the Moabite, Job and Cyrus—to name just a few. Colored people like Zipporah, the wife of Moses, the Queen of Sheba or the people of

Kuttim are valued equally with the whites. Of biblical support for Swidler's brilliant draft (*Entwurf*)—and it is indeed a great effort (*Wurf*)—there is no dearth.

In brief, without an ecumenically inspired and inspiring motivation practical measures alone will not endure over the long term. As is known, Ecumene means the whole inhabited world, which however, does not entail any kind of syncretism. Is not the Ecumene like the hand of pianist which is composed of five firm and fast but very different fingers which are capable of bringing forth totally different tones from the piano—which, however, give us the pleasure of a harmonious integration in a well-tempered symphony?

The translation of Swidler's draft into praxis will demand much effort, struggle and sweat. However, in any case, let us not sit with our hands in our lap. On the contrary! Let us encourage and support each other!

Lastly, the Ten Commandments or the Sermon on the Mount will not be diminished because we men and women unfortunately have not yet been able to integrate them fully in our lives. Is it then not high time that for the sake of peace we should as well proclaim the commonalities of our religions—without mixing—after we have for so many centuries praised to the sky all the differentiating elements?

A final suggestion: For the fostering of a more human living together, completely in the sense of Swidler's "Global Ethic," all of us, politicians, bureaucrats, and all others as well, should diligently practice the five ancient virtues:

1. Capacity for conflict-resolution—to overcome controversies fairly and without violence, and without burning bridges.

2. Readiness for dialogue—in all areas of society, from religion to politics.

3. Willingness to compromise—with ourselves first, but also with every opponent, for whom, however, hostility must be dismantled.

4. Empathy—in head and heart for the opponent, whose pain threshold must not be transgressed.

5. Patience—which comes from the insight that this world is neither saved nor un-saved, but is really salvageable—if we all are determined to make it happen. And we should strive as much as possible with the unshakable calm of that Rabbi who said: Every dispute, deeply observed, has *three* sides: Your side, my side—and the right side.

Translated from German
by Leonard Swidler

XVI. TOWARDS A UNIVERSAL DECLARATION OF A GLOBAL ETHIC A CHRISTIAN COMMENT

John Hick

Leonard Swidler is undoubtedly right—as also is his colleague Hans Küng—in thinking that the time is ripe to begin the world-wide process of formulating a basic global ethic; and we must be grateful to them for having taken the initiative embodied this draft. For we are all conscious today that our world has become a virtual communicational unity, that its nations and regions are increasingly economically interdependent, and that war is insanely destructive. The survival and flourishing of the human family requires at this moment in history the articulation of at least a basic ethical outlook, and if possible a set of ethical principles, on which all the major streams of human culture concur, and which can be used to influence their behavior. We need to uncover and cultivate the ground of human unity beneath the multiplicity of nations, cultures, social systems, religions and ideologies among which and between which conflicts are so common.

The difficulty in offering a distinctively Christian comment on Leonard Swidler's draft is that it is already in an important sense a Christian document. For since the European "Enlightenment" of the eighteenth century Western Christianity has been increasingly suffused with the individualistic, democratic, liberal, historically-minded, science-oriented outlook of the Enlightenment, an outlook that constitutes what can comprehensively be called the ethos of "modernity." Indeed Christianity, as a cultural influence, is identified in the minds of many Christians, particularly when they make comparisons with other religions, with these liberal ideals of modernity.

From an historical point of view, this is paradoxical. For what has happened is that secular modernity has transformed the outlook of most of the Christian world, rather than that Christianity has out of its own distinctive religious resources introduced these modern liberal values into Western culture. Indeed during much the greater part of its history Christianity has been neither democratic, nor liberal, nor science-oriented, nor historically-minded or individualistic in the modern sense. In saying, then, that Leonard Swidler's is a Christian draft I merely mean that it comes out of contemporary Western Christianity and embodies the spirit of post-Enlightenment culture. Anyone reading it can readily identify its provenance, reflecting as it does the concerns and presuppositions of modernity. (Let me add at this point that the currently fashionable notion of "post-modernity" has been given such different meanings by different writers and schools of thought that its use would merely be confusing in the present context, and I recommend that we avoid it).

Christianity, as an historical-cultural movement, has through the centuries absorbed and been changed by a series of external cultural forces—neo-Platonism in the early centuries, then the revival of Greek learning and of the enquiring rational spirit in the Renaissance, later the Enlightenment and the impact of modern science, then Darwinism and also the historical study of ancient scriptures in the second half of the nineteenth century, and liberal secularization in the twentieth century. All these influences have as their present end-product the modern Western outlook that is roughly coterminous with the vaguely Christian culture of North America and Europe and some of their colonial extensions.

The fact that modernity developed first in the West, and has largely remade the social ethos of Christianity in its own image, is basic to our situation today; whilst the correlative fact that this modern ethos is linked to Christianity through the contingencies of history, rather than being intrinsically Christian in any exclusive sense, may be crucially relevant to the project of a global ethic.

For it may be that some at least of the same influences are at work throughout our increasingly unified world, transforming the other religious, and also officially anti-religious, cultures of the earth, so that the kind of ethic proposed in Leonard Swidler's draft may prove to be acceptable more or less universally.

But on the other hand this may prove to be only very partially the case. Some, but not all, of the influences that have gone into the formation of the Christian version of modernity are affecting the other traditions. And there may well be yet other influences upon them that have not affected Christianity. There may thus be significant variations of outlook within an increasingly "modern" global mind-set. And these variations may quite possibly affect the basic framework and structure of a global ethic and the presuppositions that are reflected in it.

For this reason this first draft, produced by Leonard Swidler (and likewise the basically similar draft produced by Hans Küng), must not stand as the one official draft which is to be amended, added to, and developed by contributions from the rest of the world. It is essential that as early in the process as possible other independent initial drafts be forthcoming from within the cultures of China, Africa, Russia, India, the Islamic world, the Buddhist world, the "primal" life-streams. Only then, with the comparison and interaction of these perhaps significantly different drafts, will the movement towards a genuinely global Declaration be able to proceed beyond its present initial state. At least as important, then, as the organizing of intensive discussion of our Western draft must be the eliciting of Asian, African, Pacific and other drafts.

To set this wider and more pluralistic process in motion obviously requires resources. Might UNESCO be the agent? Or might an initiative be taken by religious leaders (the Pope, the Dalai Lama...), or by academics? Or might some major sponsor concerned with the larger welfare of the world be approached—the Aga Khan, or one of the major U.S. Foundations, or the Spanish Fundacion BBV...? Or several of these in collaboration? I can, alas, only ask but cannot answer these questions.

The West today is largely secular, with only a marginal religious influence in addition to that which has floated down through the culture. Much of the rest of the world is much more strongly religiously influenced. But in the West as well as elsewhere the main voice of moral consciousness, formulating and propagating whatever ethical principles we recognize, remains that of the religions. Their teachings thus constitute the natural starting point for the search for a global ethic. The recognition (which Leonard Swidler emphasizes in his Introduction) that all the major traditions teach a form of the "Golden Rule" of treating others as one would oneself wish to be treated, is thus enormously important. This will almost certainly become recognized globally as the basic principle of morality. For it seems to be a virtually universal human insight that to be a moral person is to regard others as having essentially the same value as oneself. The differences in ethical outlook then consist in different assumptions about who the "others" are—family, tribe, caste, nation, religious community, human species?

In his section 4 Leonard Swidler formulates ethical principles which follow from the Golden Rule. His eight Basic Principles sound right to me, as one sharing his modern Western liberal outlook. But I should (as I am sure Leonard Swidler would also) like to see independent attempts from within the Chinese, Indian, African and other cultures to spell out the implications of the Golden Rule. It could be that these will all be broadly consonant with his draft. Or it could be that significant differences will emerge, which would then give rise to important dialogues. And, as Leonard Swidler says in his Introduction, a Universal Declaration of a Global Ethic "must be arrived at by consensus through dialogue."

Swidler's ten Middle Principles also sound right to me. For, once again, they reflect our modern Western cultural ideals. Do they also reflect a universal point of view, common to the peoples of all cultures? I do not know. This is something that only a wider inter-cultural dialogue can establish. For the aim of a Universal Declaration must be to express an existing, or now forming, common outlook, not to impose that of one culture upon others. It may turn out that the existing common outlook does not at present go so far as some of Swidler's Middle Principles. Or it may be that it does; or again, that in the process of dialogue it might develop in that direction. Or it may be that some quite different principles will emerge.

I return in conclusion to my main point. In this first stage of the search for a global ethic, rather than getting the peoples of other cultures to debate our Western draft, agreeing or disagreeing with it as the only document on the table, we should say: "Here is the kind of draft that comes naturally to us in the industrialized West. What kind of draft comes naturally to you, and to you, and to you?" And then the next stage beyond this should be to bring a plurality of drafts together and see what comes out of the interaction between them.

I do not think that in any of this I am differing from what Leonard Swidler has in mind. I want particularly to stress, however, the need to move as soon as possible from a one-draft to a multi-draft situation. So long as we only have a modern Western draft there will be the danger of the whole project looking like an act of Western cultural imperialism. This has never been the intention. And the danger can be avoided by directing every effort to get people from within the other great cultural streams of human life to participate in the search from their own independent points of view.

It cannot count as a legitimate criticism that the search for a global ethic has originated in the West; for it had to originate some-where! And the West probably contains more abundantly than elsewhere the practical resources required to launch and promote the process. But it would be a ground for legitimate criticism if the search remained concentrated around our Western contribution to it. The challenge is now to find ways of opening the discussion up on an equal basis within all the great traditions of the earth.

XVII. LEONARD SWIDLER'S
DRAFT OF A GLOBAL ETHIC
A MUSLIM PERSPECTIVE

Khalid Duran

For a commentator it may be the wrong thing to do, but I should like to say right at the start that I fully support Leonard Swidler's project of drafting a global ethic and winning acceptance for it, global acceptance, if possible.

Islam, as we know, is not only a faith with a theology, philosophy and mysticism, but also a culture and a social phenomenon of global character—with a history of more than fourteen hundred years. If today one speaks of "the Islamic perspective," further information is needed in order to know what is meant. Hence, when I as a Muslim say that I have no difficulties with Leonard Swidler's presentation of a universal global ethic, then of course I must add that I represent only one of many possible perspectives within the Islamic spectrum. Indeed, there is the famous saying of our Prophet, according to which: One day his community will be splintered into 72 sects; only the 73rd will be saved. Now, fortunately I belong to that 73rd!—but of course my representativeness is thereby limited. On the other hand, as a historian of religion I believe I am in a position to say some things at least partially authoritative about Islam and a universal global ethic.

I believe that there are a number of reasons for Muslims to endorse a universal global ethic, first and foremost being the fact that Islam itself was originally intended as something like a global ethic. The Prophet Muhammad did not wish to found a new religion. He was driven by the desire to bring people back to the original faith of Abraham. He understood that the various types of Christianity and sects of Judaism all sprang from the same source. Since they had come to differ amongst themselves considerably, he saw his task in re-establishing the original Abrahamic religion, called Islam. This may sound odd to someone who associates the word *islám* with the religion of Islam as we know it today, or even with the world community of Islam as a social phenomenon. We might forget about Islam in this sense for a moment and bear in mind that the word *islám* has a meaning in Arabic. It signifies submission to the will of God, and peace. In that sense *islám* is the same as *salám*, which is the same as the Hebrew *shalom*, meaning peace, with the special connotation of soundness, wholesomeness.

Muhammad made it his mission to bring people back to *islám* in that original sense. He did not intend to convert people to his own religion; he wanted to convert them to the religion of Abraham. To this end the prototype of Abrahamic religion had to be reconstructed, and that became the religion of Islam as we know it today, at least in its ideal sense, as enshrined in the revelation of *Al-Qur'án* (Koran). Hence, I must once again emphasize that the Prophet Muhammad originally did not think of the creation of a new faith community. He was first of all concerned to unite the various groups of believers in God on a platform that was common to all. He proceeded on the assumption that the various sects of Jews and Christians as well as the other monotheists all formed a single family which through unfortunate accidents fell into dispute with one another. Consequently, he took as his task the reestablishment of that prototype of Abrahamic religion, monotheism.

It is in my opinion no accident that a new religion like that of Baha'i grew specifically out of Islam. It is similar with the Sikh religion, despite its "local color," for behind the Indian facade is hidden an original drive for unity, for a synthesis of Islam and Hinduism. As already earlier with Muhammad, so also with Guru Nanak in India and Baha'ullah in Persia, nothing came from this drive—nothing of this bringing together of the different faith communities. In each case a new religion arose, that is, precisely the opposite of what was at first aimed at. Nevertheless, this original motive, the unity of all believers, never was completely lost, at least not in the mystical tradition.

Sufism, with many regional differences, was for a long time dominant in the Islamic world. Today as well Sufism is still stronger that militant Fundamentalism. Wherever Sufism plays a roll, the unity of all religions is on the agenda. In this sense Sufism and Fundamentalism are diametrically opposed to each other. The Fundamentalists put up fences, dividing walls, they separate, preferably with an Iron Curtain. On the contrary, the Sufis seek to tear down everything that divides.

In interreligious dialogue, therefore, there is a problem of a particular sort with many Muslims, and especially those who are Sufi-oriented. Interreligious dialogue definitely does not wish to work syncretically. Indeed, it has a special need to differentiate itself from syncretic streams, to defend itself against the accusation of syncretism. The fear of syncretism is a restrictive limit for many who otherwise are

235

fully in favor of dialogue. Hence, the *Dialogue Decalogue* of Leonard Swidler to a large extent excludes syncretism.

Many Muslims, on the other hand, especially those who are Sufi-oriented, ask themselves, what is really so terrible with syncretism? For many the ideal is *wahdat al-wujúd* (the "unity of all being"). Others have difficulties with the pantheism that is implied therein, but would like to stress the essential unity of all religions. Hence, there is the revision that is dominant among our mystics: *wahdat ash-shuhúd* (the "unity of witnesses").

Why do I relate all this? I am concerned to illustrate the fundamental readiness to accept the drafted universal ethic. The current exclusivist positions fought for by a strengthened Fundamentalism, the cultural Apartheid striven for by the Islamists (Muslim Fundamentalists), the anti-Western xenophobia of our fanatics are all factors which easily can give the impression that Muslims *qua* Muslims are less open to such universalist goals.

I do not hesitate to maintain that precisely the opposite is the case. Islamism, that is, Fundamentalism, has indeed increased in strength, but it still remains a minority phenomenon. The majority of Muslims are especially receptive to universalistic undertakings—with, naturally, differences conditioned by specific historical experiences and varying interpretations of Islam. As a rule, however, a draft like this universal global ethic will not only encounter open ears but will also stimulate religious echoes.

"Come here for a word which is in common between you and us," it says in the Qur'an. There we have a literal translation of "dialogue," i.e., a "word between" (*dia-logos*) conversation partners. And there also we have the presentation of a common platform of all believers; for the special word between the believers of all religions, that word which is common to all of them is the confessing of God.

From this expectation Muslims can only welcome the hoped-for establishment of a universal global ethic. It doesn't need any theological tricks. For this one needs no new theology.

Islam was to do justice to both major purposes with which the term religion is usually associated, viz. an explanation of the world and an ethics. In Islam, as in Judaism, the emphasis is a little more on ethics. Given the fact that Islam, in its capacity as the reborn faith of Abraham, was meant to be a platform for Jews, Christians and other monotheists, it had to be universal. It was not a message to any particular people, not a religion for Arabs exclusively. Quite the contrary, the basic assumption underlying Muhammad's message, one that is clearly and frequently stated in *Al-Qur'án*, is that God sent messengers to all peoples. Every people has had its messenger. Jesus was understood as a messenger to the Jews primarily. Finally there was to be a messenger for all humanity, Muhammad.

Accordingly, the ethics of this prototype of Abrahamic religion *had* to be universal. The express purpose was to do away with particularisms. Not without reason have anthropologists accused Muslims of cultural levelling and creating a *homo islamicus*, enforcing a high degree of uniformity on otherwise very diverse parts of our world.

From the viewpoint of a cultural anthropologist it is certainly regrettable that the national costumes of many peoples have come to be replaced by a set of Middle Eastern gowns, creating monotony in place of creativity. I personally share this regret and seek solace in the fact that many local traditions have been able to hold their own despite that monotonous Middle Easternization following in the wake of Islam's advance.

I relate all this to illustrate what is meant by the creation of a *homo islamicus*, a kind of uniform human being, more conditioned by Islam than by any other tradition or particularism. Many scholars hold the view that it is law which has brought about that uniformity more than anything else. Islamic law, the *sharí'a*, is in fact much more than law as Westerners today understand law. The *sharí'a* is rather a comprehensive code of behavior. A modern slogan calls the *sharí'a* "complete code of life." That is not wrong, although our Fundamentalists misuse this slogan in such a way that many Muslims have become allergic to it.

A complete code of life comprises ethics, and many common believers in various parts of the Muslim world do in fact understand the term *sharí'a* to be roughly equivalent with *akhláq*, the Arabic word for ethics. I guess this problem of distinguishing, or not, between law and ethics exists in other cultures too. In the case of Islam, ethics came first. The law was formulated later in order make ethics prevail. That is a rather complex affair because in the course of time these two tend to drift apart. Among Muslims that has been a debate for centuries. We have our scholars of the law, *sharí'a*, and we have scholars of ethics,

237

akhláq. There is an age-old conflict between the scholars of the law and the teachers of ethics who feel that stagnation of the law has led to what are, from an ethical point of view, absurdities.

We might speak of a history of revolt against the law in Islam, a revolt in the name of ethics, a series of uprisings of the proponents of *akhláq* against the professors of *shari'a*. This is what comes to mind immediately upon hearing Leonard Swidler talk of global ethics. Muslims who put ethics above and the law beneath will be thrilled to hear of this project. Those who take the *shari'a* as their shield without understanding the difference between *shari'a* and *akhláq* will be apprehensive.

It will not be easy for any Muslims, including the Islamists, to say an outright "no" to such a project of a global ethic. However, the *shari'a* advocates will want the *shari'a* to be the global ethic. Confusing the law with ethics, they cannot but seek to impose their exclusivist vision on others. To sum up, there will be Muslims truly committed to the project and others who will seek to exploit it as a means of proselytizing.

What good is there in a global ethic, the defenders of the *shari'a* will argue, if it is not enacted—in other words, if the ethical principles or teachings are not converted into a law? At the same time they cannot accept any law other than the *shari'a*. Perhaps I am stating an extreme. We do of course have many scholars of the law who hold very rational views about the *shari'a*, who approach it from a historical angle and analyze it as a product in the making of which many outstanding personalities participated over a span of at least two centuries. In actual fact, the *shari'a* is the product of what was then an Islamic melting pot of races and cultures. Our Islamists, however, claim divine origin for the *shari'a*. What is divine is superior to what is human-made. Leonard Swidler's project of a global ethics can only result in a human-made product—hopefully a product made by as many women and men as possible.

Further difficulties lie, in my opinion, in the details of any universal global ethic, that is, in the difficult balance between universality and its specific binding force. Nothing is easier than to line up universal principles and have them approved. Then everyone goes about their implementation in his or her own manner. For example, we have just experienced with the collapse of the Soviet block how every concept has received a new meaning: The "peoples friendship" between East Germany and Poland was not the same as the "peoples friendship" between West Germany and France. The "freedom of the press" of the Communist *Neues Deutschland* was like the "freedom of the press" of the Nazi *Völkischer Beobachter*, but had nothing to do with the "freedom of the press" of the West Berlin *Spandauer Volksblatt*, etc.

We cannot avoid conceptually specifying the general principles and thereby going somewhat into detail. If tomorrow in Tajikstan the "Peoples' Democracy" were replaced by an "Islamic Democracy" à la Iran, we would have an experience of still more democratic rigamorole, but we would have even less of the substance of democracy. Today, however, we are passing through a phase not very different from that of Soviet rule when a particular brand of Communism was enforced. Under that ideology many terms of our vocabulary became perverted. Rather than admit that they could not care less for democracy, the Soviets insisted on being the best of democrats, and more than that, "people's democrats." This was imitated by not a few Muslim countries. A dictatorial regime in Algeria proclaimed a "Democratic and Popular Republic." Linguistically speaking that means the same thing three times. The Libyan People's *Jamáhiriya* means one and the same thing—a dozen times.

As for our Islamists, we are better off with the radical ones who openly say that there is "no democracy in Islam" and "Western" concepts of human rights cannot be reconciled with Islam. Much worse are those who speak of an "Islamic democracy" and "Islamic republic," but mean essentially the same that the Communists meant while talking about "popular democracy" and "people's republic." A group of so-called moderate Islamists even drafted an "Islamic Declaration of Human Rights." As a Muslim I would be less hesitant about signing a "Hindu Declaration of Human Rights" or a "Jewish Declaration of Human Rights." I know that there are Islamists around who just wait for someone like Leonard Swidler to hijack his global ethics.

No one has proclaimed in words so loudly in favor of the emancipation of women as the *Mullahcracy* in Iran. The most radical devotee of radical feminism could learn something from them. Even the German radical feminist publication *Emma* could not keep up with Khomeini. But what does that mean in practice? Almost the exact opposite. As gun-toters and as prison guards the women of Iran and the

Sudan are good. That then is lifted up as progress beyond the traditionalist society, which never had such. Under the aegis of the *New Ideology of Islamism*, which is everything other than the *Old Religion of Islam*, a complete emptying of concepts of their content takes place. There in the name of the Islamic Republic and its emancipation of women women are sprayed with acid because a single lock of hair slipped out a little from under the required head covering.

Saudi Arabia has no state constitution because it allegedly needs none. We have the Qur'an, it is said. That is a fatuous fiddling with the Holy Book. This forces us, then, to really define, in pedantic manner, what we are claiming and what we want to achieve. Otherwise the same will happen to us as to those concerned with human rights. For example, it is insisted that no religious minority has it so good as do the Christians of Pakistan. This ideal solution is expressed in separate election lists: Muslims may vote only for Muslim candidates, Christians only for Christian. A Hindu may not receive any more votes than there are Hindu voters, even if the majority of the Muslims might prefer to vote for him because he is the most capable candidate, because he is more honest than the Muslim candidate.

Perhaps some Germans still remember Adolf Hitler's *Mein Kampf*, where it is so beautifully stated: "The male stork goes to the female stork, the male wolf to the female wolf, house mouse to house mouse and field mouse to field mouse."[1]

In the "ideological state" of the Islamists the rights of women are better maintained than in any other system, and specifically through the fact that a few women were named as representatives of womanhood in the parliament. Men elect only men and women only women, if at all. Women Prime Ministers such as Khalida Zia in Bangladesh, Benazir Bhutto in Pakistan, Tansu Çiller in Turkey are symptoms of a devilish Westernization, *gharbzadegi*, as the Islamists say. *Gharbzadegi* means something like "being dazzled by the glitter of the West and giving oneself over as a slave to it," with the resulting immorality.

The proponents of Islamism, the ideology of the nineties, would gladly be the first to sign the draft of a universal global ethic, as long

---

[1]"Der Storch geht zur Störchin, der Wolf zu Wölfin, Hausmaus zu Hausmaus und Feldmaus zu Feldmaus."

as a long series of individual issues were not specified therein. They are also eagerly the first to engage in interreligious dialogue, to monopolize it so other Muslims—for instance, "heretics" like us—cannot participate. Afterwards in their publications in Arabic and Urdu, concerning interreligious dialogue they proclaim: That is the latest trick of the Christian missionaries after all other means to convert the Muslims have failed. Concerning the draft of a universal global ethic, their comments behind closed doors would hardly be other.

What to do? A draft of global ethics cannot go into too much detail as this would jeopardize universal acceptance. But if it remains too unspecified, too vague, it will lead nowhere, because the first ones to sign will be the perpetrators of genocide, such as Miloshevich and Karajich, Rafsanjani and Turabi. How, then, can one work out in detail such a global ethic and be just to all sides—I do not mean here the Islamists or similar Fundamentalists among Jews, Christians, Buddhists, Hindus and others. Let us leave that marginal group on the side, for it is already extraordinarily difficult to reach a consensus among the majority streams. An yet, it should be attempted. We should not limit ourselves to safe ground, but rather venture further—otherwise nothing will be gained. There is no longer a lack in our global village of well-intentioned declarations by the most various of committees of different concerns on the fundamental issues of the world community.

I mean that Leonard Swidler's initiative deserves to be taken seriously, that is, consistently worked out—which of course demands an immense amount of work, which would presume world-wide intensive discussions in buddhist monasteries, in the Vatican, in the Qarawiyí (Morocco's theological university with an influence throughout West Africa), in the 'Ulamá Academy of Lahor in Pakistan, among Hindu Pundits and Chinese Party Ideologues.

For this purpose we must wrestle with the question whether the different cultures really think in thought categories which are different from one another, as the Fundamentalists on all sides eagerly maintain. In my opinion it makes an immense difference whether one speaks of the differing concepts of the different cultures, or of different thought categories. One can translate concepts or at least find approximate correspondents in other cultures. With thought categories it is more difficult.

241

I do not wish categorically to deny that there are such fundamentally different thought categories. On the contrary, everything which enriches human thought should be welcomed. But I have experienced how the slogan of different thought categories can be misused, how every discussion can be made impossible, how every understanding of one another can be sabotaged, for our Fundamentalists obstinately insist that "true Islam" cannot be understood or analyzed with the help of Western structures of thought. Nevertheless, they propose an unanalyzable unity which can be grasped only with their own categories—not, of course, through the comparative method.

Now and again all this will be presented in a significantly more learned manner than I am doing here. But the end effect is always the same, namely, the tireless pursuit of the distortion of the meaning of concepts and the dislocation of all such universalistic attempts as that by Leonard Swidler.

I gladly grant that as a Sufi-influenced Muslim I am not especially concerned about my uniqueness. However, I believe I can bring a certain understanding for those who in their religion are first of all concerned to maintain their uniqueness and their distinctness from others. The overcoming of this hurdle is certainly the most difficult barricade on the path to a global ethic, for with many there arises the fear that through such a global undertaking they could lose something of substance, could lose holding on to "their own." That is not absolutely the same as the above-mentioned rejection of syncretism. Rather, it is a very simple question: If we all contribute something, how much from me, then, will be taken up, how will it maintain itself alongside the other elements, will it play any role at all, or will it be hardly visible any more among the multiplicity of contributions?

I once wrote a dissertation on a modern Egyptian historian and language reformer who was also a religious scholar and reform thinker. During the forty years of his activity as editor of the cultural periodical *Ath-Thaqáfa*, Ahmad Amín (d. 1954) concerned himself tirelessly with the thought of a "global marriage" of East and West ("Islamic Orient and Christian Occident"). In this he constantly asked about what would be brought along. What in our cultural heritage is appropriate to be taken up into the family community? What do we posses which we do not wish to give up, or indeed cannot give up? How do we adapt and how do we maintain our identity?

Those are all questions which will unhesitantly be posed. Even when we give our signature to the draft because we have nothing further to add, we nevertheless would like to be visible in the final version.

I should like to explain a little more why I, as a Muslim, feel so affirmative about this project. After all, I am not a contemporary of the Prophet Muhammad, when *islám* was still to be written with a small "i," as the prototype of Abrahamic religion, not *Islam* with a capital "I," the world community of today, fourteen centuries later.

Our philosophical tradition knows of a famous parable which inspired three great minds who all wrote a book on Hayy Ibn Yaqzán, an Arabic name which in English means *The Living One Son of the Wake*. Being of Andalusian ancestry, I feel closest to the version presented by our twelfth century philosopher Ibn Tufail. His Hayy Ibn Yaqzán is a human being growing up on an uninhabited island, reared by animals ever since he was placed there as a baby. In the course of a long life he discovers many laws of nature by sheer observation and by dint of his natural intelligence. Observation of animal life teaches him the rules of society and the reasons of social conduct. He becomes a deeply ethical being.

Late in his life *The Living One Son of the Wake* finally manages to get to another island with a large population and a social hierarchy. Society over there abides by a code of ethics taught to them by a prophet who had received it in the form of revelations from God. Hayy Ibn Yaqzán is wonderstruck to discover that those revelations say exactly the same as the conclusions he arrived at during his contemplations in complete solitude.

Ibn Tufail and the other philosophers wanted to tell us that ethics, to be true, must be universal. Whether we see their origin in the laws of nature or in divine revelations, the test of their truth is their universality. It is also a way of telling us to respect the ethics of other peoples, no matter whether they originate in a revelation from on high or whether they are the product of the human genius which, after all, we believe to be of divine grace too.

Without wanting to stretch the argument too far, I have sometimes asked myself whether there was not, at the back of our philosophers' minds, a realization of the oneness of humanity. As Muslims they had to believe in that anyhow, but it was a matter of taking practical steps in that direction. Islam had become yet another

243

religion. Though it had brought a large chunk of humanity together, it was no longer exactly the platform for all to stand on, as the Prophet had envisioned it. It is now one more faith, in addition to those that always existed, plus some even younger ones. What, then, about the primordial aspiration to provide a common base for all?

I cannot vouchsafe that philosophers such as Ibn Tufail, Ibn Síná and As-Suhrawardi, who all wrote about *The Living Son of the Wake*, felt that the recognition of other peoples' ethical thought as equal with ours could be such a platform. Much less can I aver that they, and other Muslim philosophers, aimed at something like a global ethic. But at least I see no rejection of such a project. On the contrary, they were apparently heading in that direction.

I do expect objections to this project from a different corner, and that may be both Muslim and Non-Muslim. Leonard Swidler is a Catholic and an American. He is the Editor-in-Chief of the *Journal of Ecumenical Studies* and the author of the *Decalogue Dialogue*. As I have noted, Islamists eagerly participate in interreligious dialogue while warning against it in their Arabic and Urdu press as the latest trick of Christian missionaries wishing to convert Muslims. They tell their followers to participate in interreligious dialogue in order to use it against the Christian missions, in order proselytize for Islam. It is important to be aware of this attitude because this is precisely the spirit with which they will approach the global ethic project. It may be possible to convince one or the other amongst them that the intention underlying the project is a very different one, but it would fallacious to entertain any illusions and to be taken in by Islamist professions of interest in the project. Their wrongly conceived misgivings about it need to be addressed again and again.

Others will allege that such a project is typical of the rich North that can engage in such pastimes. Whether they call the United States "the West" or "the North," there will be objections to the project's provenance: The much maligned West/North never ceases to impose itself culturally on the underdogs in the East/South. This widespread notion will cause much resistance to the project, resistance that would not exist if Leonard Swidler were a native of Chad or a Hindu divine from the Tamil part of Sri Lanka. It seems advisable to preempt such antagonisms by addressing them beforehand.

A Muslim Comment

Leonard Swidler and his collaborators from the Christian West simply should above all not allow themselves to be driven onto the horns of a dilemma. The protests against Western patronizing which are raised by some against his draft really appears to me to be rather threadbare. I *know* that many in the world of Islam, indeed, probably the majority, fundamentally have no problem with the project. Naturally there are also those who react to it allergically simply because it comes from America or from an American. However, we should not overreact, we should not thereby allow ourselves to be deterred. From the USA there comes not only Patriot and Stinger Missiles but also healing experiments in thought. The sooner people outside of America learn that, the better.

XVIII. HOW TO USE THIS BOOK

Denise Lardner Carmody and John Tully Carmody

1. General Suggestions

Perhaps the key to using this book well, and so grasping how it invites us to move from the theory of interreligious dialogue among the three Abrahamic faiths to their adherents' practice of common action for social justice and common worship, is to understand the source and nature of the materials between these covers.

The background of these materials is a series of meetings held from 1988-1994 by a group now known as ISAT: International Scholars' Annual Trialogue—Jewish, Christian, Muslim. At our meeting in Graz, Austria, in 1993, we studied major papers by Arthur Green, Paul Mojzes, and Fathi Osman on the concept of the good in their respective religious traditions—Jewish, Christian, and Muslim. We also discussed fully the topic of a global ethic, rooted in the religious heritage of all the world's major religious faiths. This latter topic had the specific focus of the upcoming Second Parliament of the World Religions, to be held in Chicago at the end of the summer, on the centenary anniversary of the first Parliament in 1893.1 Finally, because our meetings in Graz were occurring only an hour away from the rapes and other forms of ethnic cleansing that Serbs were then inflicting on Bosnian Muslims, the lethal potential in our religious traditions, along with the dire necessity for all peoples of good faith to collaborate in effective counter-political action, made our group less prone to lose itself in academic distractions than sometimes we had been, more inclined to favor vigorous practice of our religious convictions.

What the reader now finds in this volume reflects both the overall history of our group and its recent confrontations with political violence, indeed sobering political evil. Our meeting in 1994 in Jerusalem was less traumatic than the prior year's meeting in Graz, but even with winds of hopeful change blowing in Israel, due to the discussions of peace between the Israeli government and the PLO, we still met many signs of deep-seated hatred—much evidence that a stable peace, a happy coexistence, among Palestinians and Israelis remains a long range, perhaps a messianic dream.

The final contributions to this volume, along with the last editing, reflect this most recent experience of our group. After meeting with local Israeli leaders (including President Ezer Weitzman), local

Palestinian Muslims, local Palestinian Christians, and a few marvelous ecumenical associations such as the Rainbow Coalition in which at least two of these three groups come together regularly, we have had to present our findings, and our speculations, about the potential benefits of dialogue among the Abrahamic faiths with considerable modesty. We remain completely committed to such dialogue, and deeply impressed by the riches of all three Abrahamic traditions. But the violence of fundamentalists, and the bitter memories of many more sensible believers, remind us how painful, how bloody, a history our three faiths share. As we children of Abraham try to move from theory to practice, this history dogs our every bit of progress.

Before offering some suggestions about how best to use the specific papers presented in this volume, let us conclude our general advice by assuring the reader that the materials gathered here not only represent solid, advanced work on the state of relations among the Abrahamic faiths nowadays but that they also lay out some truly creative, hopeful pathways for future progress. If perhaps half the papers take the form of either background studies or brief reports on the | current state of particular questions, another half turn in the direction of how to I think better about the problems that have divided us in the past—how to move into new images that may free our minds and affections for significant progress in the future.

Such significant progress would be political, in the sense that it would enable Jews, Muslims, and Christians to cooperate more easily in trying to solve horrible problems such as the knife-to-the-throat situation in Bosnia. Less pressingly, perhaps, but ultimately at least as significantly, with at least as much potential for changing human consciousness profoundly, such progress would also free Jews, Christians, and Muslims to worship together more easily as brothers and sisters, spiritual neighbors and religious friends.

As we learn more about one another's senses of God, we children of Abraham tend to find, not that our religious experiences are identical, but that b they overlap sufficiently to make the substance of most of one group's experience available to its co-Abrahamists. Another way of putting this is to say that we find, when we reflect on our experiences of worship sensitively, openly, with the will to share them that good dialogue engenders, that God so beckons to become our surpassing treasure, and thereby overshadow what is only passing, partial, and self-centered in our lives, that for the moment our common creaturehood, and our common calling to live by faith, can loom as far more important than our particular traditions, histories, even grievances against one another.

This is a crucial point, one well worth tracking carefully through this volume as a key to its practical utility. The single, sometimes called "global" or "planetary," culture that has been building on the earth since World War II (and certainly will dominate the beginning of the twenty-first century) requires that we find images of humanity that make the common weal bulk much larger than any partial, local, particular prosperities. Certainly, concommitant with the rise of a global consciousness, an ecological, political, and economic sense of the priority of the whole, we find a centrifugal movement toward nationalisms, ethnicisms, tribalisms of various sorts. But nowadays only the culturally blind do not see that these centrifugal movements are merely cries of protest against a possible loss of identity, only poignant if sometimes virulent fears that who "we" are, who "we" have long been, will dissolve in the acids of post-modernity--the huge forces of international trade, technology, and politics now moving seemingly inexorably to make a new phase of human consciousness. Far from establishing the argument that we can narrow our horizons to the problems within our own national borders, such particularist tendencies merely remind us that any fully healthy, 1 truly viable common weal has to provide, dialectically, for the many as well as the one, the particular as well as the universal, the Serb and the Croat as well as the Bosnian Muslim. Planetization is not, properly, a process of leveling all peoples to a bland common denominator (most easily achieved by considering all as simply consumers of material goods). Most properly understood, planetization is a process of inviting all peoples, both individuals and groups, to think of themselves as citizens of the one earth, from which we all draw our sustenance, as children of a single mother, for whom we all carry a huge responsibility, to whose flourishing we all long to contribute our talents, offer our help, even dedicate our sufferings.

We have no other home. We all come from the dusty bosom of the one earth and return there with astonishing speed. If all human beings have always felt an innate, inalienable love of the earth, nowadays we can know with new and considerable ecological sophistication how powerful the interactions between our human intelligence and the material matrix on which our species labors can turn out to be. For, nowadays, we can know, if we are willing to open our eyes, that we are on the verge of destroying the matrix of life, the habitat of our spirit, the single motherly earth, through the technologies that our wonderful ingenuity has devised. We need only sniff the air, taste the waters, finger the dirt to sense a gathering sickness.

The common worship easy to glimpse in Abrahamic dialogue as a great future boon for humanity as a whole attacks the problems of ecological mayhem and political conflict lying across our way to a planetary common weal more directly than anything else in the human repertoire. For such worship relativizes all the political, economic, and other cultural ventures of the different tribes and nations, setting them under a truly ultimate, comprehensive horizon, where they become immensely more manageable. That horizon is God: the Lord, the Father of Jesus Christ, Allah. Under each Abrahamic name, God is infinite, sole, without limit—the one Ultimate reality and good. There is no other—Creator, final Lawgiver, Redeemer, Sovereign. This is the only pole star.

Consequently, there is no other source of radical freedom, both ideal and practical, because nothing other than the ultimate met in authentic worship (full response, self-return, to the divine mystery from the heart) removes the debris of our idols, dragging us out from under the partial allegiances we have absolutized. Consequently, when the children of Abraham worship together well, they experience together a renewal of spiritual space, an expansion of room in their hearts, to move creatively to make peace—drop old hatreds and try new friendships. In the measure that their common worship is genuine, alive and actually engaging them with the sole true God, it makes all things on their horizon new. For they sense once again that their sole true God is a future with virtually no constraints, as open, as rich with possibility, as the entire universe was at the moment before the Big Bang, when all was what might be, if unlimited energy were to take spark.

People who pray with the authenticity, the honesty, inculcated by any of the three Abrahamic faiths do meet the sole, unlimited God, at least from time to time. A cloud of Jewish, Christian, and Muslim witnesses testifies that this is so. And when they meet this, their God, however occasionally, they cannot for that moment participate in the evils of warped religion, such as we have witnessed recently in the former Yugoslavia (though, unfortunately, not there alone, by any means). The people attempting to perpetrate genocide in Bosnia simply cannot have been worshiping authentically.

Certainly, a full, scholarly estimate of the history and present politics of the former Yugoslavia would require numerous, perhaps nearly endless, entries for nuance and qualification, when it comes to religious analysis. But engross, as a summary religious estimate, we present authors find it legitimate, even necessary, to say that the leaders of all three groups—Orthodox Serbs, Catholic Croats, and Muslim Bosnians—have failed to bring their people to anything like an authentic worship and so religious practice. The fruits of religious hatred and the regular commission of heavy evils witness that the Abrahamic God has been dead in large numbers of these peoples' hearts, and so that large numbers have de facto been idolaters, able to hate and kill without measure, in the delirium of bloodlust and vengeance that sets the human spirit in hell, because they have indulged gods other than God. Such idolaters have failed, egregiously, to be human, because they have failed to be authentically religious, despite any pratings to the contrary that cultural reflexes or political opportunism may have generated.

Consequently, such abusers of religion have reminded most peoples with ears to hear, certainly our little ISAT group, that what we attempt to clarify when we discuss common Abrahamic worship, and even more when we practice it, is utterly basic to the future practical peace of large parts of our planet. The only radical way out of the guerilla violence that defaces the doors to the twenty-first century is to find in spirit a common greater cause. Only the absolute God, the divinity we can never idolize in good conscience, offers us a common cause, a common humanity, sufficiently great to compel all our hearts and so move us passionately into a viable future. There is no healthy future but God, who alone has no limits.

Though it is sad, even terrifying, to contemplate the likelihood that only a small fraction of our nearly six billion fellow human beings now actually, authentically, hold this truth about the soleness of God and the centrality of worship as their heart's besetting treasure, it is immensely encouraging to realize that God is always doing God's part. The divine mystery never deserts us. Always it is as near as the pulse at our throats, as imperative as our defense against warfare and death,

250

our response to joy and creativity. We cannot, simply cannot, be human without it, and we will not, in the long run, live by perversion alone—the perversion of forgetting or denying that humanity is our inmost calling.

So consider carefully the implications for common worship, as a wellspring for common political practice, that run through these papers. Muse imaginatively about the new sympathies, intuitions, nearnesses that the single sole God, first clarified for Jews, Christians, and Muslims in the figure of Abraham, bids fair to raise up nowadays, if we members of three Abrahamic faiths show ourselves wise enough, brave enough, to approach him, her, with open hands and hearts. Hushed to reverent silence, chastened by the memory of our many failures in the past, we might easily find in such simple prayers as the Jewish Shema, the Christian Credo, and the Muslim Shadadah all that we need to regain right spiritual order and so begin to make a world much freer of the disorders of hatred and war than the one in which so often we have to work nowadays.

2. Suggestions for Specific Readings

Readers new to interreligious dialogue can find in Leonard Swidler's opening essay, on "The Dialogue Decalogue," virtually all that they need to position themselves, mentally, for maximal profit from both the materials that l are to follow here and any ecumenical dialogues arising in their own lives. The ten commandments that Swidler elucidates summarize the findings, the gains, that professional practitioners, among whom Swidler himself is highly visible, have attained in the past thirty years, sometimes painfully.

It takes considerable time for people who have long felt themselves to be strangers, perhaps in many ways antagonists, to grope their way forward to friendship. It takes great patience, courage, and faith. Inevitably, there are stops and starts, failures of nerve, fears that they are betraying their own heritage, their own truth, even their own God. Commandments such as these ten indicate images, ways of thinking, restraints of biases that can mitigate such potential dangers to, destroyers of, ecumenical progress. As a challenge and gift to both our minds and hearts, this decalogue presents imperatives for spiritual life. So heed it well, applying its commandments to all the materials in this volume, and also to your own spirit, the index of ecumenical readiness that a sober examination of conscience now discloses in your own breast.

John Hick's essay, "Do We All Worship the Same God," is one of the most creative and relevant in this entire volume, getting to the nub of the theological issue most crucial to Abrahamic dialogue, with both dispatch and clarity. For though our confessions of faith suggest that we children of Abraham live under the same divine soleness, our histories show that we have understood this soleness quite differently, generating different theologies as well as different cultural complexes. The One God whom we have come to worship with gratitude to Abraham has not kept us from becoming alien to one another, often to the point of murderous warfare. So we need new images, ways out of past impasses and forward into a less fearful, less self-aggrandizing future. Hick offers us several. For example, Hick implies that if we think that we need to retain traditional convictions about our Jewish chosenness, or about the uniqueness of the incarnation of divinity in Jesus, or about the finality of the revelation given in the Qur'an, so as to retain our identity as Jews or Christians or Muslims, we should at least try to soften the edges of these convictions, to open new, permeable membranes, so that they do not isolate us from others, turning them into lesser children of God.

In fact, creative theologians in all three traditions are working hard to show how strong claims such as these longstanding ones need not become absolutist in the sense of necessarily condemning those who do not live by them to second-rate status—outer darkness, where there is the weeping and gnashing of the unsaved, the only partially human and loved by God. In few places will the reader find so succinct and clear an analysis of this capital issue as in Hick's present essay on the ways in which we Abrahamists do and do not worship the same God. It is a golden primer.

Gordon Kaufman's study of the contributions of the Abrahamic faiths to both war and peace summarizes another central issue quite well. The fact is that we Jews, Christians, and Muslims have through the centuries made a great deal of war and a great deal of suffering. Again and again we have given our detractors, who at their best have simply been defenders of the ordinary human beings whom we have turned into victims, carloads of evidence that religion is one of the worst features of the human psyche (*corruptio optimi pessimum*).

When people take their passion for God, which presses to become the absolute ardor of their spirits, and apply it to the annihilation of those they consider enemies of God, foes of the Absolute, infidels, they usually make themselves into fanatics—people unhinged, out of balance, terribly dangerous. In their dementia, which they can easily think is the purest form of religious allegiance, they can disgrace the name of God among sane people, as though trying to throw pitch over the shining uncapturable mystery, or as though God were no longer compassionate and merciful, slow to anger and abounding in steadfast love. "God" becomes angry, irrational, cruel, because that is what their own psyches are projecting onto heaven. They are disgruntled, ashamed of their present worldly status, afraid that history is passing them by. They think that they have survived by keeping boiling age-old enmities, hatreds, dreams of revenge, and so they forget the terrifying biblical maxim: "Vengeance is mine," saith the Lord.

Gordon Kaufman revisits this sobering historical and psychological ground, to remind all the children of Abraham that their past is not simon-pure. Indeed, in the context of today's nuclear arsenals, he forges a powerful call to make any religious claims so clearly the servant of humanity's future peace that "war" and "Abrahamic faith" might become antonyms. You could scarcely use this essay more profitably than by paying close attention to Kaufman's analysis and judging how chastening a challenge it sets before all current and future interreligious dialogue.

John Cobb's study of the relationships between the historical phenomenon known as the Enlightenment, when what European culture calls "modernity" came into being, and Christian faith is important for more than its assessment of this capital intellectual event. Much of the current discussion of human rights takes place against the background of the Enlightenment, and with more or less explicit awareness that the views of human nature, perhaps especially of human reason, that developed during the Enlightenment shape the mainstream of the current debates about the possibility of a universal declaration of human rights.

Inasmuch as the Enlightenment was a child, or a rebel, begotten from Western Christian culture, the ties between modernity and Christianity have been complex. Cobb reminds us of this heritage, both its assets and its liabilities. As we move into the future of interreligious dialogue, when many cultures besides European Christian will come into play, we can only profit from being aware that "human" and "rights" have to be so defined to give all parties to the dialogue their due.

In another of the studies in this volume that one might underscore as especially precious because hard to find in other places, Lakhsassi takes up the problem that Cobb has elucidated in terms of the Enlightenment, but through the lens of the Qur'an. In dealing with the "other," the non-Muslim (especially the People of the Book—Jews and Christians), the Qur'an had to enter the thickets of such questions as (1) God's plan of election to salvation and (2) the unity of human nature. The rights of outsiders, non Muslims, raised questions about the superior rights of Muslims, while the superior rights of Muslims raised questions about the lesser rights of outsiders. Lakhsassi's indication of the rich tradition of scholarly Qur'an commentary on this theme reminds us that Muslims have been grappling with it profoundly for centuries. The more fully our future interreligious dialogue can draw on this tradition of Muslim reflection, the more likely it is to deal with the question of human rights in ways pleasing to the nearly billion citizens of our one earth who now take their primary spiritual orientation in life from the Qur'an. Especially relevant are Lakhsassi's comments on the views of recent, reformist Muslim thinkers, who have moved between the Qur'an and Western notions of human rights, trying to achieve a synthesis that will bring out the best in each tradition.

The three papers that follow Lakhsassi's study deal with the notion of the good in the three Abrahamic traditions. The "good" is what a tradition lays before its adherents as their goal, that for which they ought to strive, whose achievement will make their overall lives, including their exercise of their inalienable human rights, a success. To miss the good, fail to achieve it, is to wander away from one's calling, both human and religious. However variously each tradition has characterized its sense of the good, usually its Scriptures have played a major in the formation of this sense, representing it to the faithful generation after generation. Thus what Arthur Green describes for Judaism, Paul Mojzes describes for Christianity, and Fathi Osman describes for Islam goes back to Torah, the New Testament, and the Qur'an. Readers might profit most from trying to get as firm a hold on these scriptural foundations as possible. By tracing down the biblical texts that these three authors provide, and then musing about how later conceptions of the good evolved from these scriptural beginnings, readers could come away with a fairly sophisticated appreciation of the inevitable development in religious doctrines, both theological and ethical.

The reflective essay that we present writers have developed under the title, "Synthesis and Implementation," bears principally on the results of the three proceeding papers on the good. Moving back for an overview, we have tried to indicate (1) where the Abrahamic traditions largely agree about the core of a successful human venture under God, (2) where their histories have made each group distinctive, (3) the political cooperation that one might reasonably think could come in the future from this combination of agreement and distinctiveness, (4) the fuller sharing in worship that this combination might stimulate, and (5) the future intellectual exchanges, including more intimate participation in each other's theological reflections, that this combination of overlap and distinctiveness in convictions about the good might encourage. Our essay is tentative and speculative, in the nature of the case, but in working it out we found ourselves greatly encouraged. Because the good life, as people formed by the faith of Abraham and Sarah tend to conceive it, reposes directly in the unabridgeable goodness and freedom of God, virtually all good things are possible. Specifically, this faith allows Jews, Christians, and Muslims to hope that none of their past enmities need keep them from fully effective political cooperation, common worship, and intellectual sharing in the future.

Leonard Swidler's statement, "Toward a Universal Declaration of a Global Ethic," envisions the entire span of the world religions, not just those that have derived from the biblical figure of Abraham. Nonetheless, the nearly 40% of the world's population that gives at least nominal allegiance to the Abrahamic faiths obviously constitutes a large fraction of the constituency that any universal declaration of ethical principles has to target.

Moreover, as the study of John Cobb that we have described suggests, and the study of John Hick to which we shall soon come entails, the relationship between modern Western Christian experience and the Enlightenment views to which Swidler's Declaration carries large debts begs full acknowledgment. Critically, one has to ask whether this Declaration has a sufficiently broad base in overall, global human experience to merit its ambitious claims to be "universal." Many questions of definition and interpretation hedge the way to answering this question, but Swidler does all readers a great service by laying out in considerable specificity a model for, one possible articulation of, the sense of the good, and the concommitant sense of the human rights both required to prosecute the good and seen to flow from it, that our global culture is now pressing us to publish, as a guide for our common life in the twenty-first century.

The Jewish, Christian, and Muslim commentaries that follow on Swidler's Universal Declaration illustrate the reception that it is likely to receive among the Abrahamic communities nowadays. Naturally, commentators other than Lapide, Hick, and Duran might react significantly differently, creating quite a different impression. But these three veterans of interreligious dialogue probably represent their traditions in a centrist manner, speaking not simply from their own personal likes and dislikes but with full awareness of how their fellow religionists, both past and present, would tend to respond. The generally favorable, positive tenor of their remarks is therefore encouraging. Whatever the infelicities, Swidler's overall project, like the parallel project of Hans Küng[1], receives much backing. The time seems ripe for expressions of what the world religions have to contribute to the platform of values, the consensus about goods and rights, that planetary, global civilization is now begging us to provide. The groups with the best developed interreligious dialogues are the ones most likely to respond to this importuning and feed to the worldwide human spirit, so hungry for justice and peace, bread from heaven and perseverance.

In the final analysis, though, the best way to use this book, in whole or part, is probably with the greatest freedom. Apart from the rare cases where readers have come in search of specific, even technical aid in the transition from interreligious dialogue to praxis, the most profitable readings are likely to be those most personal, leisurely, and thorough. The model of spiritual reading sometimes called lectio divina comes to mind. In many traditional manuals about how to use religious scriptures or classical texts, the essential advice is to clear one's mind of any pragmatic agenda and pay close attention to what the Spirit of

---

[1] See Hans Küng and Karl-Josef Kuschel, eds., *A Global Ethic: The Declaration of the World's Religions* (New York: Continuum, 1993); also Joel Beversluis, *A Sourcebook for the Community of Religions* (Chicago: The Council for a Parliament of the World's Religions, 1993).

God raises up. If a passage warms one's heart, one should linger with it, following the invitation it offers to flow into the largess of God, loving and praising God from the center of one's being.

Conversely, if a passage is daunting, challenging, one should also take it to heart, but as a potentially profitable warning—a call to examine one's conscience, be sure that one is not overlooking or neglecting some important religious obligation. In the spirit of the Psalmist's refrain that the beginning of wisdom is fear of the Lord, one should take the occasion of a challenging passage to reinvigorate one's sense of the holiness of God and the completeness of the divine sovereignty. If the soleness of God is the nonpareil source of human freedom, kicking us free of the idols that would tie us down, the soleness of God is also the measure to which we have to offer ourselves again and again, if we are to remain free—be people of full, whole-hearted faith. Reading for this measure, using these essays to move into the infinity of the One God once again, we can come away at least somewhat reconverted to the liberation summarized in the figure of Abraham.[2] Truly, that would be a significant result.

---

[2] For a suggestion of the spiritualities (the lives embracing both theoria and praxis) implied in the founding figures of the Buddha, Confucius, Jesus, and Muhammad, see Denise Lardner Carmody and John Tully Carmody, *In the Path of the Masters* (New York: Paragon House, 1994).

AUTHORS

Jews

Professor Nancy Fuchs-Kreimer (Reconstructionist Jewish [American]), Professor of Interreligious Relations, Reconstructionist Rabbinical College, Philadelphia, PA, and a Board Member of the Association for Religion and Intellectual Life, received her Ph.D. from Temple University Department of Religion. She has published a number of articles and is at work on a book on "Jewish Views of Paul."

Professor Arthur Green (Conservative Jewish [American]), Professor of Judaica at Brandeis University was previously the President of the Reconstructionist Rabbinical College, and before that Professor of Judaica at the University of Pennsylvania. He is the author of several books, especially in the field of Jewish mysticism.

Professor Pinchas Lapide (Orthodox Jewish [Israeli]), was born in Vienna, made *aliya* to Israel in the 1930s, fought with the British Army's Jewish Brigade in Egypt and Italy, taught in Israeli (Bar Ilan) and German (e.g., Tübingen) universities, has published numerous books both on his own (e.g., *The Sermon on the Mount. Utopia or Program for Action?* and many in bi-lateral dialogues with leading Christian thinkers, e.g., Karl Rahner, Hans Küng, Jürgen Moltmann. Ruth Lapide (Orthodox Jewish [German]) is the close collaborator, researcher and writer with Pinchas Lapide.

Christians

Professors Denise and John Carmody (Catholic [American]); John Carmody was Senior Research Fellow in Religion at Santa Clara University, received his B.A. and M.A. from Boston College, a licentiate in philosophy from Weston College, a Bachelor of Divinity from Woodstock College, and his Ph.D. from Stanford University. He died on September 23, 1995. Denise Carmody is the Bernard J. Hanley Professor at Santa Clara University, where she also chairs the Religious Studies Department. She received her M.A. and Ph.D from Boston College. Together and alone, they wrote over sixty books, including, *Ways to the Center: An Introduction to World Religions.*

Professor John B. Cobb, Jr. (Methodist [American]), born and raised in Japan, Professor (Emer.) of Process Theology at Claremont Graduate School of Religion, founder of the "Society for Buddhist-Christian Dialogue," is the author of numerous books, including *Christ in a Pluralist Age* (Westminster, 1975), *Beyond Dialogue* (Fortress, 1982), and with Leonard Swidler *Death or Dialogue. From the Age of Monologue to the Age of Dialogue* (Trinity, 1990).

Professor John Hick (Presbyterian [English]), winner of the 1991 Grawemeyer Award for the most significant new thinking in religion during the past five years, is a Fellow of the Institute for Advanced Research in the Humanities at Birmingham University, UK, and Danforth Professor of the Philosophy of Religion, emeritus, at the Claremont Graduate School, California. He is the author of many books on theology and the philosophy or religion, including *An Interpretation of Religion; Faith and Knowledge; Problems of Religious Pluralism; Arguments for the Existence of God; Three Faiths--One God: A Jewish, Christian, Muslim Encounter*; and *God and the Universe of Faiths.*

Professor Gordon Kaufman (Mennonite [American]), the Edward Mallinckrodt, Jr. Professor of Divinity at Harvard Divinity School, received the Ph.D. from Yale University in 1955. Before coming to Harvard in 1963 he taught at Pomona College, Claremont, CA and Vanderbilt Divinity School. He has published many articles and nine books, the most recent being *In Face of Mystery: A Constructive Theology* (Harvard University Press, 1993).

Professor Paul Mojzes (Methodist [Yugoslav]), Professor of Religion at Rosemont College (a Catholic college near Philadelphia), Co-Editor of the *Journal of Ecumenical Studies*, co-founder of "Christians Associated for Religious Relations with Eastern Europe" (CARREE), author of eight books and many articles in the interreligious dialogue area, including *Christian-Marxist Dialogue in Eastern Europe* (Augsburg, 1981) and co-editing with Leonard Swidler, *The Uniqueness of Jesus* (Orbis Books, 1997).

Professor Leonard Swidler (Catholic [American]), Professor of Catholic Thought and Interreligious Dialogue at Temple University, Co-Founder with his wife Professor Arlene Anderson Swidler, and Editor of the *Journal of Ecumenical Studies*, is the author/editor of sixty books, including *Bursting the Bonds. A Jewish-Christian Dialogue on Jesus and Paul* (Orbis, 1990), *After the Absolute. The Dialogical Future of Religious Reflection* (Fortress, 1990), and *Muslims in Dialogue* (Mellen, 1992).

Muslims

Professor Fathi Osman (Muslim [Egyptian]), past Professor of Religion, Temple University, Professor of Islamics, University of Riyadh, Editor of *Islam* (an international circulation monthly out of London), now Scholar in Residence at the Islamic Institute of California, is the author of many scholarly books on Islam and Byzantine Christianity in Arabic and many articles on Muslim dialogue with Christianity and Judaism.

Professor Khalid Duran (Muslim [Spanish]), received the Ph.D. from the Free University of Berlin, was Associate Professor for seven years in Islamic history at the Islamic Research Institute, Islamabad, Pakistan, and for eight years Senior Research Officer, Deutsches Orient-Institut in Hamburg, and Visiting Professor at Temple University, University of California, American University, Catholic University of America and the University of Louisville. He is the author of several books and many articles on Islam and interreligious dialogue, including *Islam und politischer Extremismus* (Deutsches Orient-Institute, 1985), and since 1995 is the Founder and Editor of the quarterly *TransStateIslam*.

Professor Abderrahmane Lakhsassi (Muslim [Moroccan]), Professor of Islamic Thought and Civilization, Philosophy Department, Mohammed V University in Rabat, Morocco, received the B.A. (1971) from the American University of Beirut, the Maitrice from the Sorbonne and the Ph.D. from the University of Manchester (1982), with a thesis on the epistemology of Ibn Khaldun, and recently was Visiting Professor at Hartford Theological Seminar, Hartford, CN. He has published a number of articles on Berber Islamic literature, his most recent publication being a contribution to the forthcoming *The Routledge History of Islamic Philosophy* (London).

INDEX

Abraham 3, 5, 7, 42, 109, 111, 113, 122, 131-134, 185-187, 188, 189, 191, 193-198, 224, 234-236, 247, 249, 252, 253, 255, 257

Abrahamic 2, 6-9, 58, 60, 62, 74, 114, 185-192, 194-200, 234, 235, 237, 243, 246, 247, 249-255, 256

Agape 147, 162

Aggadah 126, 128

Allah 22, 42, 45, 46, 48, 49, 56, 57, 64, 94, 99, 102, 106-108, 186, 190, 191, 249

Anawati, Georges 172, 174, 175, 177, 180

Antisemitism 52

Arkoun, Mohammed 14, 114

Askari, Hasan 18, 19

Balic, Smail 13, 36

Bosnia 36, 247, 250

Buber, Martin 121, 137

Buddhism 6, 7, 9, 29, 207, 209

Calvin, Jean 160

Catholic 3, 5, 30, 32, 39, 59, 81, 149-151, 153, 154, 159, 161, 213, 244, 250, 258-260

Christ 10, 33-35, 45, 47, 50, 51, 58, 77, 78, 81, 86, 145, 148, 152, 153, 157, 158, 191, 196, 249, 259

Christianity 3, 6-11, 19, 23, 28-30, 33, 35, 37, 43, 45-47, 49, 51, 52, 57-59, 71, 73-75, 78, 79, 81, 83-87, 99, 105, 139, 142, 144, 146, 147, 156, 157, 158, 163, 187, 190, 202, 229, 230, 234, 253, 254, 260

Constantinian 157, 158, 160, 162, 163

Dhimmis 88, 89, 92

Dialogue 1-12, 14, 17-37, 39-41, 71, 85, 111, 118, 189, 190, 195, 196-199, 202-204, 212, 217, 220, 221, 227, 232, 235, 236, 241, 244, 247, 249, 251, 252-254, 256, 259, 260

Duran, Khalid 19, 20, 31, 36, 37, 39, 40, 234, 256, 260

Enlightenment 11, 71-75, 77, 82-87, 152, 229, 230, 253, 254

Environment 2, 55, 86, 220, 225

Feminism 141, 142, 239

Feminist 22, 142, 152, 239

Fundamentalism 235, 236

Golden Rule 26, 206-211, 216, 217, 231

Graz 1, 2, 5, 6, 35, 36, 40, 212, 246

Hadith 17, 52, 97, 107, 108, 113, 174, 208

Halakhah 122, 126-129

Hassan, Riffat 7, 19-22, 36, 37, 39

Heschel, Abraham 122

Hinduism 6, 7, 9, 27, 28, 235

Holocaust 10, 60, 140-142

Human Rights 7, 17-19, 21, 22, 71, 73, 82, 86, 108, 182, 194, 205, 211, 212, 214, 215, 239, 240, 253, 254, 256

Ibn Khaldun 40, 98, 100, 114, 115, 117, 174, 176, 178, 179, 260

ISAT 1, 2, 5, 7, 30-33, 36-41, 147, 212, 246, 250

Islam 6-13, 15-23, 27, 30, 33, 35-37, 40, 43, 45-49, 52, 57, 58, 71, 88-95, 99-106, 108, 110, 113-116, 136, 162, 166-168, 172, 174, 176, 177, 180, 181, 186, 187, 190, 201, 234, 234-236, 237, 238, 239, 240, 242-244, 254, 260, 260

Islamism 105, 204, 236, 240

Jerusalem 6, 37-42, 50, 111, 125, 131, 135, 174, 246

Jesus 7-10, 12, 34, 42, 45, 46,

48-50, 52, 57-59, 75, 77, 90, 101, 113, 137, 145, 151, 152, 155, 157, 158, 186, 188-190, 193, 196, 208, 224, 225, 226, 237, 249, 252, 257, 259, 260

Jihad 22, 95, 100-102

Journal of Ecumenical Studies 6, 7, 12, 14, 17-19, 31, 244, 259, 260

Judaism 6-10, 23, 29, 30, 33, 37, 43, 44, 46, 47, 49, 52, 57, 71, 99, 119-126, 130, 136, 137, 139-143, 145, 157, 166, 167, 174, 186, 187, 190, 208, 234, 236, 254, 260

Kant, Immanuel 54, 55, 72, 209

Khan, Agha 13, 39, 231

Küng, Hans 16, 30, 59, 155, 164, 212, 230, 256, 258

Luther, Martin 153, 160

Magisterium 149

Messiah 10, 34, 42

Middle East 22, 40, 100, 192

Midrash 119

Mishnah 125, 128, 136

Mission 19, 20, 106, 131, 223, 235

Mohammed 7, 17, 35, 91, 114, 208, 260

Monotheism 7, 43-45, 47, 52, 88, 112, 140, 172, 235

Mu'tazila 172, 173, 178, 179

New Testament 8, 9, 33, 34, 42, 43, 45, 75, 77, 117, 145, 147, 150, 157, 186, 189, 254

Orthodox 11, 31, 89, 97-99, 115-117, 124, 139, 147-149, 159, 196, 213, 250, 258

Panikkar, Raimundo 26, 28

Peace 1, 2, 5, 15, 30, 34, 36-41, 53, 59-61, 69, 90, 100, 121, 126, 128, 147, 156, 186, 191, 194, 212, 214, 220, 222-224, 224,

225, 234, 246, 249, 250, 252, 256

Pluralism 11, 20, 160, 184, 192, 259

Protestant 17, 30, 32, 59, 86, 150, 153, 155, 160, 161, 213, 223

Qutb, Sayyid 93, 94, 105-108, 118

Rahman, Fazlur 12, 15, 16, 88, 93, 94, 99, 108-110, 109-111, 113, 118

Razi, F. 94-97, 99-102

Rosenzweig, Franz 121

Secularism 20, 204

Shalom 5, 39, 121, 132, 224, 225, 234

Shari'a 175, 179, 181, 183

Sufi 16, 177, 178, 181, 186, 235, 236, 242

Sufism 176-178, 180, 181, 235

Taha, Mahmoud 16, 17, 93

Talbi, Mohamed 7, 17, 100

Torah 33, 42, 44, 48, 49, 52, 112, 115-117, 119, 121-123, 126-132, 134, 135, 167, 188-191, 193, 197, M, 208, 254

Trialogue 1, 6, 7, 10, 12, 19, 20, 30, 32,35-38, 147, 161, 197, 212, 246

Ulama 99, 175, 178-180

Ummah 8, 47, 93, 96-98, 102, 111, 112, 114, 117

UN 29, 89, 92, 228

UNESCO 30, 231

Vatican Council II 3, 11, 27, 32, 159

Worship 3, 5, 42, 43, 46, 47, 54, 56, 69, 76, 101, 134, 168, 169, 177, 185, 188, 190, 191, 194-197, 246, 247, 249-251, 252, 255

Yahweh 8, 42-46, 48, 56, 57

Yugoslavia 1, 31, 250

262

PRINTED ON PERMANENT PAPER • IMPRIME SUR PAPIER PERMANENT • GEDRUKT OP DUURZAAM PAPIER - ISO 9706

ORIENTALISTE, KLEIN DALENSTRAAT 42, B-3020 HERENT